EASY cuisine

meals in minutes

300 quick and delicious recipes for you to enjoy

Patricia M. Butkus

BORDERS®

EASY cuisine

meals in minutes

300 quick and delicious recipes for you to enjoy

*This book is dedicated to the readers who embrace healthy living,
a healthy lifestyle, and a healthy diet. I respect their dedication to
cooking and creating memorable moments around the dining table.*

An Everything® Series Book.
Everything® and everything.com® are registered trademarks of F+W Publications, Inc.

Published by Adams Media, an F+W Publications Company
57 Littlefield Street, Avon, MA 02322 U.S.A.
www.adamsmedia.com

ISBN 10: 1-59869-219-4
ISBN 13: 978-1-59869-219-8
Printed in China.

J I H G F E D C B A

Library of Congress Cataloging-in-Publication Data
available from the publisher.

This publication is designed to provide accurate and authoritative information with regard to the subject matter covered. It is sold with the understanding that the publisher is not engaged in rendering legal, accounting, or other professional advice. If legal advice or other expert assistance is required, the services of a competent professional person should be sought.
—From a *Declaration of Principles* jointly adopted by a Committee of the American Bar Association and a Committee of Publishers and Associations

Easy Cuisine: Meals in Minutes is intended as a reference volume only, not as a medical manual. In light of the complex, individual, and specific nature of health problems, this book is not intended to replace professional medical advice. The ideas, procedures, and suggestions in this book are intended to supplement, not replace, the advice of a trained medical professional. Consult your physician before adopting the suggestions in this book, as well as about any condition that may require diagnosis or medical attention. The author and publisher disclaim any liability arising directly or indirectly from the use of this book.

Many of the designations used by manufacturers and sellers to distinguish their products are claimed as trademarks. Where those designations appear in this book and Adams Media was aware of a trademark claim, the designations have been printed with initial capital letters.

Previously published as *The Everything® Healthy Meals in Minutes Cookbook*.

Contents

Acknowledgments

Many people have helped in the development of this book. I would like to thank my office staff, including Paula, Jim, and Caryn. Fritz, Zoe, and Zeke gave moral support and Betsy saw the whole process through to its completion. Kent Roberts from Low Carb Chicago gave insight to new products and trends.

Introduction

WELCOME TO THE WORLD of quick and easy healthy cooking and eating. This is an exciting time for research of carbohydrates, protein, and fats and how they impact your metabolism and affect weight control. Many popular diet plans today, such as the 30/40/30 food balance plan, the South Beach diet, and the Atkins low-carb diet, emphasize the importance of higher-protein/lower-carb eating. If you are interested in eating a low-carb diet, the recipes in this book are a good jumping off point—each one contains a low to moderate number of carbs, and carb counts are given for each recipe. Increasing your protein intake as you reduce the "bad carbs" (carbs that have a high glycemic index, which causes blood sugar levels to spike rapidly) is another way to help you in your weight loss goals; protein and fat values are listed too for each recipe.

All the recipes and tips in this book are focused on healthy eating based on the general principles of balancing your intake of carbs, fat, and protein—plus they are quick and easy! Explore different ethnic markets, fresh farmers' markets, restaurant supply stores, gourmet grocers, specialty butchers, and delicatessens. As you expand your knowledge about healthy eating, you'll find a number of new horizons for new products, gadgets, and convenience items. There are many resources on the Internet to provide the nutritional statistics and data for your diet plan. It's also very important to involve your primary-care physician in your diet planning. There are a number of nutritional supplements being developed specifically to complement most diets. Read the labels, and also make sure you

let your physician know of any supplements you are planning to incorporate into your diet plan. It is important to have a concise review of all supplements and medications you are taking to avoid any drug interactions.

One of the keys to any successful diet plan is support. You'll find that entering the venture of a controlled diet plan is really more of a lifestyle change. It is important that you have friends or family that support your commitment. You'll also find that you'll share success stories, enjoy outdoor activities in a group, and most important, have memorable dining experiences.

Easy Cuisine: Meals in Minutes provides recipes that will stimulate your own creative ideas for the foods that you enjoy. This book is meant to be a workbook as much as a reference guide. Mark your notes and changes in the margins. Rate the recipes as you try them! There is no universal spice or flavor that works for everyone. Cooking is an adventure that lets you explore and develop your tastes and favorite flavor combinations. The best way to remember the successful (and not so successful) results is by taking concise notes. There's nothing better than reading notes for a recipe that makes your mouth start to water and brings back fond memories of a pleasurable dining event.

There are several other simple steps that can enhance the atmosphere of your dining event and not necessarily add to the preparation time. Pick out a new CD or plan the appropriate background music. A classical CD for a romantic dinner or a compilation of 60s rock for an outdoor barbecue can set the tone for the occasion. Also, many supermarkets have beautiful floral departments; consider adding a few fresh flowers if it fits in your budget. Last, consider your beverage selection. Wines are a traditional standby, but there are a number of nonalcoholic and low-carb combinations that are flavorful and may be the perfect complement for your meal. There are several great-tasting sugar-free juice mixes on the market that can easily be dressed up for an adult spritzer with a bit of imported sparkling mineral water and a slice of fresh citrus. If you're avoiding artificial sweeteners, consider adding 2 tablespoons of pomegranate juice to a sparkling mineral water for a satisfying beverage alternative. It has 4 grams of carbohydrates but provides a dose of antioxidants and is a flavorful adult drink.

Quick and easy cooking means efficiency of your time and efforts. You'll develop a specific working methodology that is particular to your workspace. I always enjoy group dinners where everyone is preparing a dish in my kitchen. I love to watch other people see my workspace from their perspective and I learn from the efficiencies and different prep methods they bring to the party. What a fun learning experience!

Every recipe in this book contains the nutritional statistics for carbs, fats, and proteins. These statistics are rounded to the nearest full gram and are not modified in any way for fiber. Using a reputable, nationally recognized computerized nutritional analysis program, I determined the total carb count on a per serving basis. Several of the current popular programs for calculating carbs subtract the fiber content before reporting the carb count, so counts may seem lower than they really are. My analysis is based on the full carb amount; no compensations have been made.

LOW—These recipes all contain 10 grams or fewer of carbohydrates per serving.

MODERATE—These recipes all contain between 10 and 20 grams of carbohydrates per serving.

The recipes in this book are designed to complement your lifestyle. Use thi book as a reference and a guide to create new and memorable dining moments and recipe favorites on your new adventure into a healthy life. The key to success in any new endeavor is to explore and have fun. Enjoy!

Chapter 1: **Fit and Fast**

WELCOME TO THE WORLD OF QUICK AND EASY COOKING! There are many new conveniences available to the consumer to make your time in the kitchen the most efficient. This chapter gives you a few hints on how to take advantage of your supermarket to reduce your time in the kitchen. It also outlines the basics to making your kitchen an efficient workspace.

The Fat/Protein/Carb Balance

Proteins, fats, and carbohydrates are known as "macronutrients" because people need large amounts of these nutrients in their diets. Achieving the right balance of the three is the focus of many diets.

Protein is used by the body to build and repair bone, muscles, connective tissue, skin, internal organs, and blood. Protein also makes up your hair, nails, and teeth. Hormones, antibodies, and enzymes, which regulate the body's chemical reactions, are all composed of protein. Protein helps wounds to heal and blood to clot. Protein can be found in meat, poultry, fish, eggs, milk, cheese, yogurt, and soy products.

Fat is another macronutrient vital to a healthy diet. Fat helps carry, absorb, and store the fat-soluble vitamins (A, D, E, and K) in your bloodstream. Fat can also be used as an energy source. Body fat also helps to cushion your organs and protect them from injury and to supply insulation to help regulate body temperature.

Carbohydrates are essentially fuel. The word carbohydrate is based on the combination of carbon, hydrogen, and oxygen. Carbohydrates are a primary means of storing or consuming energy—other forms of energy storage and consumption are fat and protein.

Carbohydrates are high-energy chemical compounds that are found in foods like breads, pasta, cereal, and vegetables. There are two types of carbohydrates—sugars (also called *simple carbohydrates*) and starches (or *complex carbohydrates*). Simple sugars are absorbed directly into the bloodstream fairly quickly after you eat them. That's why you get a quick burst of energy from a candy bar, followed by a crash as your blood sugar level drops once the sugars are absorbed. Starches are digested into simpler sugars, which are further converted into glucose. Glucose is the main source of energy for the cells of the human body. Because it takes longer for the body to break down and digest these carbohydrates, the sugars enter the bloodstream at a fairly constant rate.

Your body uses the energy it needs and stores the rest for later use. When you eat more carbs than your body needs, the high glucose levels cause your body to produce more fat to store the excess energy. Diets that consistently contain more carbohydrates than the body needs can lead to health problems such as obesity and, in some cases, diabetes. Research has also suggested that diets high in starch contribute to atherosclerosis and heart disease, the number one cause of death in the United States.

Remember that calories count and it's important not to lose perspective of your food intake. The Calorie Control Council at *www.caloriecontrol.org* can provide basic straightforward dialogue about portion sizes and caloric intake. The recipes in this book contain a variety of foods including fruits, vegetables, seeds, and nuts to complement your high-protein entrée selections.

What Is Quick and Easy Cooking?

Quick and easy cooking starts from the moment you write your shopping list and ends with the cleanup. The actual cooking component is just a portion of the quick and easy cooking experience. A big part of quick and easy cooking is making the most of your time to produce the highest-quality meals. The recipes in this book are designed to be completed in 30 minutes or less. This time does not include shopping time or time to assemble the ingredients for preparation. The ingredient description generally includes the required preparation work. Take, for example, "½ cup sliced red onions." If you have a red onion in your pantry, you know that it will need to be sliced. If you are going to add red onion to your shopping list, list it as ½ cup sliced red onions and buy it at the salad bar. The salad bar may seem expensive based on a price per pound, but it can be an economical option when you consider the time you save and the lack of waste (you can buy exactly the amount you need).

Getting Organized

Professional chefs have a philosophy called *mis en place*, which means "everything in its place." Quite simply, it's organization. Before you go shopping, it always wise to write a list of the things you'll need to purchase, and it's helpful to consider the best places to buy the ingredients you'll be using. You have a lot of options to explore these days with so many specialty food stores opening. You'll also want to take into account the before and after of making a meal—setting up your workspace and serving the meal.

Shopping

Read a recipe in its entirety at least once before starting your shopping list. Write your list to take advantage of items at the salad bar for prepped produce, the deli counter for sliced meats and cheeses, the produce counter for cleaned greens, the freezer section for prepped vegetables, and the dairy counter for specialty cheeses. As you get more familiar with your grocery store, you can begin to write your shopping list in the same organization as the store, grouping dairy together, produce together, deli together, and other categories.

Never shop on an empty stomach. Many stores now offer tastes and samples of a variety of food products, and you won't be worrying about carb counts if someone offers you a sample of pizza when you're starving. While shopping can be fun, the goal is to buy what you need and not have leftovers. Packaging and storing leftovers are added steps and are not part of the quick and easy philosophy.

Know your stores. There are so many specialty stores including gourmet shops, cheese shops, ethnic markets, butchers, restaurant supply houses, and local supermarkets. Plan to stop at one new store on shopping expeditions when you have time, and you'll be amazed at the different foods and products that are designed to save you time. There are also "low-carb stores" opening in populated areas and these stores offer a variety of products targeted to make life easier for those who choose to follow a more intensive low-carb plan. There are literally hundreds of time-saving products and creative food ideas in addition to a well-stocked research and information area in low-carb stores. Check your area; if a store has not yet opened, chances are that there will be one in the near future.

Setup

A clean work area is a pleasure to be in. Give yourself counter space. Make sure your sink and dishwasher are clean; have a couple of clean cutting boards on hand, and you're set. Your products should be arranged in the order listed in the recipe—this is also the order in which you'll use them. Premeasure where possible, prepare baking pans if specified, preheat your oven when needed, and bring refrigerated items to room temperature if required. Now take a step back and put away anything that you're not going to be using including spice jars, dairy containers, canisters, pans, or bowls. Trimmings and scraps should go into the garbage and dirty dishes should go into the sink; preferably in hot, soapy water to make cleanup easy. Good planning may seem like work, but it's just a way to establish good habits that save time in the long run. Now is also a good time to think ahead and chill salad plates and warm serving platters.

Cooking

Your area is clean and your ingredients are prepared and you're ready to start. Take a minute and read the recipe in its entirety one more time. The worst time to realize you forgot something is in the middle of cooking. Have a few extra tasting spoons available and make sure there are paper towels and dishcloths easily accessible—just in case.

It's always a good idea to wash a few pots and pans when you have a minute, but don't let yourself become distracted from your priority, which is cooking. Follow the steps in the recipe and follow the visual indicators in addition to the suggested times provided for each step. If your fish is golden brown and cooked through in 6 minutes even though the recipe says 9 minutes, take it off the heat. The visual indicators supersede the suggested times. Each oven and stovetop cook differently, pans cook differently, and meats, poultry, fishes, and vegetables each cook differently depending on age. Let your senses guide you, not the clock.

Serving and Presentation

Even if you're cooking for just yourself, use a plate and sit at the table to enjoy your meal. It's just no fun to stand at the stove and eat your food from the pan. You deserve to be served, even if you're the one serving. Take a minute to chill salad plates and soup cups, if appropriate, and warm your dinner plates and serving platters.

Make sure you have a spot in the kitchen or a clean dishwasher so you have somewhere to put dirty dishes if you're serving a multicourse meal. It's better to have a place to put them temporarily than to leave them on the table.

Cleanup

Cleanup is a necessary evil. Try not to leave everything for the end; put dirty dishes in the dishwasher as you use them. If you're going to leave a dirty pot on the stove to save sink space, fill it partway with hot soapy water so it can soak while you're enjoying your meal.

Restaurant supply houses, many of which are now open to the public, and larger discount chains sell a variety of aluminum disposable pans at a reasonable cost. Use these pans for any dishes that will be potentially messy due to sauces, broiling, or roasting. You can run them through the dishwasher, and if they don't come out clean, toss them in the garbage. Place your broiler rack on a small rimmed baking sheet with sides or a small baking pan filled halfway with water—the drippings will fall into the pan, reducing your broiler cleaning time by at least half. Clean your broiler and grill after each use; it's disheartening to start preparing dinner and realize the broiler or grill was never cleaned from the previous use.

Kitchen Essentials

Your kitchen is where quality outweighs quantity when it comes to equipment. Your kitchen equipment will determine the efficiency of your workspace, which produces time savings in prepping, cooking, and cleanup. Having the right appliances make your cooking experience efficient and easy. The right utensils for the right job also play a big role in how smoothly everything goes. Everything from what you use to cook to how you get rid of the scraps shapes the outcome of your cooking.

Basic Equipment

Freezer containers, food storage bags, freezer bags and refrigerator bags in a variety of sizes, parchment paper, plastic film, and aluminum foil are staples that you should not be without. Ideal for storing leftovers for short or long periods of time, these items make it easy to handle any food that doesn't get eaten and provide versatility for storing depending on the type of food you're working with. For strainers and colanders, buy two different sizes of the metal type and you won't need to worry about heat resistance. A metal steamer basket is perfect for preparing vegetables, and the quality is usually consistent from brand to brand. Cutting boards are also helpful tools. Ideally, you should have two or three on hand. It's good to differentiate one board for fruits, one for onions, garlic, etc., and one for meat and poultry. You can also have one for fish. Proper maintenance is mandatory, so be sure to follow the manufacturer's directions. They're available in wood and plastic, but the difference is simply one of personal preference.

A good cookware store will work with you to explain the pros and cons of each type of cookware for pots, pans, and bakeware. There are many manufacturers and each brand has its advantages. You'll know the types of foods you'll be preparing most and your style of cooking—braising, broiling, stovetop grilling, and sautéing. Invest in the cookware that you'll be using most. There are many cost-effective cookware sets on the market, but make sure you analyze your storage space before bringing home that twenty-two-piece set that was just too good to pass up. Check with people you know who cook—ask what they use and what their likes and dislikes are and what they would do differently if purchasing a cookware set again.

Food Processors

Mini–food processors are huge timesavers for mincing garlic, shallots, herbs, and a number of other items. Many are now under $25, and if you watch for sale specials, you can get an extra work-bowl at no charge. You can also use a full-sized food processor. Prices have come down on these appliances, so research before you buy to get the most for your money. Simpler is better than complex—pay only for the accessories that you'll actually use. These appliances come with helpful manuals that provide tips for using them to get certain desired results. It's worth taking the time to get acquainted with the different ways you can use these products so that you know different ways to prepare food. In the end, these tips will make cooking much easier and save you time!

Handy Gadgets

One tool that every kitchen and cook should have is a hand mixer. Invest in a quality mixer with good motor speed. Several models also include a number of accessories including "wands" that are invaluable for puréeing soups, sauces, and fruit smoothies.

Citrus graters, which are also called *rasps*, are incredibly efficient tools that are excellent for grating the rinds of fruits for zest, and the larger version can be used for cheeses. Vegetable peelers are helpful, too. Buy two—you'll be glad you did (especially when you forget to run the dishwasher!). Can openers, whether manual or electric, are another must-have for any kitchen. A quality manual one is just as easy to use as an electric one, and does the job all the same—it just depends on your preference. Pick one that's easy to hold and has rubberized handles. Instant-read thermometers are a sure way to test temperatures and doneness. Many thermometers now have the proper temperatures for meat and poultry printed right on them or their cover. Timers are also a must-have—it's just too easy to get distracted and a timer can save you from making countless mistakes.

Useful Equipment

When it comes to what you use to measure your ingredients, what you'll cook them in, and where you'll store them, there are some basic items that you'll need. Liquid measuring cups are essential. Don't count on just one big glass measuring cup to do everything. Have a variety of sizes and use the size that fits the job. There are several sets that nest, which saves on storage space. There is a difference between dry and wet measuring equipment, too. Dry measuring cups are available in plastic or metal. One advantage to plastic is that it's microwavable, but it will eventually stain. Metal cups are more durable, but lack the convenience of being microwavable.

In addition to measuring cups, you'll need measuring spoons. One set works for both liquid and dry measures and the metal spoons are worth the investment.

Utensils

It's important to have a variety of spoons available. There are many different types, such wooden and metal, slotted and nonslotted, big and little. Using the right tool makes everything easier and potentially saves on spills and accidents. Knives are also a personal preference. Check out several different manufacturers, and test them for weight and balance. A good cookware store will let you try out several types by cutting a potato or other vegetable to see if you like the feel. Paring knives are invaluable, as are a good midsize (8 to 10 inches) chef's knife, an 8-inch serrated knife, and an 8- to 10-inch carving knife for slicing roasts. Your choice of knife sizes and types is a personal preference. Knives can be quite costly, so take time to do the research before investing. The most important part of your knife kit is a sharpener. Learn how to use it, and have your knives professionally sharpened a few times a year. Dull knives cause accidents.

Garbage cans are one of the most used pieces of equipment in your kitchen. They range from the simplest plastic open container to mechanical stainless steel gizmos that require an instruction manual to understand. Check to make sure that it's easy to get the garbage in and easy to take the bag out. Most of all, it has to be easy to clean.

Also necessary, but less commonly considered, are tools such as ladles, spatulas, tongs, and whisks. It's nice to have a small (2-ounce) and a medium-sized (6-ounce) ladle on hand for hot liquids and skimming. There are two different types of spatulas available—the mixing type and the turning type. For the mixing type, have several sizes of heat-resistant quality. That way you can use your spatulas for any application, hot or cold. Use good-quality metal spatulas for the turning type. Make sure the handle is heat resistant so it won't melt when you rest it on the edge of a hot skillet. There is also a specialty spatula called a *fish-turner.* This tool is very helpful if you prepare a fair amount of fish. You should also have a few heat-resistant plastic spatulas to protect the surface of nonstick pans, if you own them. For tongs, purchase two or three good-quality aluminum ones in different sizes. Check the locking mechanism before purchasing—some of the mechanisms are cumbersome. Wire whisks come in handy when making sauces and homemade vinaigrettes. You should have at least one good whisk on hand.

Supermarket Tricks

Knowing your supermarket layout is a good start. You've got the produce section, the frozen food sections, the salad bar, and the deli section—the four areas that offer the best array of products for quick and easy cooking. The more familiar you become with these sections of your supermarket, the more you'll see that each has a lot to offer as far as cooking ingredients are concerned.

Some produce counters offer prepared greens, vegetables, herbs, and fruits. Mentally inventory what's available and ask the produce manager how they handle seasonal specialty items. The salad bar is waste-free purchasing at its best. Check that salad bar for sliced onions, peppers, mushrooms, scallions, cabbage, and buy the specific quantity listed in the recipe; that way you won't need to worry about waste and leftovers. The deli counter has the same benefits as the salad bar but with meats and cheeses. It's also easy to be lulled into purchasing a few of the vast array of salads now available, but ask for a copy of the nutrition information first.

Moving on to the freezer section, which is often overlooked, there are a number of frozen vegetables that are almost as nutritious as fresh veggies—and some are even more nutritious, depending on how long the fresh vegetables have been sitting on the shelf at your supermarket. It doesn't hurt to have a bag of chopped onions, chopped peppers, green beans, and broccoli, or your personal favorites, in the freezer. They're easy to use in a pinch and are true time savers.

Meat and Seafood Counters

Also don't forget your meat, poultry, and seafood counters. Check premarinated meats for nutrition information, as they often contain sugars and starches. The fishmonger will shuck oysters, trim and clean mussels, bone fish, and let you know what's on sale. The butcher will trim and bone meats for you and tell you what's the best buy. Getting to know your supermarket staff is the biggest time-saver of all. Find one quality market that can take care of the majority of your needs. If the closest market always has outdated produce and you find that you're driving to the next market anyway, it's time to switch your primary supermarket. Don't ever get into the habit of compromising quality for your supermarket purchases.

A Word about Sugar Substitutes

Some recipes in this book call for a sugar substitute, leaving the choice of which substitute to use up to the reader. There are a few on the market. Splenda is excellent for your baking needs, because it holds up better under heat than others, and it measures just like sugar. For any recipe that calls for "sugar substitute equal to 1 teaspoon of sugar," you can simply use 1 teaspoon of Splenda. Equal also measures the same as sugar. Stevia, another popular substitute, can be harder to measure precisely, so you may have to practice to determine how much (or how little) to use to achieve the right level of sweetness.

For a substitute for brown sugar, substitute Splenda combined with a small amount of dark molasses (the darker it is, the fewer carbs it has).

Ginger Cashews

Serves 12

Carb Level: Moderate

Per serving:

Carbohydrate: 11g

Protein: 5g

Fat: 16g

You can substitute pecans halves for the cashews—it will reduce the carb count but will also dramatically change the texture and flavor.

3 cups cashews

Sugar substitute equal to
  ¼ cup granulated sugar

1 teaspoon kosher salt

1½ teaspoons ground ginger

1 tablespoon honey

1½ tablespoons water

2 teaspoons vegetable oil

1. Preheat oven to 300°. Place the nuts in a single layer on 2 baking sheets lined with parchment paper. Toast until fragrant, about 6 to 8 minutes. Stir and turn the nuts at least 2 times during the roasting process. Be very watchful during the last half of baking, as the nuts can burn quickly. Remove the nuts from the oven and set aside.
2. Combine the sugar substitute, salt, and ginger in a small bowl; mix until evenly blended and set aside.
3. Combine the honey with the water and the oil in a large saucepan and bring to a boil. Reduce heat and add the toasted cashews. Cook, stirring frequently to coat the cashews evenly, until all the liquid is evaporated, about 3 minutes.
4. Transfer the nuts to a large bowl, add the ginger mixture, and toss to coat evenly. Spread the nuts on a single layer of parchment to cool. The cashews may be kept in an airtight container at room temperature for up to 4 days.

Food for Thought

When planning an appetizer reception, plan on 4 appetizers per person per hour. Also make sure your menu includes a mix of beef, poultry, seafood, and cheese or a vegetarian offering.

Hot Crabmeat Dip

8 ounces cream cheese, at room
  temperature
7½ ounces canned crabmeat
2 tablespoons finely chopped
  yellow onion
2 tablespoons whole milk

1 teaspoon prepared horseradish
⅛ teaspoon seasoned salt
Freshly cracked black pepper, to
  taste
⅓ cup sliced almonds

1. Preheat oven to 375°.
2. Combine the cream cheese, crabmeat, onion, milk, horseradish, salt,
   and pepper in a medium-sized bowl; mix until well blended.
3. Transfer the crabmeat mixture to a 9-inch pie plate or ovenproof dish
   and sprinkle with the sliced almonds. Bake uncovered for 15 minutes
   until hot and bubbly. Serve hot.

Serves 10

___

Carb Level: Low
Per serving:
Carbohydrate: 2g
Protein: 7g
Fat: 11g

Serve as
a dip with
raw veg-
etables and
whole-wheat
crackers.

Grapes with Roquefort

10 ounces blanched almonds,
  toasted and chopped
8 ounces cream cheese,
  at room temperature
⅛ pound Roquefort cheese,
  at room temperature

2 tablespoons heavy cream,
  at room temperature
1 pound green seedless grapes,
  rinsed and dried, plucked from
  stems
Freshly cracked black pepper

1. Place the nuts in a small bowl and set aside.
2. In a medium-sized bowl, combine the cream cheese, Roquefort, and
   heavy cream; use an electric mixer to beat until smooth.
3. Use a toothpick to spear a grape; dip it into the cheese mixture and
   then into the nut mixture.
4. Season with freshly cracked black pepper and place the grapes on a
   tray lined with parchment paper. Refrigerate until ready to serve.

Serves 12

___

Carb Level: Moderate
Per serving:
Carbohydrate: 11g
Protein: 7g
Fat: 21g

It may take
a couple of
tries to get
the hang of
dipping and
rolling the
grapes.

Tuna and Avocado on Cucumber Slices

Serves 8

Carb Level: Low

Per serving:

Carbohydrate: 3g

Protein: 8g

Fat: 13g

This delicious recipe also makes a great spread with crudités and whole-wheat crackers.

1 cucumber, seedless variety
1 avocado
¼ cup mayonnaise
¼ cup sour cream
2 tablespoons fresh-squeezed lemon juice
1 tablespoon roughly chopped scallions
1 tablespoon Worcestershire sauce
6½ ounces canned tuna, packed in oil, drained
1 tablespoon capers
¼ teaspoon seasoned salt
Freshly cracked black pepper, to taste

1. To prepare the cucumber, rinse under cool running water and pat dry. Trim off and discard about 1 inch from each end (the ends are often bitter). You can either peel the entire cucumber or "stripe" it by leaving alternating strips of green peel. Cut the cucumber into slices and place in a single layer on paper towels.
2. Cut the avocado in half, discard the pit, and spoon out the flesh into the bowl of a food processor fitted with a metal blade. Add the mayonnaise, sour cream, lemon juice, scallions, and Worcestershire sauce; process until smooth, scraping down the sides of the bowl as needed.
3. Transfer the mixture to a medium-sized mixing bowl and add the tuna, capers, salt, and pepper; blend well using a fork. Adjust seasoning to taste if necessary.
4. Arrange the cucumber slices on a serving platter. Use a small teaspoon to mound about ¾ teaspoon of the tuna and avocado mixture in the center of each slice. Garnish with fresh cracked pepper.

Preparing Cucumbers

To help the topping stay seated, cut the cucumber into slices about ¼ inch thick and use a melon baller to scoop out a small hollow in the center of each slice. You can also use a small teaspoon. Make sure you don't cut the entire bottom out. For cucumber cups, cut the slices about 1 inch to 1¼ inches thick and use the melon baller to scoop out the center, about ¾ inch deep.

Cucumber Rounds with Smoked Salmon

1 cucumber, seedless variety
8 ounces smoked salmon
2 tablespoons finely diced red
  onion
1 tablespoon roughly chopped
  capers

1 teaspoon snipped fresh chives
  or dill, plus extra for garnish
1 tablespoon olive oil
Freshly cracked black pepper

Serves 8

Carb Level: Low
Per serving:
Carbohydrate: 1g
Protein: 5g
Fat: 3g

---

1. To prepare the cucumber, rinse under cool running water and pat dry. Trim off and discard about 1 inch from each end (the ends are often bitter). You can either peel the entire cucumber or "stripe" it by leaving alternating strips of green peel. Cut the cucumber into slices and place in a single layer on paper towels.
2. Trim off and discard any dark section from the center of the salmon, if needed. (These sections are somewhat bitter in taste.) Dice the salmon into medium-sized cubes and transfer to a medium-sized bowl. Add the remaining ingredients and lightly mix with a fork until the olive oil is evenly distributed.
3. Arrange the cucumber slices on a serving platter. Use a small teaspoon to mound about ¾ teaspoon of the salmon mixture in the center of each slice. Garnish with the snipped chives or dill and serve.

The mix of textures and the cool crispness of this dish make it a delicious summer appetizer. You can make the salmon mixture several hours in advance—just cover and refrigerate until ready to use.

Cucumber Tips

The zesty crunch of cucumbers makes them a perfect carrier for hors d'oeuvres of any variety, especially seafood, vegetables, and certain tangy cheeses. Try using a "seedless" or "English" cucumber, as they have fewer seeds than the traditional garden variety. Always slice them just before assembling your hors d'oeuvres so they are fresh and crisp.

Smoked Whitefish Mousse on Cucumber Slices

Serves 8

Carb Level: Low

Per serving:

Carbohydrate: 1g

Protein: 8g

Fat: 5g

You can substitute smoked trout if white-fish is not available. The mousse can be made several hours in advance—cover and refrigerate until ready to use.

1 cucumber, seedless variety

4 ounces cream cheese, at room temperature

¼ cup roughly chopped scallions

2 tablespoons snipped fresh dill, plus extra for garnish

8 ounces smoked whitefish, skinned and boned

¼ cup heavy cream

4–6 drops (or to taste) hot sauce

Freshly cracked black pepper, to taste

1. To prepare the cucumber, rinse under cool running water and pat dry. Trim off and discard about 1 inch from each end (the ends are often bitter). You can either peel the entire cucumber or "stripe" it by leaving alternating strips of green peel. Trim the cucumber into slices and place in a single layer on paper towels.
2. Combine the cream cheese, scallions, and dill in the bowl of a food processor fitted with a metal blade; process until well blended. Add the smoked whitefish and process until smooth.
3. While the machine is running, slowly pour the cream through the feed tube. Process until the mixture is soft and creamy, scraping down the sides of the bowl as needed. Season to taste with the hot sauce and pepper.
4. Arrange the cucumber slices on a serving platter. Use a small teaspoon to mound about ¾ teaspoon on the mousse mixture in the center of each slice or use a pastry bag fitted with a star tip to pipe a rosette in the center of each slice. Garnish with the snipped dill and serve.

Recognize a Good Cucumber

When you purchase cucumbers, they should be firm, including the ends. Cucumbers are best kept refrigerated in the produce drawer of your refrigerator until ready to use.

Bacon, Lettuce, and Tomato Cups

2 cucumbers, seedless variety
4 strips bacon
½ cup finely chopped romaine
   lettuce
⅛ cup finely diced tomato, flesh
   only, no seeds
⅛ cup shredded Cheddar cheese

¼ cup mayonnaise
¼ teaspoon seasoned salt
Freshly cracked black pepper, to
   taste
Chopped fresh parsley, for
   garnish

Serves 6

Carb Level: Low
Per serving:
Carbohydrate: 4g
Protein: 7g
Fat: 18g

This recipe
is very easy
to prep,
even though
it requires
some chop-
ping. Once
everything
is chopped
and lined up,
assembly is a
breeze.

1. To prepare the cucumbers, rinse under cool running water and pat dry. Trim off and discard about 1 inch from each end of both cucumbers (the ends are often bitter). You can either peel the cucumbers entirely or "stripe" them by leaving alternating strips of green peel.
2. Prepare 12 cucumber cups by cutting the cucumbers into slices about 1 to 1¼ inches thick; use a melon baller to scoop out the center of each slice, about ¾ inch deep. Place the cups upside down in a single layer on paper towels for about 10 minutes before using.
3. Place several layers of paper towels on a microwave-safe plate or tray and place the bacon strips in a single layer on top. Cover the bacon with a paper towel to prevent spattering. Microwave on medium-high at 1-minute intervals for a total of 3 to 4 minutes or until the bacon is crispy. Rotate the bacon ¼ turn at each cooking interval. (If cooking bacon on stovetop, cook until crispy and transfer to paper towels to drain.)
4. Chop the cooked bacon into a medium dice and transfer to a medium-sized mixing bowl. Add the lettuce, tomatoes, Cheddar, mayonnaise, salt, and pepper; lightly blend with a fork until evenly mixed. The mixture should be tossed until just combined, not mashed down with the fork.
5. To assemble, arrange the cups on a serving platter. Use a teaspoon to fill each cup with the bacon mixture until nicely mounded on the top. Garnish with chopped parsley and serve.

Herbed Goat Cheese and Black Olive Cucumber Cups

Serves 6

Carb Level: Low

Per serving:

Carbohydrate:	5g
Protein:	18g
Fat:	22g

Goat cheese crumbles are featured here, but feel free to substitute another favorite such as feta or blue cheese crumbles.

2 cucumbers, seedless variety
12 ounces herbed and seasoned goat cheese crumbles
4 ounces canned, pitted black California olives, drained and medium diced

2 tablespoons chopped fresh parsley, plus extra for garnish
2 tablespoons julienned fresh basil
Freshly cracked black pepper, to taste

1. To prepare the cucumbers, rinse under cool running water and pat dry. Trim off and discard about 1 inch from each end of both cucumbers (the ends are often bitter). You can either peel the cucumbers entirely or "stripe" them by leaving alternating strips of green peel.
2. Prepare 12 cucumber cups by cutting the cucumbers into slices about 1 to 1¼ inches thick; use a melon baller to scoop out the center, about three-fourths of the way down. Place the cups upside down in a single layer on paper towels for about 10 minutes before using.
3. Combine the goat cheese crumbles, olives, parsley, basil, and pepper in a medium-sized mixing bowl; toss with a fork until just combined.
4. To assemble, arrange the cups on a serving platter. Use a teaspoon to fill each cup with the goat cheese mixture until nicely mounded on the top. Garnish with chopped parsley and serve.

Are Cucumbers Nutritious?

A whole cucumber has only 2 grams of carbohydrates and 1 gram of protein with just a trace of fat. It is a highly efficient diet food.

Spicy Fiesta Chicken in Cucumber Cups

2 cucumbers, seedless variety
⅔ cup diced rotisserie chicken
⅓ cup shredded pepper jack or
    equivalent Mexican cheese
½ cup Frontera brand hot
    habanero salsa or equivalent
    quality spicy salsa

½ cup finely chopped romaine
    lettuce
2 tablespoons chopped fresh
    cilantro, plus extra for garnish
⅓ cup finely diced red onion
¼ teaspoon garlic salt

Serves 6

Carb Level: Low
Per serving:
Carbohydrate: 5g
Protein: 7g
Fat: 3g

---

1. To prepare the cucumbers, rinse under cool running water and pat dry. Trim off and discard about 1 inch from each end of the cucumbers (the ends are often bitter). You can either peel the cucumbers entirely or "stripe" them by leaving alternating strips of green peel.
2. Prepare 12 cucumber cups by cutting the cucumbers into slices about 1 to 1¼ inches thick; use a melon baller to scoop out the center, about three-fourths of the way down. Place the cups upside down in a single layer on paper towels for about 10 minutes before using.
3. Combine the chicken, cheese, salsa, lettuce, cilantro, onion, and garlic salt in a medium-sized mixing bowl; toss with a fork until just combined.
4. To assemble, arrange the cups on a serving platter. Use a teaspoon to fill each cup with the chicken mixture until nicely mounded on the top. Garnish with chopped cilantro leaves and serve.

Rotisserie chickens are now available in most medium-sized supermarkets. They are economical and usually provide enough for two full meals and leftovers.

Expand Your Storage Space

If you're having a party and you're limited on space, especially freezer and refrigerator space, consider using your washing machine as an ice chest. Fill the washer's basket with ice, cans, and bottles and you have a beverage replenishment center. After the party, run the spin cycle to drain the water.

Petite Salami Tortas

Serves 8

Carb Level: Low

Per serving:

Carbohydrate: 1g

Protein: 5g

Fat: 13g

These tortas
are easy
to make in
advance—just
cover and
refrigerate
until ready
to serve.
You can use
any variety
of imported
salamis,
including
mortadella.

*6 ounces cream cheese, at room
   temperature*
*4 teaspoons finely chopped oil-
   packed sun-dried tomatoes,
   with a touch of the oil*

12 slices Genoa salami
¼ cup julienned fresh basil
Freshly cracked pepper, to taste
16 toothpicks

1. Combine half of the cream cheese with the sun-dried tomatoes in a mini–food processor and process until smooth and evenly blended.
2. Lay out 4 of the salami slices on a work surface. Spread the sun-dried tomato mixture on top of the salami, dividing it evenly between the 4 slices. Top each with another piece of salami.
3. Divide the remaining cream cheese into 4 equal portions and spread on top of the salami "sandwiches." Sprinkle with the basil and top with the remaining salami slices. (Each salami torta should have 3 layers of salami and 2 layers of cream cheese.)
4. Use a serrated knife to cut each torta into quarters and spear each quarter with a toothpick. Garnish with fresh cracked pepper. Arrange on a serving platter and serve.

Spice It Up

Invest in a quality pepper grinder. The flavor of freshly cracked pepper is much cleaner and more intense than store-bought ground pepper. Read the directions on the pepper grinder, as many models are adjustable for the size of the grind.

Party Cheese Spread
with Blue Cheese and Olives

8 ounces cream cheese, at room temperature
4 ounces blue cheese crumbles
1 cup pitted canned black olives, drained
3 ounces scallions, dark green leaves removed, roughly chopped
1 tablespoon fresh-squeezed lemon juice
Freshly cracked black pepper, to taste
Chopped parsley, for garnish

Serves 8

Carb Level: Low
Per serving:
Carbohydrate: 3g
Protein: 5g
Fat: 16g

> You can make this spread in advance and form it into a ball or log and refrigerate until set.

1. Place the cream cheese, blue cheese, olives, scallions, lemon juice, and black pepper in a food processor fitted with a metal blade and process in pulses until just coarsely blended.
2. Use a spatula to transfer the mixture to a serving bowl if serving immediately. If you're preparing the spread in advance, transfer the mixture to a work surface lined with plastic wrap; form the spread into a ball or log and refrigerate until ready to serve. Garnish with fresh-chopped parsley and serve with carrot and celery sticks and whole-wheat crackers.

Serving Cheese

It is important to serve cheese at the proper temperature. Soft cheese should be taken out of the fridge about an hour before serving and hard cheeses should come out a little earlier. Do not put them by the oven or other heat source. Take out only as much cheese as will be eaten at one time, as repeated temperature changes alter the taste.

Curry Cayenne Peanuts

Serves 12

Carb Level: Low

Per serving:

Carbohydrate: 8g

Protein: 10g

Fat: 18g

The key to success here is a premium-quality curry powder and freshly shelled peanuts.

1 large egg white
2 tablespoons curry powder
1½ teaspoons kosher salt

Sugar substitute equal to 1
*   teaspoon granulated sugar*
¼ teaspoon cayenne pepper
3 cups unsalted peanuts, shelled

1. Preheat oven to 300°. Line 2 baking sheets with parchment paper.
2. In a medium-sized bowl, whip the egg white until frothy. Add the curry powder, salt, sugar substitute, and cayenne pepper; whisk until evenly blended. Add the peanuts and stir until evenly coated.
3. Spread the nuts in a single layer on the prepared baking sheets. Roast, uncovered, for about 20 minutes until the nuts are dry and toasted. Stir and turn the nuts at least 2 times during the roasting process. (Be very watchful during the last half of baking, as the nuts can burn quickly.) Remove the nuts from the oven and transfer them to a sheet of parchment paper to cool.

Fall Endive Spears

Serves 4

Carb Level: Low

Per serving:

Carbohydrate: 5g

Protein: 3g

Fat: 6g

This is an attractive hors d'oeuvre for a predinner reception.

8 Belgian endive spears
⅓ cup blue cheese crumbles
1 tablespoon roughly chopped
*   dried cherries or cranberries*

3 tablespoons roughly chopped
*   pecans*
¼ cup watercress sprigs

Fan the endive spears on a serving platter. Equally divide the blue cheese crumbles among the 8 spears, placing the cheese nearer to the base. Add a pinch of the dried cherries (or cranberries) and top with the chopped pecans. Garnish each spear with a sprig of watercress, and serve immediately.

Endive Spears with Herb Cheese

12 Belgian endive spears
6 ounces flavored Boursin cheese

Chopped fresh parsley or watercress sprigs, for garnish

Fan the endive spears on a serving platter. Spread about 1 teaspoon (½ ounce) of the Boursin cheese at the base of each spear. Garnish with chopped parsley (or watercress sprigs) and serve.

Got Boursin?

Boursin is a white, buttery triple-cream cheese that is very easy to spread and is usually flavored with herbs, garlic, or cracked pepper. If your supermarket does not carry Boursin cheese, substitute a flavored soft cheese.

Serves 6

Carb Level: Low
Per serving:
Carbohydrate: 3g
Protein: 3g
Fat: 12g

Make sure the endive spears are fresh, not brown at the edges.

Endive Spears with Hummus and Sprouts

16 Belgian endive spears
8 ounces traditional hummus or
flavored hummus

2 ounces sprouts (alfalfa or
radish)

Fan the endive spears on a serving platter. Spoon a teaspoonful of hummus on the base of each spear. Garnish with sprouts and serve.

Good Sprouts

There are a variety of sprouts available in the produce section—use a very fine sprout with a hint of green leaves, such as an alfalfa or radish sprout. Make sure you rinse them well under cold, running water and dry thoroughly with paper towels before using.

Serves 8

Carb Level: Low
Per serving:
Carbohydrate: 6g
Protein: 3g
Fat: 3g

There are many flavored hummus selections available at most super-markets.

Herb-Broiled Oysters

Serves 8

Carb Level: Low

Per serving:

Carbohydrate: 6g

Protein: 10g

Fat: 8g

The herb topping can be made a day in advance and kept refrigerated; bring to room temperature before using for ease of handling.

2 cloves garlic
1 tablespoon roughly chopped fresh parsley
1 tablespoon roughly chopped fresh tarragon
¼ teaspoon roughly chopped fresh thyme
¼ cup fresh bread crumbs
¼ cup butter, at room temperature
¼ teaspoon celery salt
3 cups coarse salt
16 oysters, shucked and on the half shell
Freshly cracked black pepper, to taste

1. Use a mini–food processor to mince the garlic cloves. Add the herbs, bread crumbs, butter, and celery salt; process until mixed. (Alternately, mince the garlic by hand and blend the ingredients with a fork.)
2. Position broiler rack about 4 inches from the heat source. Preheat oven broiler to medium.
3. Pour the coarse salt into a large ovenproof baking dish (or use a disposable tinfoil pan). The salt should be in an even layer about ½ inch thick. Place about 1½ teaspoons of the herbed butter mixture on top of each oyster. Place the oysters in a single layer, evenly spaced, in the salt bed, keeping them as level as possible.
4. Place the dish in the oven and broil for about 4 to 5 minutes until bubbly and just starting to brown. Garnish with fresh cracked pepper. Serve hot.

Entertaining Tip

You can supplement an hors d'oeuvres offering by including bowls of olives, nuts, and a simple presentation of cheeses. These healthy foods are all low in carbs and make great party food for anyone cutting carbs.

Shrimp Skewers with Pineapple

¾ pound cooked shrimp, peeled
   and deveined with tail on
   (about 16 pieces of 21–25
   count)
1 (8-ounce) can pineapple
   chunks in juice, drained

2 cups whole spinach leaves
16 skewers or toothpicks
1–2 tablespoons teriyaki sauce
Freshly cracked black pepper, to
   taste

Serves 8

Carb Level: Low
Per serving:
Carbohydrate: 5g
Protein: 9g
Fat: Trace

1. Wrap 1 shrimp and 1 pineapple chunk in a spinach leaf, with the shrimp tail sticking out, and fasten with a small skewer or toothpick. Repeat with the remaining skewers.
2. Arrange the skewers on a serving platter. Drizzle with teriyaki sauce and sprinkle with pepper. Use any leftover spinach leaves as a garnish on the serving platter, and serve immediately.

The Right Skewers

Try to find a fancy skewer to dress up the presentation. There are several types of decorative cocktail skewers on the market that are made from a bamboo twist or that have tiny ornaments glued on the ends. Since this is a no-cook recipe, you don't need to soak the skewers or worry about the decorations being heat proof.

Use a premium-quality teriyaki sauce; they vary widely in quality and carbohydrate counts. Also, try to use fresh-cooked shrimp instead of frozen if possible.

Asian Sesame Chicken Skewers

Serves 8

Carb Level: Low

Per serving:

Carbohydrate: 1g

Protein: 20g

Fat: 4g

You can make the marinade and trim the chicken a day ahead. Cook just before serving. This goes great with Thai Peanut Sauce (see page 29).

24–30 (6-inch) wooden skewers
½ cup canned low-sodium chicken stock
¼ cup chopped fresh cilantro, plus extra for garnish
2 tablespoons tamari or low-sodium soy sauce
2 tablespoons sesame oil
2 garlic cloves, minced
4–5 drops (or to taste) hot sauce
1½ pounds boneless, skinless chicken breasts (about 6 halves)
2 tablespoons (approximately) black sesame seeds, for garnish

1. Place the wooden skewers in a tall glass of water to soak for at least 15 minutes while preparing the chicken. (This will help prevent them from burning under the broiler.)
2. To make the marinade, combine the stock, cilantro, tamari, sesame oil, garlic, and hot sauce in a medium-sized bowl; whisk until blended.
3. Rinse the chicken under cold, running water and pat dry with paper towels. Cut the chicken into ½-inch-wide strips the length of the breast. You should have about 18 to 24 strips. (The strips will vary somewhat in size.) Add the chicken strips to the marinade, cover, and refrigerate for 15 minutes.
4. Just before preparing to serve, lightly oil a broiler rack and position it about 4 inches from the heat source. Preheat oven broiler to medium.
5. Remove the chicken strips from the marinade and discard the marinade. Thread one strip on a presoaked wooden skewer. Thread the remaining chicken on the remaining skewers. (Threading the chicken in the form of an S will help them stay on the skewer.)
6. Place the skewers on the broiler rack and broil for about 3 minutes. Turn the skewers over and broil for another 3 to 4 minutes, until the chicken is no longer pink. Remove from the oven and sprinkle with sesame seeds and chopped cilantro. Serve hot.

Thai Peanut Sauce

2 tablespoons water
¼ cup creamy peanut butter
2 tablespoons tamari
1 teaspoon red pepper flakes

2 teaspoons sesame oil
2 tablespoons chopped unsalted
   peanuts, for garnish (optional)

1. Place all the ingredients (except the peanuts) in the bowl of a food processor fitted with a metal blade or in a blender (or blend by hand with a sturdy whisk); cover and process until smooth. Add a little more water if necessary to adjust the consistency.
2. Place the sauce in a small serving bowl and garnish with the chopped peanuts.

Serves 4

Carb Level: Low
Per serving:
Carbohydrate: 8g
Protein: 11g
Fat: 21g

This is a great sauce for grilled or broiled chicken or beef skewers.

Spicy Roasted Garbanzos

2 tablespoons olive oil
½ teaspoon each: ground
   coriander, ground cumin, and
   red pepper flakes

¼ teaspoon seasoned salt
2 cups canned garbanzo beans
   (also called chickpeas), rinsed
   and drained

1. Preheat oven to 400°. Spray a nonstick baking sheet with nonstick spray and set aside.
2. Combine the oil and seasonings together in a medium-sized bowl. Add the garbanzo beans and toss until evenly coated. Spread out the beans in a single layer on the prepared baking sheet and place in the oven. Shake the pan every 10 minutes to make sure the beans are cooking evenly. Bake for 20 to 30 minutes, until crisp and golden. Let cool slightly before serving. Can be made the day before and kept in an airtight container.

Serves 8

Carb Level: Moderate
Per serving:
Carbohydrate: 14g
Protein: 3g
Fat: 4g

A little higher in carbs but a delicious fix to satisfy a craving for legumes.

Sweet and Spicy Mixed Nuts

Serves 12

Carb Level: Moderate

Per serving:

Carbohydrate: 13g

Protein: 6g

Fat: 22g

This is a great recipe for a party. The nuts are easy to make in quantity and can be stored in an airtight container.

¼ cup honey

1 tablespoon red pepper flakes

2 tablespoons olive oil

1 teaspoon kosher salt

½ teaspoon cayenne pepper

3 cups mixed nuts

1. Preheat oven to 300°.
2. Line a baking sheet with parchment paper and lightly oil the paper. Set aside the baking sheet.
3. Place all the ingredients except the mixed nuts in a medium-sized nonstick skillet over medium heat. Cook uncovered, stirring frequently, until the mixture reaches a syrup consistency, about 2 to 3 minutes. Add the nuts and gently fold them into the syrup mixture until evenly coated. Use a rubber spatula to make the mixing easier and take care not to break up the nuts.
4. Transfer the nuts to the prepared baking sheet and spread out in an even layer. Bake for about 20 minutes, stirring and turning the nuts about every 6 to 8 minutes. Be very watchful during the last half of baking, as the nuts can burn quickly. Serve warm or at room temperature.

How to Store Nuts

Store all nuts in the freezer in an airtight container. Nuts will hold in the freezer up to 4 months. Always taste nuts before using to make sure that they aren't on the verge of turning.

Ham Pinwheels with Ricotta and Almonds

½ cup ricotta cheese
¼ cup chopped parsley
½ teaspoon seasoned salt

Freshly cracked black pepper
½ pound deli ham, thinly sliced
¼ cup slivered almonds

Serves 4

Carb Level: Low
Per serving:
Carbohydrate: 3g
Protein: 15g
Fat: 19g

Roll these up
a day early—
wrap tightly
with plastic
wrap and
refrigerate.

1. Place the ricotta, half of the parsley, the seasoned salt, and pepper in a bowl and mix until just blended.
2. Place a ham slice on a work surface. Spoon the cheese filling in a line along one side of the slice, about 1 inch from the side nearest to you. Sprinkle with the slivered almonds and lightly press the nuts into the cheese mixture. Starting from the side nearest to you, roll the ham over the filling to form a cylinder. Insert the toothpicks at ½-inch intervals.
3. Just before serving, use a serrated knife to cut through the roll at the midpoint between each toothpick. Arrange the pinwheels on a platter and garnish with the remaining chopped parsley.

Trio of Caviar

2 ounces each: lumpfish caviar, salmon roe, and golden whitefish caviar
1 lemon, cut into 4 wedges, seeds removed

4 slices of bread, crusts removed and lightly toasted, cut into triangle quarters
¼ cup crème fraîche or sour cream
4 teaspoons minced white onion

Serves 4

Carb Level: Moderate
Per serving:
Carbohydrate: 16g
Protein: 13g
Fat: 13g

One spoonful
of caviar pro-
vides all the
daily require-
ment of B_{12}
for an adult.

1. Chill 4 salad plates. Just before you are ready to assemble the appetizer, remove the plates from the refrigerator. Place ½ ounce of each type of caviar on each plate, with each dollop just touching the others on the plate. Place a lemon wedge on each plate.
2. Stack 4 toast points on each plate and add a dollop of crème fraîche and 1 teaspoon of minced onion. Chill until ready to serve. Each of the 4 plates should look exactly alike for presentation.

Water Chestnuts and Bacon

Serves 4

Carb Level: Low

Per serving:

Carbohydrate: 1g

Protein: 9g

Fat: 14g

This is a great dish for a "stand-up" reception, as there is no sauce to worry about dripping.

1 (8-ounce) can whole water chestnuts, drained

¼ pound bacon, cut into 1-by-4-inch strips

1 teaspoon peeled, grated fresh ginger or jarred minced ginger

1. Preheat broiler.
2. Wrap each water chestnut with a piece of bacon, and fasten with a toothpick. Place on a baking sheet and dab a little of the ginger on each. Broil on the top rack for about 3 minutes or until the bacon is crispy, turning once. Arrange on a serving platter and serve hot.
3. To cook in the microwave, line a microwaveable plate or tray with several layers of paper towels. Place bacon-wrapped water chestnuts on the paper towels, evenly spaced. Place in the microwave and cover with a few paper towels to keep the bacon from spattering. Microwave on high in 30-second intervals until the bacon is crisp. Rotate the plate ¼ turn at each interval to ensure even cooking.

Storing Bacon

To store unused, uncooked bacon, roll each piece up lengthwise and freeze in a plastic bag. You can then remove only the number of pieces you'll need for the next recipe.

Farmers' Market Radishes with Watercress Butter

10 radishes, washed and dried
4 tablespoons unsalted butter, at room temperature
1 cup watercress leaves
1 garlic clove

⅛ teaspoon salt
Freshly cracked black pepper, to taste
Pastry bag and plain tip

Serves 10

Carb Level: Low
Per serving:
Carbohydrate: Trace
Protein: Trace
Fat: 5g

1. Wash and trim the root end from each radish. Trim the stems from the top of the radish, leaving a few stems and leaves for decoration only if they are fresh and look appealing; otherwise, trim off the stems to the top of the radish. Split the radishes in half from top to bottom (stem end to root end). Trim a small slice from the rounded bottom of each radish so they will sit upright.
2. Blend the remaining ingredients in a mini–food processor or blender until thoroughly mixed and smooth.
3. Fill a pastry bag with the butter mixture and pipe a thin line down the center of each radish half. If you do not have a pastry bag, use a very small pastry knife or butter knife to spread a thin layer of the butter across the radish half. Complete the process with the remaining radish halves. Serve immediately.

The watercress butter can be stored in the freezer, tightly wrapped, for up to two weeks.

Radish Variety

There are many varieties of radishes available at the summer farmers' market and specialty produce stores. The watercress butter is especially good when paired with French breakfast radishes.

Cocktail Pecans

Serves 8

Carb Level: Low

Per serving:

Carbohydrate: 5g

Protein: 2g

Fat: 21g

Buy nuts in
bulk and store
unused or
uncooked nuts
in an airtight
container in
the freezer
for up to two
months.

2 tablespoons unsalted butter
1½ tablespoons Worcestershire
  sauce
2 cups pecan halves

1 teaspoon kosher salt
Freshly cracked black pepper, to
  taste

1. Preheat oven to 350°. Line a baking sheet with parchment paper and set aside.
2. In a medium-sized nonstick skillet, melt the butter and add the Worcestershire. Add the nuts, salt, and pepper. Cook over medium heat, stirring frequently, until the nuts are evenly coated.
3. Transfer the nuts to the prepared baking sheet and roast for 8 to 10 minutes, shaking the baking sheet frequently to cook the nuts evenly. Transfer to several layer of paper towels to drain. Adjust seasoning as needed. Let cool, and store in an airtight container until ready to serve. If the nuts need to be "crisped," place them on a baking sheet and bake in a preheated 350° oven for about 3 minutes, shaking the baking sheet once or twice.

Write It Down

Keep an inventory list on the outside of your freezer door. It will save on energy because you won't have to open the door to look for items. The list is easily updated whenever you add or use something. Tie a string to a pen and attach it nearby for convenience.

Beef Tenderloin Bites with Creamy Horseradish Sauce

¼ cup prepared horseradish
½ cup sour cream
2 (6-ounce) filet mignon steaks
1½ tablespoons olive oil
¼ teaspoon kosher salt

Freshly cracked black pepper
12 Asian soup spoons
12 toothpicks
Chopped fresh parsley,
  for garnish

1. In a small bowl, mix together the horseradish and sour cream. Set aside.
2. Cut each steak into 6 pieces as evenly sized as possible. Transfer to a medium-sized bowl and toss with 1 tablespoon of the olive oil, salt, and pepper until evenly coated.
3. Heat the remaining ½ tablespoon of olive oil in a nonstick sauté pan over medium-high heat. When very hot, but not smoking, add the beef cubes and sear on each side for about 1 minute per side for rare, about 1½ minutes per side for medium.
4. Transfer the meat to a plate and tent with tinfoil to keep warm. Let rest for about 7 minutes to allow the juices to reabsorb.
5. To serve, arrange the spoons on a serving platter. Use a toothpick to spear a piece of meat and place it on one of the spoons; continue with the remaining pieces. Drizzle any remaining beef juices over each piece. Add a dollop of the horseradish sauce just to the side of each piece of beef. Garnish with the chopped parsley and serve warm.

This is a delicious and impressive appetizer—well worth the cost. The horseradish sauce can be made a day or two in advance and kept refrigerated.

How Do You Like It?

The beef tenderloin can be bought in 6-ounce steaks, already trimmed and ready to cook. If you like your beef rare, leave the steaks in the refrigerator until ready to cook. If you like your beef more well done, let the steaks come to room temperature before cooking. The internal temperature of the meat before cooking will help control the final outcome.

Sesame Shrimp with Seaweed Salad

Serves 6

Carb Level: Low

Per serving:

Carbohydrate: 1g

Protein: 12g

Fat: 3g

This is a flavorful and colorful appetizer—best of all, no cooking required. Seaweed salad is available at many large supermarkets and Asian specialty stores.

12 Asian soup spoons
12 toothpicks
¾ pound cooked, peeled, and deveined shrimp, tail on (21–25 count)

1 tablespoon toasted sesame oil
⅓ cup seaweed salad
Freshly cracked black pepper
Black sesame seeds

1. To serve, arrange the spoons on a serving platter.
2. Use a toothpick to spear each shrimp and place one on each spoon. Top each shrimp with several drops of toasted sesame oil to taste, then top with a dollop of seaweed salad and a sprinkling of pepper. Garnish with sesame seeds and serve.

Serve It on Spoons

Spoons are an attractive and easy carrier for a variety of elegant appetizers. If there is a local Chinatown or Asian market in your area, stop by and see their offerings. Even the Asian grocery stores offer a selection of ceramics and kitchen supplies. The flat-bottomed Asian soup spoons work as an hors d'oeuvre server and are available in plastic or ceramic, ranging in price from about a quarter to $3 each. Find a pattern that you like and buy a dozen or so to have on hand. They're reusable and most are dishwasher safe. They are great carriers for a bite of meat with a sauce. Remember to use a toothpick for larger bites of meat or seafood.

Sausage Bites with Mascarpone Pesto

1 clove garlic
½ cup fresh basil leaves, stems
*   removed*
3 tablespoons olive oil
2 tablespoons shredded
*   Parmesan*
3 ounces unflavored mascarpone
*   cheese or cream cheese, at*
*   room temperature*

1–2 tablespoons heavy cream
⅛ teaspoon salt
Freshly cracked pepper, to taste
1 pound hot Italian sausage
*   links, cut into 12–18 even-*
*   sized pieces*
12–18 toothpicks
12–18 Asian soup spoons
Julienned fresh basil

Serves 6

Carb Level: Low
Per serving:
Carbohydrate: 2g
Protein: 12g
Fat: 39g

These bites
are served
hot from the
pan with
a creamy
mascarpone
pesto sauce.
Substitute
cream cheese
if mascar-
pone is not
available.

1. Fit the bowl of a food processor with the metal blade. With the motor running, drop the garlic clove through the feed tube. Add the basil, olive oil, and Parmesan, and process until somewhat smooth. Add a little more oil if needed. The basil should be a pastelike consistency. Add the mascarpone and process, scraping down the sides of the bowl as needed. With the motor running, add 1 tablespoon of the cream, the salt, and pepper. The pesto should be thick but pourable. Add more cream, little by little, until the proper consistency is achieved. Taste and adjust seasoning as needed. Set aside.
2. Heat a medium-sized nonstick sauté pan over medium-high heat. Add the sausage pieces and cook, stirring occasionally to prevent sticking. Cover the pan and cook through, about 12 to 14 minutes.
3. To serve, spear each sausage piece with a toothpick and place it on one of the spoons. Drizzle about 1 teaspoon of the mascarpone pesto over each sausage piece. Garnish with julienned basil and serve warm.

Keep Herbs Fresh

To store fresh herbs for maximum life, remove them from their store container and snip the ends of the stem. Fill a small jar with cold water and add the herbs, just as you would put flowers in a vase. Store in the refrigerator and change the water at least every other day.

Oysters with Horseradish

Serves 4

Carb Level: Low

Per serving:

Carbohydrate: 2g
Protein: 2g
Fat: 6g

Many fish markets sell fresh-shucked oysters, which eliminates just about all the work for this recipe.

⅛ cup prepared horseradish
¼ cup heavy cream
⅛ teaspoon seasoned salt
12 fresh-shucked oysters

Freshly cracked black pepper, to taste
12 Asian soup spoons
1 lemon, cut into wedges and seeded

1. Combine the horseradish, cream, and seasoned salt in a small bowl; mix until blended and set aside.
2. Just before serving, place an oyster with a few drops of its liquor on each spoon. Add a dollop of the horseradish cream to the top of each oyster. Top with a few turns of fresh-cracked pepper. Serve with lemon wedges on the side.

Buying Fresh-Shucked Oysters

Make sure the oysters are fresh; ask the clerk when they were delivered. They should have a clean smell. Make sure you gently "sort" through the oysters to check for any stray pieces of shell. It's advisable to wear latex gloves when working with and serving raw seafood, and make sure the oysters stay chilled throughout the process. You can place the oyster container on an ice-filled bowl to ensure they stay cold.

Five-Spice Tuna with Wasabi Aioli

1 teaspoon five-spice powder
2 tablespoons olive oil, divided
¾-pound tuna steak
1 teaspoon wasabi powder

¼ cup mayonnaise
12 toothpicks
12 Asian soup spoons
1 tablespoon tamari

Serves 6

Carb Level: Low
Per serving:
Carbohydrate: Trace
Protein: 14g
Fat: 15g

1. Combine the five-spice powder and 1 tablespoon of the olive oil in a medium-sized bowl and set aside.
2. Place the tuna on a very clean work surface and cut into 12 evenly sized pieces, cutting against the grain where possible. Transfer the tuna pieces to the five-spice mixture and toss until evenly coated; place in the refrigerator.
3. In a small bowl, combine the wasabi powder with a few drops of water until blended. Add the mayonnaise and mix until evenly blended. Set aside.
4. Heat a medium-sized nonstick skillet over medium-high heat and add the remaining tablespoon of olive oil. When very hot, but not smoking, add the tuna pieces. Quickly sear on each side, stirring frequently. The inside should be rare and the outside should be seared.
5. Transfer the tuna to a clean bowl. Spear each piece of tuna with a toothpick and place on a spoon. Sprinkle the tuna with a few drops of tamari and a dollop of the wasabi aioli. Serve warm.

Buy the best-quality tuna steak for this recipe. This is a very simple recipe and the quality of the products really shows through.

Stay Sharp

If you store your knives in a knife block, always keep them cutting-side up. If the cutting side is down and against the wood, you'll dull them a little bit each time you remove them. This storage method will also save wear and tear on your knife block.

Greek Islands Feta and Herb Spread

Serves 6

Carb Level: Low

Per serving:

Carbohydrate: 3g

Protein: 6g

Fat: 13g

This tangy Greek-inspired dip is delicious with sliced jicama chips. Add toasted pita chips if this is for a mixed dietary crowd.

2 tablespoons olive oil
2 teaspoons fresh-squeezed lime juice
½ teaspoon chopped fresh rosemary
1 teaspoon dried Italian seasoning
¼ teaspoon garlic salt
Freshly cracked black pepper, to taste
6 ounces crumbled feta cheese
8 ounces plain yogurt
Chopped fresh parsley, for garnish

1. Combine the olive oil, lime juice, rosemary, Italian seasoning, garlic salt, and pepper in a serving bowl. Set aside at room temperature for 20 minutes to allow the flavors of the dried herbs to blossom.
2. Add the feta and yogurt to the seasoning mixture and combine thoroughly. Refrigerate until ready to use. Sprinkle with chopped parsley just before serving.

Freeze!

How much ice will you need when entertaining? You can calculate 1 pound of ice per person for a cocktail reception. This does not include ice that you'll use to chill beverages beforehand.

Deli Turkey Cobb Salad with Vinaigrette

Serves 4

Carb Level: Moderate

Per serving:

Carbohydrate:	14g
Protein:	52g
Fat:	60g

Microwave the bacon and have a few hard-boiled eggs in the fridge.

6 cups chopped romaine hearts
¾ pound honey-roasted turkey breast, sliced and cut into ½-inch strips
¾ pound ham, sliced and cut into ½-inch strips
½ cup cooked bacon crumbles
¾ cup blue cheese crumbles
¾ cup seeded and diced tomatoes
¾ cup diced hard-boiled eggs
Freshly cracked black pepper, to taste
1 cup Cobb Salad Vinaigrette (see below)

Place the lettuce in a large salad bowl or on a large serving platter. Arrange the meats, cheese, tomatoes, and eggs on top of the lettuce in neatly arranged rows. Sprinkle with pepper. Serve the dressing on the side and enjoy!

Cobb Salad Vinaigrette

Serves 8

Carb Level: Low

Per serving:

Carbohydrate:	1g
Protein:	Trace
Fat:	18g

Homemade vinaigrettes just taste better than the store-bought varieties.

¼ cup cider vinegar
2 tablespoons fresh-squeezed lemon juice
Sugar substitute equal to 1 teaspoon granulated sugar (optional)
½ teaspoon salt
½ teaspoon freshly cracked black pepper
1 tablespoon Dijon mustard
⅔ cup extra-virgin olive oil

Combine the vinegar, lemon juice, sugar substitute (if using), salt, pepper, and mustard in a container or jar with cover and shake vigorously to combine. Add the oil and shake until emulsified. Alternatively, combine all the ingredients in a food processor and process until creamy. Use immediately or refrigerate overnight. Bring to room temperature before using.

Greek Feta Salad

3 tablespoons fresh-squeezed
   lemon juice
½ cup olive oil
½ tablespoon dried
   Mediterranean spice blend
¼ teaspoon salt
Red pepper flakes, to taste
1 cup crumbled feta cheese

2 cups peeled, seeded, and sliced
   cucumbers
¼ cup thinly sliced scallions
½ cup pitted kalamata olives
½ cup pepperoncini, drained, whole
6 cups romaine hearts, chopped
½ cup halved cherry tomatoes

In a large mixing bowl, combine the lemon juice, oil, spices, seasonings, and cheese; mix until well combined. Add the remaining ingredients and toss until evenly coated. To serve, divide equally among 4 chilled salad plates.

Serves 4

Carb Level: Moderate
Per serving:

Carbohydrate:	17g
Protein:	12g
Fat:	44g

Add a pound of cooked gyro meat on top of this salad for a hearty one-plate meal.

Watercress, Basil, and Goat Cheese Salad

2 tablespoons raspberry vinegar
½ teaspoon Dijon mustard
2 tablespoons extra-virgin
   olive oil
¼ teaspoon kosher salt
Freshly cracked black pepper

1 tablespoon sliced black olives
1 cup watercress leaves, stems
   removed
1 cup fresh basil leaves, stems
   removed
2 ounces goat cheese, crumbled

In a medium-sized bowl, whisk together the vinegar, mustard, olive oil, salt, and pepper. Add the olives, watercress, basil, and goat cheese; lightly toss to combine. Taste and adjust seasoning as needed.

Serves 2

Carb Level: Low
Per serving:

Carbohydrate:	2g
Protein:	7g
Fat:	15g

An elegant salad when served with a piece of grilled fish.

Fennel Salad with Garlic Oil

Serves 4

Carb Level: Low

Per serving:

Carbohydrate: 3g

Protein: 1g

Fat: 27g

This is an elegant entrée salad when topped with a skewer of grilled shrimp or a trio of pan-sautéed scallops.

½ cup olive oil, divided
2 garlic cloves, peeled and lightly
   crushed
1 cup sliced fennel bulb

¼ teaspoon kosher salt
Freshly cracked black pepper
1 teaspoon lemon zest
4 cups baby spinach greens

1. Combine half the olive oil and the garlic in a small nonstick skillet over medium heat. Cook until the garlic begins to sizzle. Remove the garlic with a slotted spoon and discard. Add the fennel and quickly stir-fry to coat with oil and just warm through, about 1 to 2 minutes.
2. Remove the skillet from the heat and add the remaining oil, the salt, pepper, and lemon zest to the hot oil.
3. To serve, equally divide the greens among 4 salad plates. Use a slotted spoon to remove the fennel. Equally divide the fennel and place in the center of the greens. Serve the garlic oil on the side.

Green Facts

Occasionally greens are very sandy. The quickest way to clean greens is to fill a large bowl with cold water, add the greens, and gently swish them around until the sand settles on the bottom. Change the water and repeat the process until the water stays clear.

Iceberg Lettuce with Blue Cheese Dressing

½ pound iceberg lettuce, cored
    and cut into 6 wedges
3 ounces blue cheese,
    crumbled
¼ cup buttermilk
¼ cup sour cream
¼ cup mayonnaise
1 tablespoon white wine
    vinegar

¼ teaspoon honey
⅛ teaspoon garlic powder
½ teaspoon seasoned salt
¼ teaspoon ground black pepper
1 cup peeled, seeded, and sliced
    cucumber
2 cups medium-ripe tomato
    wedges

Serves 6

Carb Level: Low
Per serving:
Carbohydrate: 6g
Protein: 5g
Fat: 14g

Serve this salad with a grilled steak and creamed spinach. If you don't have a food processor, you can use a fork to blend the dressing in a small bowl.

1. Rinse the lettuce wedges under cold water. Keep the lettuce in wedges and place on a cloth towel to dry.
2. Combine the blue cheese, buttermilk, sour cream, mayonnaise, vinegar, honey, garlic powder, salt, and pepper in the bowl of a food processor fitted with a metal blade. Pulse until blended but some blue cheese crumbles still remain.
3. To serve, place a lettuce wedge on each salad plate. Arrange the cucumber slices and tomato wedges around the lettuce. Spoon dressing over each wedge of lettuce. Serve immediately.

Storing Greens

Never store greens with rubber bands, twist ties, tape, or twine. These restraints cut the circulation of nutrients through the leaves and speed up decay. Remove the shipping restraints and remove and discard any discolored or damaged leaves. Wrap in slightly damp paper towels in a perforated plastic bag.

Chinese Chicken Salad

Serves 4

Carb Level: Moderate

Per serving:

Carbohydrate:	12g
Protein:	12g
Fat:	24g

This is a hearty salad and an excellent use for leftover chicken. Serve on a bed of baby greens with a drizzle of the extra dressing on the side.

¼ cup bean sprouts
⅓ cup rice vinegar
¼ cup peanut oil
1 tablespoon soy sauce
3 tablespoons hoisin sauce
1 tablespoon minced fresh ginger
¾ pound cooked skinless chicken, cut into ⅓-inch dice

2 cups sliced napa cabbage (cut crosswise into ¼-inch-thick shreds)
¼ cup sliced scallions
¼ cup sliced water chestnuts, rinsed and drained
½ cup chopped unsalted dry-roasted peanuts

1. Place the bean sprouts in a bowl of ice water to cover. Combine the vinegar, oil, soy sauce, hoisin, and ginger in a large bowl and whisk to combine. Remove ½ cup dressing from the bowl and set aside. Add the chicken, cabbage, scallions, and water chestnuts to the bowl and mix to combine. Add more dressing as needed to achieve desired consistency.
2. Transfer the bean sprouts to paper towels to drain. To serve, divide the chicken salad among 4 salad plates. Garnish with bean sprouts and chopped peanuts. Serve any extra dressing on the side.

Salad Additions

Consider adding a tablespoon of toasted sunflower seeds on top of your salad in place of croutons. One tablespoon of sunflower seeds is worth 1g of carbohydrates. Roasted pumpkin seeds are worth 2g of carbohydrates for a 1-tablespoon serving.

Warm Calamari Salad with Tomatoes

½ cup olive oil, divided
1 tablespoon minced garlic
1 pound calamari
½ teaspoon kosher salt
Freshly cracked black pepper, to taste
½ cup dry white wine

⅛–¼ cup fresh-squeezed lemon juice
1 cup seeded and diced tomatoes (about ½-inch dice)
¼ cup chopped fresh parsley
4 cups baby spinach salad leaves

Serves 4

Carb Level: Low
Per serving:
Carbohydrate: 8g
Protein: 19g
Fat: 19g

Squid should be purple to white in color, have a clean smell, and the skin should be shiny. The frozen calamari on the market is usually quite good.

1. Preheat oven to 350°.
2. Heat 3 tablespoons of the oil along with the garlic in an ovenproof, medium to large nonstick skillet over medium heat. Add the squid and sauté for 1 minute. Transfer the skillet to the oven to finish cooking, about 3 minutes. (Calamari is done when is evenly opaque, but tender when pierced with the tip of a knife.)
3. Transfer the skillet to the stovetop over medium heat (remember that the handle is hot). Season with salt and pepper and add the wine. Bring to a simmer, stirring frequently. Use tongs to transfer the calamari to a plate and tent with tinfoil to keep warm.
4. Add ⅛ cup of the lemon juice to the pan and simmer until reduced by half, about 3 to 4 minutes. Add the tomatoes, parsley, and spinach, and return the squid to the pan. Toss until just mixed; the spinach should be just wilted. Transfer to serving plates and drizzle with remaining olive oil. Taste and adjust seasoning as needed, adding more lemon juice if desired.

Olive Oil Facts

Extra-virgin olive oil is the first cold pressing of the olives and is only 1 percent acid. Cold pressing is the best method for extracting olive oil; it is a chemical-free process that uses only pressure, which naturally produces a low level of acidity. Virgin olive oil contains 1 to 5 percent acidity and is produced from subsequent cold pressings.

Green Beans and Jicama Salad

Serves 2

Carb Level: Moderate

Per serving:

Carbohydrate: 14g

Protein: 2g

Fat: 14g

You can use
frozen beans
in a pinch.

1 tablespoon salt
6 ounces green beans, trimmed
2 tablespoons red wine vinegar
3 tablespoons lime juice
2 tablespoons extra-virgin olive oil
1 teaspoon ground cumin

2 tablespoons chopped cilantro
¼ cup diced ripe tomato (about
   ½-inch dice)
4 ounces jicama, peeled and cut
   into matchsticks

1. Fill a medium-sized saucepan with water and add the salt; bring to a boil over medium-high heat. Add the beans and cook until bright green and crisp-tender, about 5 minutes. Drain and set aside.
2. In a medium-sized bowl, combine the vinegar, lime juice, olive oil, and cumin; whisk until blended. Add the cilantro, tomato, jicama, and beans, and lightly toss until evenly coated. Transfer to a platter for serving.

Cucumber Salad with Chicken

Serves 4

Carb Level: Low

Per serving:

Carbohydrate: 7g

Protein: 37g

Fat: 14g

You can use
store-bought
rotisserie
chicken
or substi-
tute cooked
shrimp.

¼ cup tamari
2 tablespoons unseasoned
   rice wine
2 tablespoons mirin
2 tablespoons sesame oil
½ teaspoon ground cayenne
   pepper
Salt, to taste

½ cup sliced red onion
2 cups seeded and diced English
   cucumber (unpeeled)
1 pound shredded cooked
   chicken
2 tablespoons toasted sesame
   seeds

1. Combine the tamari, rice wine, mirin, sesame oil, cayenne, and salt in a medium-sized nonreactive bowl. Taste and adjust seasoning as desired. Add the red onion and cucumber, and lightly toss to combine.
2. To serve, place the cucumber salad on a serving plate. Top with the cooked chicken and garnish with sesame seeds.

Jicama and Red Cabbage Salad

¼ teaspoon anise seeds
1 tablespoon vegetable oil
2 tablespoons fresh-squeezed
   lime juice
¼ teaspoon Dijon mustard
Pinch salt

Jicama, peeled and cut into
   matchsticks to yield ½ cup
½ cup shredded red cabbage
2 tablespoons chopped fresh
   parsley
Freshly cracked black pepper

Serves 2

Carb Level: Low
Per serving:
Carbohydrate: 6g
Protein: 1g
Fat: 7g

1. Heat the anise seeds in a small, dry skillet over high heat until fragrant, about 1 minute, flipping the seeds to avoid scorching. Transfer to a mortar and crush with a pestle or place in a sealable plastic bag and crush with a mallet.
2. In a large bowl, combine the crushed anise seeds with the vegetable oil, lime juice, mustard, and salt. Add the jicama, red cabbage, and parsley, and toss thoroughly. Sprinkle with pepper. Taste and adjust seasoning as needed.

This salad is a great addition to any grilled dinner. It's great to take to a potluck picnic, as it holds up well.

Salads and Kitchen Equipment

Invest in a quality salad spinner, sharp paring knife, chef's knife, plastic Asian mandoline, grater, and small food processor. These basic pieces will allow you to produce just about any type of salad recipe.

Arugula Salad with Summer Squash

Serves 6

Carb Level: Low

Per serving:

Carbohydrate: 6g

Protein: 13g

Fat: 26g

This takes advantage of economical zucchini and yellow squash.

¼ cup extra-virgin olive oil

2 tablespoons lemon juice

1 tablespoon minced shallot

¼ teaspoon salt

⅛ teaspoon black pepper

1 pound green and yellow summer squash, sliced

4 lightly packed cups roughly chopped arugula

¼ packed cup fresh basil leaves, torn into small pieces

5 ounces goat cheese, crumbled

Combine the oil, lemon juice, shallot, salt, and pepper in a large non-reactive bowl and whisk to mix. Add the squash, toss to coat, and let stand for 3 minutes. Add the arugula and basil and toss to combine. Arrange the salad on a serving platter or individual chilled plates and sprinkle with the goat cheese. Serve immediately.

Smoked Turkey and Hazelnut Salad

Serves 4

Carb Level: Moderate

Per serving:

Carbohydrate: 13g

Protein: 50g

Fat: 47g

You can substitute smoked chicken in this salad.

3 cups sliced smoked turkey breast

½ cup coarsely chopped skin-ned and toasted hazelnuts

1 cup thinly sliced celery

½ cup halved seedless green grapes

½ cup halved seedless red grapes

½ cup mayonnaise

¼ cup plain yogurt

1 tablespoon honey

1 tablespoon fresh-squeezed lemon juice

½ teaspoon ground ginger

⅛ teaspoon salt

Freshly cracked black pepper

1. In a large mixing bowl, combine the turkey, half the hazelnuts, the celery, and grapes. Set aside.
2. In a small mixing bowl, combine the remaining ingredients except the remaining hazelnuts. Add the dressing mixture to the turkey and lightly toss to coat. Serve on chilled plates and garnish with the remaining hazelnuts.

Filet Mignon Caesar

2 (6-ounce) filet mignons, each
    wrapped in a strip of bacon
½ teaspoon kosher salt
½ teaspoon freshly ground black
    pepper
2 cups roughly chopped hearts of
    romaine

2 tablespoons freshly grated
    Parmesan cheese
¼ cup prepared Caesar dressing
6 anchovy fillets, drained and
    rolled into pinwheels

Serves 2

Carb Level: Low
Per serving:
Carbohydrate: 8g
Protein: 41g
Fat: 59g

1. Pat the steaks dry with paper towels. Lightly season the steaks with salt and pepper. Heat an indoor grill pan or a sauté pan over medium-high heat. Cook the steaks to desired doneness, 4 to 6 minutes per side for medium-rare. Transfer the filets to a plate and tent with tinfoil to keep warm.
2. Toss together the lettuce, half of the dressing, and the Parmesan cheese. Add additional dressing to achieve desired consistency. To serve, divide the salad between 2 dinner plates. Add a hot filet and 3 of the anchovies to each plate.

Bottles Dressings Vs. Homemade

There are a number of great bottled dressings available in the refrigerated section of your grocer. Read the labels. Many of the dressings are loaded with unnecessary saturated fats and many are packed with sugars and salt. It's worth experimenting with your own homemade vinaigrettes to come up with your personal healthy favorite.

For ease and convenience, this recipe uses a commercial Caesar dressing. You can substitute your favorite homemade dressing if you desire.

Sirloin Steak Salad

Serves 2

Carb Level: Low

Per serving:

Carbohydrate:	10g
Protein:	24g
Fat:	26g

Increase the amount of steak if you have larger appetites at the table. Use a stovetop grill pan for great results for the steak and vegetables.

2 teaspoons olive oil
8 ounces top sirloin, 1 inch thick
Salt and fresh-cracked black pepper, to taste
¼ cup sliced scallions (2-inch pieces)
½ cup red pepper strips (about ¼-inch strips)
1 tablespoon soy sauce
1 tablespoon red wine vinegar
1 teaspoon sesame oil
1 teaspoon minced fresh ginger
¼ teaspoon kosher salt
4 cups salad greens, rinsed and dried

1. Heat the oil in a large nonstick skillet over medium-high heat. Season the steak with salt and pepper.
2. Place the meat, scallions, and red peppers in the hot skillet and cook until the vegetables begin to brown and the steak is medium-rare, about 10 minutes total, turning the steak once and stirring the vegetables occasionally. Transfer the cooked meat and vegetables to a plate and tent with tinfoil to keep warm. Let the meat rest for 5 minutes to allow the juices to reabsorb.
3. Combine the soy sauce, vinegar, sesame oil, ginger, and kosher salt in a salad bowl and whisk to combine. Add the greens and toss with the dressing. Divide between 2 large dinner plates.
4. Slice the meat against the grain into very thin slices. Fan the meat over the salad greens and arrange the cooked scallions and peppers alongside the meat.

Flavored Vinegars

There is a variety of fruit and herb vinegars available, including raspberry, tarragon, dill, hot chili, and other specialty blends. These flavored vinegars are generally used for specific applications.

Spinach Salad with Shrimp and Roasted Pepper Vinaigrette

¾ cup sliced almonds

9 ounces (about 8 lightly packed cups) baby spinach

5 tablespoons extra-virgin olive oil, divided

1 pound medium-sized shrimp, peeled and deveined (tail optional)

Salt, to taste

4 ounces jarred roasted red peppers, drained and cut into thin strips (about ½ cup)

¼ cup thinly sliced shallots

⅛ teaspoon ground black pepper

1½ tablespoons sherry vinegar

Serves 4

Carb Level: Moderate
Per serving:
Carbohydrate: 11g
Protein: 26g
Fat: 32g

It's important to use spinach leaves in this salad. Normal salad greens won't stand up to the warm vinaigrette dressing.

1. Toast the almonds in a large nonstick skillet over medium heat until lightly browned, about 3 minutes. Shake the pan frequently and turn the almonds to prevent scorching. Place the spinach in a serving bowl and sprinkle the almonds on top.

2. In a large skillet over medium-high heat, add 2 tablespoons of the oil, add the shrimp, and cook until just starting to turn pink, about 1½ minutes. Turn the shrimp over and cook through (the center will be opaque), about 45 seconds. Transfer the shrimp to a plate, season with salt, and set aside.

3. Lower the heat to medium and add the remaining 3 tablespoons oil, the red peppers, shallots, ¼ teaspoon salt, and pepper. Cook until the shallots soften, about 2 minutes. Remove from heat and whisk in the vinegar. Pour the warm dressing over the spinach and toss. Divide the spinach salad among 4 plates and arrange the shrimp on top. Serve immediately.

Bag It

There are many convenience packages of salad greens available in the produce section of your grocer. Take a minute to read the labels, because many of the newer greens additions are actually "kits" that contain everything to make the salad, including hidden carbs.

Antipasti Salad

Serves 4

Carb Level: Moderate
Per serving:
Carbohydrate: 12g
Protein: 18g
Fat: 27g

This recipe takes advantage of the convenience of the deli and salad bar. Substitute a few of your personal favorites for the selections here.

¼ pound Genoa salami, thinly sliced and cut into quarters
¼ pound pepperoni, thinly sliced and cut into quarters
¼ pound sopressata, thinly sliced and cut into quarters
⅛ pound mozzarella, thinly sliced and cut into quarters
⅛ pound provolone, thinly sliced and cut into quarters
½ cup pepperoncini, drained, left whole
¼ cup thinly sliced red onion
½ cup halved cherry tomatoes
¼ cup sliced black olives
½ cup assorted color bell pepper strips
½ cup sliced mushrooms
12 ounces baby spinach leaves
⅓ cup Italian dressing
Parmesan shavings
Dried Italian seasoning, for garnish

Put the meats, cheeses, vegetables, and spinach in a large mixing bowl and lightly toss to combine. Slowly drizzle with the Italian dressing, continuing to toss. The salad should be very lightly dressed (reserve leftover dressing for another use). Transfer the salad to a serving bowl and garnish with Parmesan shavings and Italian herbs.

Supermarket Convenience

Take advantage of the salad bar and the deli for preprepped vegetables for your salad. While the cost may initially seem expensive, remember: no waste, no leftovers, no prep time. It actually may be cost-effective in the long run.

Asian-Style Eggplant on Spinach

2 tablespoons soy sauce
1½ teaspoons Asian sesame oil
Sugar substitute equal to 1
   teaspoon granulated sugar
2 tablespoons thinly sliced
   scallions
3 tablespoons, plus 1 teaspoon
   peanut oil

1 pound eggplant, peeled and cut
   into ½-inch dice
1 tablespoon minced fresh ginger
2 tablespoons minced garlic
12 ounces baby spinach leaves
2 tablespoons chopped unsalted
   dry-roasted peanuts
½ lime, cut into wedges

Serves 4

Carb Level: Low
Per serving:
Carbohydrate: 8g
Protein: 4g
Fat: 14g

Try drizzling a light vinaigrette, such as the Creamy Asian Dressing (see page 60), over the spinach.

1. In a small bowl, mix the soy sauce, sesame oil, sugar substitute, and scallions; set aside. Heat 3 tablespoons of the oil in a large nonstick skillet over medium-high heat. Add the eggplant and cook until soft and browned, stirring often, about 9 minutes.
2. Make a well in the center of the eggplant and add the ginger, garlic, and the remaining 1 teaspoon of oil to the center. Cook until fragrant, about 15 seconds. Stir together with the eggplant. Remove the pan from the heat, add the soy mixture, and toss to coat.
3. To serve, place the spinach leaves on a serving platter. Spoon the warm eggplant mixture on the center of the spinach. Top the eggplant with the chopped peanuts and garnish with the lime wedges. Serve a light vinaigrette on the side.

Portion Sizes

Calculate 1½ cups of cleaned greens for each side salad portion. Plan on at least 2 cups of cleaned greens for each entrée salad portion.

Seafood Salad

Serves 4

Carb Level: Low
Per serving:
Carbohydrate: 1g
Protein: 24g
Fat: 28g

Keep the seafood cold throughout the assembly and serving stages.

½ cup minced fresh parsley
2 tablespoons capers, rinsed and drained
1 tablespoon minced garlic
½ cup extra-virgin olive oil
Pinch salt
Freshly cracked black pepper

Fresh-squeezed lemon juice
1 pound combination of cooked and/or smoked shrimp, scallops, lobster, crabmeat, mussels, clams, octopus, and/or squid

1. Combine the parsley, capers, garlic, all but a tablespoon of the olive oil, the salt, pepper, and a couple of tablespoons of lemon juice in a medium-sized nonreactive bowl. Taste and adjust seasoning as desired.
2. Just before serving, add the seafood and lightly toss to combine. Drizzle with additional lemon juice and the remaining olive oil, and serve.

Classic French Dressing

Serves 6

Carb Level: Low
Per serving:
Carbohydrate: 1g
Protein: Trace
Fat: 27g

A versatile dressing to use over mixed greens or as a marinade for chicken.

1 teaspoon seasoned salt
1 teaspoon lemon pepper
1 teaspoon dry mustard

⅛ cup fresh lemon juice
⅛ cup cider vinegar
¾ cup olive oil

Combine all the ingredients in a glass bowl and whisk to combine. Taste and adjust seasoning as desired. Remix just before serving. Refrigerate any unused portion and bring to room temperature before serving.

Herbs and Salads

Fresh herbs add a unique flavor to the traditional salad. A 2-tablespoon serving of basil, chives, or parsley has just a trace of carbs; chervil has 2g of carbs; and fennel has 1g.

Warm Cabbage Bacon Slaw with Roquefort

6 ounces thick-sliced bacon, cut
  into ¾-inch pieces
½ cup dry white wine
2 tablespoons minced shallots
¾ cup heavy cream, at room
  temperature
1½ teaspoons Dijon mustard
⅛ teaspoon seasoned salt

Freshly cracked black pepper, to
  taste
10 cups sliced red or green
  cabbage
2 tablespoons cider vinegar
4 ounces Roquefort, crumbled

Serves 6

Carb Level: Moderate
Per serving:
Carbohydrate: 16g
Protein: 24g
Fat: 41g

A hearty deli-
cious salad
packed with
flavor. Pair
this salad
with broiled
pork chops
for a hearty
meal.

1. Preheat oven to 350°.
2. Place the bacon in a medium-sized nonstick skillet over medium heat and cook until crispy, stirring frequently, about 8 minutes. Transfer the bacon to a plate layered with paper towels to drain.
3. Pour out all but 1 tablespoon of the bacon drippings; reserve excess drippings. Add the wine and shallots, and cook until reduced, about 4 minutes. Add the cream, mustard, salt, and pepper; simmer until slightly thickened.
4. In a large nonstick skillet, heat half of the reserved bacon drippings over medium-high heat. Cook half of the cabbage, stirring, until it begins to wilt, about 2 minutes. Transfer the cooked cabbage to a bowl and repeat the process with the remaining cabbage.
5. Return all the cabbage to the skillet. Add the vinegar and cook, stirring, for 1 minute. Stir in the cream mixture and cook until the cabbage is crisp-tender. Add the Roquefort, stirring until melted. To serve, divide the slaw among 4 warmed plates and sprinkle with bacon. Serve warm.

Serving Salad

Serve salads on chilled plates. Pop the plates in the refrigerator when you are prepping your ingredients and they should be chilled by the time you're ready to plate
and serve.

Herbed Goat Cheese on Mesclun Greens

Serves 4

Carb Level: Low

Per serving:

Carbohydrate: 8g

Protein: 38g

Fat: 44g

This is a delicious way to highlight quality goat cheese.

1 pound cold fresh goat cheese
¼ cup sour cream
1 tablespoon (or to taste) chopped fresh thyme

1 teaspoon minced garlic
Pinch salt
Freshly cracked black pepper
12 ounces mesclun greens

1. Combine the goat cheese, sour cream, thyme, garlic, salt, and pepper in a food processor; blend until smooth. Taste and adjust seasoning as desired.
2. Divide the greens among 4 chilled serving plates. Equally divide the cheese mixture into 4 portions. You can either place the cheese mixture in a dollop in the center of the greens or use a piping bag to pipe a rosette of the cheese in the center of each salad. Drizzle your favorite light vinaigrette over the salad.

Garlic Ranch-Style Dressing

Serves 6

Carb Level: Low

Per serving:

Carbohydrate: 3g

Protein: 1g

Fat: 12g

Drizzle over grilled fish or chicken.

2 teaspoons minced garlic
2 teaspoons garlic powder
½ cup mayonnaise
½ cup sour cream
3 teaspoons Dijon mustard

3 tablespoons fresh-squeezed lemon juice
¼ teaspoon seasoned salt
Freshly cracked black pepper, to taste

Combine all the ingredients in a small nonreactive bowl and whisk to combine. Refrigerate, up to 4 days, until ready to use.

Cilantro and Red Onion Dressing

2 tablespoons finely chopped red
   onion
½ teaspoon ground ginger
3 tablespoons slivered almonds
1 tablespoon sesame seeds
1 teaspoon anise seeds
3 tablespoons chopped fresh
   cilantro

¼ teaspoon paprika
2 tablespoons white wine vinegar
3 tablespoons fresh-squeezed
   lemon juice
½ cup extra-virgin olive oil
¼ teaspoon seasoned salt

Combine all the ingredients in a medium-sized nonreactive bowl and whisk to combine. Taste and adjust seasoning as desired. Remix just before serving. Refrigerate any unused portion and bring to room temperature before serving.

Serves 6

Carb Level: Low
Per serving:
Carbohydrate: 8g
Protein: 2g
Fat: 21g

A great dressing over fruits such as strawberries or mandarin oranges.

Green Goddess Dressing

½ cup mayonnaise
¼ cup heavy cream
¼ cup sour cream
1 tablespoon minced garlic
3 tablespoons finely chopped
   fresh parsley
3 tablespoons snipped fresh
   chives

1 tablespoon finely chopped fresh
   tarragon
1 tablespoon fresh-squeezed
   lemon juice
1 teaspoon lemon zest
⅛ teaspoon seasoned salt
Freshly cracked black pepper, to
   taste

Combine all the ingredients in a nonreactive bowl and whisk until well blended. Taste and adjust seasoning as desired. Refrigerate until ready to use.

Serves 6

Carb Level: Low
Per serving:
Carbohydrate: 2g
Protein: 1g
Fat: 21g

This dressing makes a delicious sauce for grilled fish and sturdy greens.

Creamy Avocado Dressing

Serves 6

Carb Level: Low

Per serving:

Carbohydrate: 4g
Protein: 1g
Fat: 23g

Make this dressing several hours in advance and store it in the refrigerator.

1 medium ripe avocado, halved and pitted, about ¾ cup
2 tablespoons finely chopped red onion
1 teaspoon lime zest
1 tablespoon fresh-squeezed lime juice
1 tablespoon Worcestershire sauce
½ cup sour cream
½ cup mayonnaise
¼ teaspoon seasoned salt
Freshly cracked black pepper, to taste

Spoon out the avocado meat into the bowl of a food processor fitted with a metal blade. Add the remaining ingredients and process until smooth. Taste and adjust seasoning as desired.

Creamy Asian Dressing

Serves 6

Carb Level: Low

Per serving:

Carbohydrate: 2g
Protein: 1g
Fat: 25g

Add a small amount of water chestnuts, sprouts, and scallions for added crunch.

¾ cup mayonnaise
¼ cup sour cream
2 tablespoons tarmari
1 teaspoon minced garlic
2 tablespoons rice wine
1 teaspoon honey
¼ cup thinly sliced scallion
Freshly cracked black pepper, to taste

Combine all the ingredients in a nonreactive bowl and whisk until well blended. Taste and adjust seasoning as desired. Refrigerate until ready to use.

Asian Pork Stew

Serves 4

Carb Level: Moderate
Per serving:

Carbohydrate:	15g
Protein:	40g
Fat:	16g

Store soups and stews in the refrigerator, covered for three to four days. Freeze soup in individual containers for six to eight weeks.

2 tablespoons all-purpose flour
2 teaspoons Chinese five-spice powder
1½ pounds pork tenderloin, trimmed of excess fat and cut into ¾-inch cubes
2 tablespoons olive oil
1 cup sliced celery
¾ cup sliced red onion
½ cup diced green peppers
1 tablespoon minced garlic
1 cup chicken stock
2 tablespoons hoisin sauce
2 tablespoons tamari
½ teaspoon ground ginger
8 ounces zucchini, cut into ¼-inch-thick rounds and halved
3 tablespoons toasted sesame seeds
Fresh cilantro leaves

1. Combine the flour and five-spice powder in a shallow bowl. Dredge the pork pieces in the flour and shake off the excess, reserving the excess flour.
2. Heat 1 tablespoon of the oil in a large nonstick skillet over medium-high heat. Add the pork and brown on all sides, stirring occasionally to cook evenly, about 6 minutes. Use a slotted spoon to transfer the meat to a plate and tent with tinfoil to keep warm.
3. Add the remaining tablespoon of oil and the celery, onions, peppers, and garlic. Cook until soft, about 4 minutes, stirring occasionally. Return the pork to the pan and add the stock, hoisin, tamari, ginger, and zucchini. Bring to a simmer and cook until the vegetables are crisp-tender and the meat is tender and cooked through, about 18 minutes.
4. Add 3 to 4 tablespoons of the pan juices to the reserved flour and whisk until there are no lumps. Add the flour mixture to the stew and whisk to combine. Cook and stir until thick. To serve, ladle the stew into warm shallow soup bowls and garnish with the sesame seeds and cilantro leaves.

Asparagus Soup with Truffle Oil

2½ pounds asparagus, medium-
    sized stalks
1 tablespoon butter
1 teaspoon salt

½ cup half-and-half
2 teaspoons white truffle oil
Freshly cracked pepper,
    to taste

Serves 4

Carb Level: Low
Per serving:
Carbohydrate: 8g
Protein: 4g
Fat: 9g

If truffle oil isn't available, swirl a small dollop of crème fraîche in the center before serving.

1. Snap off and discard the woody bases from each asparagus stalk. Use a vegetable peeler to peel the stalks, leaving the tips intact. Cut off the tops about 1½ inches down. Cut the stalks into 1-inch pieces. Bring a pot of salted water to a boil and cook the asparagus tips until bright green, about 2 minutes. Remove with a slotted spoon and set aside to cool.

2. Melt the butter in a medium-sized nonstick skillet over medium heat. Add the stalk pieces and salt to taste, and cook until crisp-tender, about 4 to 5 minutes. Slowly add the half-and-half and bring to a simmer; cook until the asparagus is tender, about 1 minute. Be careful not to overcook. Use a slotted spoon to transfer the asparagus to a blender or food processor fitted with a metal blade. Allow to cool for several minutes, then process until smooth. Add a few tablespoons of the hot half-and-half if needed.

3. Transfer the purée back to the pan with the half-and-half. Stir to combine, and adjust seasoning to taste. Heat through without boiling, just 1 or 2 minutes. To serve, ladle the purée into soup bowls and top with several of the vibrant green asparagus tips. Drizzle the truffle oil over each bowl and top with a few turns of freshly cracked black pepper.

Simple Suggestion

When transferring a puréed soup from a food processor, put your index finger up through the center hole in the bottom of the work bowl to secure the blade while pouring the purée to another container.

Onion and Mushroom Soup

Serves 4

Carb Level: Low

Per serving:

Carbohydrate: 6g

Protein: 12g

Fat: 9g

Use morels, chanterelles, and other domestic exotics for a flavorful presentation.

3 tablespoons butter
6 ounces assorted mushroom
  caps, thinly sliced
½ cup thinly sliced yellow onion
4 cups beef broth
¼ cup dry sherry

¼ teaspoon salt
Freshly cracked black pepper
2 tablespoons freshly grated
  Parmesan
Chopped fresh thyme

1. Melt the butter in a medium-sized nonstick skillet over medium heat. Add the mushrooms and onions; cook, stirring frequently, until translucent, about 8 minutes.
2. Add the beef broth, sherry, salt, and pepper; simmer for about 5 to 7 minutes. Taste and adjust seasoning as needed. To serve, ladle the hot soup into 4 soup bowls and garnish with a sprinkling of Parmesan and fresh thyme leaves.

Basil and Zucchini Soup

Serves 6

Carb Level: Low

Per serving:

Carbohydrate: 5g

Protein: 2g

Fat: 1g

You can add a shot of hot pepper sauce or substitute tarragon for a different twist.

6 cups sliced zucchini
½ cup fresh basil leaves
  (about 20)
3 cups chicken stock

1 teaspoon salt
2 tablespoons lemon juice
½ cup plain yogurt
Julienned fresh basil

1. Place the zucchini and basil leaves in a medium-sized saucepan with the stock and salt. Bring to a boil, reduce heat, and simmer for 10 minutes.
2. Remove the saucepan from the heat, add the lemon juice, and allow the vegetables to cool slightly. Use a slotted spoon to transfer the vegetables to a food processor fitted with a metal blade, or a blender; process to a smooth purée, adding a few tablespoons of the broth if needed. Transfer to a bowl and chill.
3. Serve in chilled soup bowls with a dollop of plain yogurt. Garnish with basil and serve chilled.

Beef Stroganoff Soup

2 pounds top sirloin steak,
    trimmed of visible fat and cut
    into ½-inch cubes
½ teaspoon salt
Freshly ground black pepper
4 tablespoons all-purpose flour
4 tablespoons butter
1 tablespoon olive oil
½ cup sliced yellow onions

3 cups sliced mushrooms
2 tablespoons minced garlic
¼ cup dry white wine
2 cups beef stock
2 tablespoons chopped parsley,
    plus extra for garnish
2 teaspoons Worcestershire sauce
½ cup sour cream

Serves 6

Carb Level: Low
Per serving:
Carbohydrate: 9g
Protein: 30g
Fat: 33g

Make sure the pan is really hot when you sear the meat to ensure the meat stays tender and the flavorful juices stay inside the meat.

1. Pat the meat dry with paper towels and season with salt and pepper. Place the flour in a shallow bowl. Dredge the meat in the flour, shaking off excess. Reserve remaining flour.
2. Melt the butter in a large nonstick skillet over high heat until bubbling. Add the meat and brown on all sides, stirring occasionally to cook evenly, about 6 minutes. Use a slotted spoon to transfer the meat to a plate and tent with tinfoil to keep warm.
3. Heat the oil over medium-high heat and add the onions, mushrooms, and garlic. Cook until soft, about 6 minutes, stirring occasionally.
4. Sprinkle the reserved flour over the vegetables. Cook and stir until thick. Add the white wine and cook until thick and reduced, about 4 minutes. Add the stock, parsley, and Worcestershire; bring to a simmer and cook until somewhat reduced, about 6 minutes.
5. Add the meat and any accumulated juices and simmer, uncovered, for 10 minutes. To serve, stir in the sour cream and heat through. Serve hot in warm shallow bowls.

Flavor Enhancer

You can use bouillon cubes to enhance the flavors of savory soups. Be careful when salting, as the bouillon cubes already contain quite a bit of salt.

Chicken Soup

2 tablespoons olive oil
½ cup sliced yellow onions
1 cup chopped broccoli
½ cup carrots, peeled and cut into ¼-inch rounds
½ cup chopped bell pepper

Salt
Freshly ground black pepper
2 cups low-sodium chicken stock
1 cup diced cooked chicken, skinless
2 tablespoons chopped parsley

1. Heat the oil in a medium-sized stockpot over medium-high heat. Add the onions and cook until soft, about 4 minutes, stirring occasionally. Add the broccoli, carrots, and peppers; cook until the broccoli starts to turn bright green, about 4 minutes. Add the salt, pepper, and stock, and bring to a simmer. Cook until the vegetables are crisp-tender, about 8 minutes.
2. Add the chicken and parsley, and return to a simmer. Serve hot.

Cheddar Cheese Soup

2 tablespoons butter
¼ cup chopped yellow onion
½ cup chopped celery
2 tablespoons all-purpose flour
½ teaspoon ground cayenne pepper

¼ teaspoon dry mustard
½ tablespoon Worcestershire sauce
1 cup whole milk
1½ cups chicken stock
2 cups shredded Cheddar cheese
Paprika, for garnish

1. Melt the butter in a medium-sized saucepan and sauté the onion and celery until tender, about 4 minutes. Add the flour, cayenne pepper, mustard, and Worcestershire, and mix to combine.
2. Add the milk and chicken stock and bring to a boil. Cook for 1 minute, stirring constantly. Reduce heat to low, add the cheese, and stir occasionally just until the cheese is melted.
3. To serve, ladle hot soup into small decorative cups and sprinkle with paprika.

Chilled Cucumber Soup with Salmon

1 cup sliced yellow onion
3 cups fish stock (or clam stock)
3 cups peeled, seeded, and diced
*   cucumber (about ½-inch dice)*
2 tablespoons chopped dill
2½ cups plain yogurt

Salt, to taste
Freshly cracked black pepper, to
*   taste*
1½ pounds salmon fillet
Snipped fresh dill, for garnish
Lemon wedges, for garnish

Serves 6

Carb Level: Low
Per serving:
Carbohydrate: 10g
Protein: 23g
Fat: 10g

1. Combine the onions, fish stock, and cucumbers in a medium-sized saucepan and bring to a simmer over low heat. Cook for about 5 minutes, until the cucumbers are tender but not mushy. Transfer the mixture to a food processor fitted with a metal blade and process until smooth. Add the dill and yogurt, and pulse until just combined. Season with salt and pepper and transfer to a bowl. Refrigerate until chilled. (The soup can be made ahead up to this point.)
2. **To cook salmon:** Preheat oven to 375°. Place salmon fillet on a tinfoil-lined pan, skin-side down. Lightly season with salt and pepper. Bake, uncovered, until cooked through, about 12 to 15 minutes.
3. When ready to serve, flake the salmon and gently stir it into the soup. To serve, ladle the soup into chilled soup cups and garnish with dill. Serve the lemon wedges on the side.

You can add a shot of cayenne pepper or hot pepper sauce if desired. Plan your schedule to allow some time for the soup to chill.

Cold Soups

When preparing chilled soups, make sure each of the ingredients is well chilled before preparing. This will substantially reduce the amount of chilling time before serving.

Chilled Zucchini Squash Soup with Basil

Serves 6

Carb Level: Low

Per serving:

Carbohydrate: 6g

Protein: 3g

Fat: 13g

This soup is best served when very chilled. You can prepare the soup in advance up to the point where you purée the vegetables.

3 tablespoons olive oil
½ cup finely chopped leeks (white and light green parts only)
4 cups thinly sliced zucchini squash
4 cups chicken stock
1 tablespoon fresh-squeezed lemon juice

½ cup half-and-half
½ cup sour cream
2 tablespoons finely chopped fresh chives
6 tablespoons finely chopped fresh basil
Salt, to taste
Freshly ground black pepper, to taste

1. Heat the oil in a large saucepan over medium heat and sauté the leeks until softened, about 5 to 7 minutes. Add the squash and sauté for another 5 minutes, or until lightly browned.
2. Add the stock, cover, and cook for about 15 minutes, until the squash is tender. Use a slotted spoon to transfer the zucchini to a food processor fitted with a metal blade or to a blender; process to a smooth purée, adding a few tablespoons of the hot stock if necessary. Transfer the soup to a bowl and refrigerate. (The soup may be made ahead up to this point.)
3. After the soup has been chilled, add the lemon juice, half-and-half, sour cream, chives, and 3 tablespoons of the basil. Season with salt and pepper. Taste and adjust seasoning as desired.
4. Serve in chilled soup bowls, garnished with the remaining 3 tablespoons basil.

Cleanup Tip

To clean the bowl of a blender or food processor after puréeing, put about ½ cup of warm soapy water in the bowl and process for about 30 seconds.

Cream of Chicken Soup

2 tablespoons butter
½ cup finely chopped celery
½ cup finely chopped yellow
   onion
¼ cup finely chopped, peeled
   carrot
1 cup sliced mushrooms
1 teaspoon salt

3 tablespoons all-purpose flour
3 cups chicken stock
½ teaspoon thyme
Freshly ground pepper
¾ cup half-and-half
1½ cups diced cooked chicken
2 tablespoons chopped fresh
   parsley, for garnish

Serves 4

Carb Level: Moderate
Per serving:
Carbohydrate: 11g
Protein: 14g
Fat: 21g

This is com-
fort food at
its best. This
really is an
entrée dish
when accom-
panied with a
green salad.

1. Melt the butter in a medium-sized saucepan over medium-high heat. Add the celery, onion, and carrots; cook until soft, about 4 minutes, stirring occasionally. Add the mushrooms and salt, and cook for about 4 to 5 minutes. Whisk the flour into the pan juices and cook until bubbly, about 4 minutes.
2. Add the stock, thyme, and pepper, and stir. Cook until slightly thickened and smooth, about 5 minutes. Reduce heat to medium-low and add the half-and-half and chicken; bring to a low simmer. Cook for about 5 minutes to allow the flavors to blend. Serve hot garnished with parsley.

Kitchen Equipment Tip

Mandolines are a great way to consistently slice or julienne vegetables. The professional stainless models will cost upwards of $130. There are smaller mandolines available such as the Berliner, a Japanese model, which is plastic with surgical steel blades and costs about $35 at Japanese markets. They are easy to handle and clean.

Creamy Avocado Soup with Chives

Serves 4

Carb Level: Moderate

Per serving:

Carbohydrate: 17g

Protein: 6g

Fat: 23g

Read the dietary label on the vegetable stock, as the carb count varies between brands.

2 large avocados, ripe
1½ cups vegetable stock (Hains is a good choice)
1 tablespoon Worcestershire sauce
¾ cup plain yogurt
¼ cup sour cream
¼ teaspoon kosher salt
Dash hot pepper sauce
⅛ teaspoon red pepper flakes
2 tablespoons snipped fresh chives

1. Cut the avocados in half and remove the pits. Use a spoon to remove the flesh from the skin and process in a food processor fitted with a metal blade until smooth.
2. Add the remaining ingredients and process until smooth, about 1 minute. Taste and adjust seasoning as desired. Refrigerate, covered, until ready to serve.

Creamy Tomato Soup

Serves 6

Carb Level: Moderate

Per serving:

Carbohydrate: 14g

Protein: 2g

Fat: 8g

This soup can be served hot or cold.

3 tablespoons olive oil
4 cups canned stewed, diced tomatoes
½ cup sliced green onions
¼ cup red pepper, seeded and chopped
2 cloves garlic, minced
2 cups chicken stock
1 teaspoon honey
¼ cup half-and-half, at room temperature
2 tablespoons chopped basil
Salt and ground black pepper
Chopped chives, for garnish

1. Heat the oil in a large saucepan and combine the tomatoes, green onions, red pepper, garlic, stock, and honey. Bring to a boil and reduce to a simmer for about 15 minutes. Remove from the heat and let cool for several minutes.
2. In a blender or a food processor fitted with a metal blade, purée the soup until smooth. Transfer back to the pan and stir in the half-and-half, basil, salt, and pepper. Heat to a light simmer and adjust seasoning to taste. Ladle the soup into serving bowls and garnish with the chopped chives.

Creamy Broccoli Soup

1½ pounds broccoli
¾ cup chopped celery
½ cup chopped yellow onion
Salt
2 tablespoons butter
2 tablespoons all-purpose flour
2½ cups chicken stock

⅛ teaspoon freshly grated
   nutmeg
Freshly cracked pepper
½ cup heavy cream, at room
   temperature
½ cup shredded Cheddar cheese,
   for garnish

Serves 4

Carb Level: Moderate
Per serving:
Carbohydrate: 16g
Protein: 10g
Fat: 22g

Pair this with
a light crispy
salad and you
have a great
weekend lun-
cheon menu.

1. Trim the woody stalks from the broccoli and chop the remaining tender stems and tops into medium dice. Combine the broccoli, celery, and onions in a medium-sized saucepan. Add just enough water to cover the vegetables, and salt generously. Bring to a boil and cook until the vegetables are tender, but not mushy, about 8 minutes.
2. Use a slotted spoon to transfer the vegetables to a food processor fitted with a metal blade (or a blender). Process until smooth, adding a few tablespoons of the cooking liquid if needed.
3. Melt the butter in a medium-sized saucepan over medium heat. Add the flour and whisk until smooth. Cook until smooth and bubbly, about 4 minutes. Slowly add the chicken stock, whisking constantly. Bring to a simmer and cook for 2 minutes until thick.
4. Stir in the broccoli purée, the nutmeg, and salt and pepper to taste; bring to a simmer and cook to allow the flavors to blend. Slowly pour in the cream, whisking to blend. Heat through but do not boil. Taste and adjust seasoning as desired. To serve, ladle soup into bowls and top with shredded cheese. Serve hot.

Soup Garnishes

The more complex the soup, the simpler the garnish should be. For hot soups, you can use chopped fresh herbs, minced scallions, a dollop of sour cream, or grated Parmesan.

Creamy Cabbage Soup

Serves 4

Carb Level: Moderate
Per serving:
Carbohydrate: 16g
Protein: 10g
Fat: 22g

You can add bacon bits or small pieces of cooked smoked sausage and turn this rich soup into a hearty entrée.

1½ pounds cabbage
¾ cup chopped celery
½ cup chopped onion
Salt, to taste
2 tablespoons butter
2 tablespoons all-purpose flour
2½ cups chicken stock

⅛ teaspoon freshly grated nutmeg
Freshly cracked black pepper
½ cup heavy cream, at room temperature
½ cup shredded Cheddar cheese, for garnish

1. Cut the cabbage in half and cut out the core. Shred or cut the cabbage into ⅛-inch strips. Combine the cabbage, celery, and onions in a large saucepan. Add just enough water to cover the vegetables, and salt generously. Bring to a boil and cook until the vegetables are tender, but not mushy, about 6 minutes.
2. Use a slotted spoon to transfer the vegetables to a food processor fitted with a metal blade (or a blender). Process until smooth, adding a few tablespoons of the cooking liquid if needed.
3. Melt the butter in a medium-sized saucepan over medium heat. Add the flour and whisk until smooth. Cook until smooth and bubbly, about 4 minutes. Slowly add the chicken stock, whisking constantly. Bring to a simmer and cook for about 2 minutes, until thick.
4. Stir in the cabbage purée, the nutmeg, and salt and pepper to taste. Bring to a simmer and cook to allow the flavors to blend. Slowly pour in the cream, whisking to blend. Heat through but do not boil. Taste and adjust seasoning as desired. To serve, ladle soup into bowls and top with shredded cheese. Serve hot.

No Boiling!

Don't boil cream soups; it will affect the taste. Reheat cream soups on medium heat and bring to a gentle simmer. Cook for 2 minutes to heat through.

Cucumber and Shrimp Soup

1 pound cooked peeled shrimp,
  cut into medium dice
1 pound cucumbers (about 3
  medium), peeled, seeded, and
  cut into medium dice
1 tablespoon mayonnaise
3 tablespoons minced fresh dill,
  divided
Salt
1 tablespoon minced garlic

3 cups buttermilk
⅓ cup sour cream
1 teaspoon Dijon mustard
⅛ teaspoon hot pepper sauce
Sugar substitute equal to 1 ¼
  teaspoons granulated sugar
Freshly cracked black pepper, to
  taste
Lemon wedges, for garnish

Serves 6

Carb Level: Low
Per serving:
Carbohydrate: 9g
Protein: 21g
Fat: 5g

You can
substitute
crabmeat
or flaked
cooked, skin-
less, boned
salmon for
the shrimp,
if desired.
Makes an ele-
gant summer
luncheon.

1. Combine the shrimp, cucumbers, mayonnaise, and 1 tablespoon of the dill in a medium-sized bowl. Taste and adjust seasoning as desired and refrigerate until needed.
2. Combine the remaining ingredients (except the lemon wedges), including 1 teaspoon of salt and black pepper to taste, in a blender and blend until smooth, about 1 minute. Taste and adjust seasoning as desired. Refrigerate until ready to use.
3. To serve, ladle the soup into chilled shallow bowls. Spoon a large dollop of the shrimp and cucumber mixture in the center of each bowl. Serve chilled.

Chilling Additions

Chilled soups can be garnished with whole cooked shrimp, a spoonful of caviar, chopped hardboiled eggs, a dash of sherry, a dollop of crème fraîche, or a few paper-thin slices of radish.

Curried Cauliflower Soup

1 tablespoon olive oil
½ cup chopped yellow onion
Sugar substitute equal to 1
  tablespoon granulated sugar
2 teaspoons curry powder
4 cups chopped cauliflower florets

¼ pound Yukon gold potatoes,
  peeled and cut into ½-inch dice
3½ cups chicken stock
Plain yogurt, for garnish
Chopped fresh mint, for garnish

1. Heat the oil in a large saucepot over medium-high heat. Add the onions and cook until soft, about 4 minutes. Stir in the sugar substitute and curry. Add the cauliflower and potatoes, and stir. Add the stock and bring to a boil; reduce heat to medium-low and simmer until the vegetables are tender.
2. Use a slotted spoon to transfer the vegetables to a food processor; process until smooth. Transfer back to the saucepot and heat through, stirring constantly. Serve garnished with a dollop of yogurt and the mint.

Quick Gazpacho

1½ cups tomato juice
½ cup peeled, seeded, and diced
  cucumber
½ cup seeded and diced green
  pepper
¼ cup chopped yellow onion
2 tablespoons lemon juice

1 tablespoon olive oil
2 cups seeded and chopped ripe
  tomatoes
Salt, to taste
Freshly cracked black pepper, to
  taste
Snipped fresh dill, for garnish

Combine all the ingredients in a blender or food processor fitted with a metal blade. Process until somewhat smooth. Transfer to a mixing bowl sitting in an ice bath. Stir occasionally until chilled. To serve, ladle soup into small cups and garnish with fresh snipped dill.

Home on the Range Soup

1 tablespoon vegetable oil
1 pound lean ground beef
1 cup chopped yellow onion
½ cup chopped carrot
⅛ teaspoon garlic salt
Freshly cracked black pepper

¼ cup garbanzo beans (also
   called chickpeas)
3 cups beef stock
1 cup salsa (spiciness to taste)
¼ cup sour cream

Serves 4

Carb Level: Moderate
Per serving:
Carbohydrate: 18g
Protein: 5g
Fat: 8g

Kids love
this soup.

1. Heat the oil in a large heavy-bottomed saucepan over medium-high heat. Add the ground beef, onion, and carrot; cook until the meat is browned, about 7 minutes, stirring frequently. Break up the larger pieces of meat while cooking. Season with garlic salt and pepper.
2. Add the beans, stock, and salsa, and bring to a simmer. Cook for 2 to 3 minutes. Serve toppped with a dollop of sour cream.

Italian Sausage and Vegetable Soup

2 tablespoons olive oil
1 tablespoon minced garlic
½ cup chopped yellow onion
8 ounces hot Italian sausage, cut
   into ½-inch pieces
12 ounces bacon, cut into 1-inch
   pieces

1 cup sliced white mushrooms
1 cup sliced zucchini
1 teaspoon garlic salt
4 cups baby spinach leaves
3 cups chicken stock
1 cup half-and-half, at room temp

Serves 4

Carb Level: Low
Per serving:
Carbohydrate: 9g
Protein: 39g
Fat: 80g

Use mild sau-
sage if you're
serving to a
mixed crowd.

1. Heat the oil in a large saucepan over medium-high heat. Sauté the garlic and onions until soft. Do not allow to brown or burn. Add the sausage and bacon and brown fully, about 8 minutes, stirring often.
2. Add the mushrooms, zucchini, and garlic salt, stirring often, and cook until tender. Add the spinach and cook until slightly reduced, about 5 minutes. Add the chicken stock and bring to a simmer. Reduce heat to medium-low. Slowly add the half-and-half, stirring constantly, and heat through..

Oyster Stew

Carb Level: Low

Per serving:

Carbohydrate: 8g

Protein: 7g

Fat: 54g

Have the fish monger shuck the oysters for you. You also need the oyster liquor.

3 tablespoons unsalted butter
¼ cup minced shallot
¼ cup finely chopped celery
2 teaspoons all-purpose flour
½ cup dry white wine
2 cups heavy cream, warmed
1 tablespoon dry sherry
1 teaspoon fresh lemon juice

1 teaspoon finely chopped fresh
   parsley
1 teaspoon finely snipped chives
Pinch ground cayenne
Salt, to taste
25 raw oysters, shucked, with
   1 cup oyster liquor reserved

1. Melt the butter in a large saucepan over medium-low heat until foaming. Add the shallot and cook, stirring frequently, until fragrant and translucent, about 5 minutes. Add the celery and cook until slightly softened, about 2 minutes. Stir in the flour and cook until bubbly, about 20 seconds, stirring constantly. Stir in the wine and simmer until thickened and bubbly, about 20 seconds.

2. Stir in the cream and return to a simmer. Simmer to blend the flavors and cook the flour, about 5 minutes. Add the sherry, lemon juice, parsley, chives, cayenne, salt to taste, oysters, and oyster liquid. Return to a simmer. (The oysters will be cooked at this point. The oyster edges will ruffle and curl when cooked.) Taste and adjust seasoning as desired. Serve hot.

For Maximum Flavor

Add fresh herbs at the end of cooking time. Fresh herbs lose their flavor and intensity when cooked for a long period of time.

Stracciatella

2 quarts chicken stock
6 large eggs
½ cup grated Parmesan cheese
¼ cup chopped basil or parsley

Pinch freshly grated nutmeg
Salt, to taste
Freshly ground black pepper

Serves 8

Carb Level: Low
Per serving:
Carbohydrate: 2g
Protein: 6g
Fat: 4g

The fresh herbs add a nice flavor to this old-time favorite.

1. Bring the stock to a simmer in a large saucepan over medium-high heat. Combine the eggs, cheese, basil, and nutmeg in a medium-sized mixing bowl and beat with a fork until well blended.
2. Stir the simmering stock with a large spoon so it is moving in a circle. Keep stirring as you pour the egg mixture into the stock in a slow, steady stream so that shreds of egg form; cook for about 1 minute. Once all the eggs have set, break up the pieces with a fork. Season to taste with salt and pepper. Serve hot.

Reuben Soup

2 tablespoons butter
½ cup chopped yellow onion
1 tablespoon all-purpose flour
4 cups beef stock
⅛ teaspoon caraway seeds
1 bay leaf
1 teaspoon salt

½ teaspoon dried thyme
Freshly cracked black pepper
1 cup sauerkraut, rinsed and drained
¾ pound extra-lean corned beef,
   thinly sliced
1 cup grated Swiss cheese
4 rye crisp crackers

Serves 4

Carb Level: Low
Per serving:
Carbohydrate: 10g
Protein: 23g
Fat: 27g

This delicious soup offers a tasty alternative to the Reuben sandwich.

1. Melt the butter in a large saucepot. Add the onions and cook until soft, about 4 minutes, stirring occasionally. Sprinkle the flour over the onions and stir to mix. Add the stock, bring to a simmer, and cook until slightly thickened. Add the caraway, bay leaf, salt, thyme, pepper, and sauerkraut. Bring to a simmer and cook for 5 minutes.
2. Remove and discard the bay leaf and add the corned beef. Bring to a simmer and cook for 2 minutes. Ladle the soup into warm shallow soup bowls. Sprinkle the Swiss cheese and place a cracker on top.

Sauerkraut and Kielbasa Soup

Serves 4

Carb Level: Moderate

Per serving:

Carbohydrate: 13g

Protein: 17g

Fat: 37g

You can substitute different sausages, but kielbasa provides a rich smoky flavor to this hearty soup.

2 tablespoons butter
1 pound kielbasa, cut into
*   ¼-inch half-moons*
¾ cup sliced yellow onion
¾ cup peeled and diced red-
*   skinned potato (about*
*   ¼-inch dice)*
¼ cup chopped celery
¼ cup finely chopped peeled
*   carrot*

4 cups beef stock
½ cup flat beer (such as lager)
1 bay leaf
1 teaspoon caraway seeds
Salt, to taste
Freshly cracked black pepper, to
*   taste*
1½ cups sauerkraut, rinsed and
*   drained*

1. Melt the butter in a large saucepan over medium-high heat. Add the sausage and cook until well-browned, about 6 minutes, stirring frequently. Use a slotted spoon to transfer the sausage to a plate. Set aside.
2. Add the onions and cook until soft, about 4 minutes. Add the potatoes, celery, carrots, stock, beer, bay leaf, caraway, salt, and pepper; bring to a simmer and cook until the potatoes are tender, about 15 minutes.
3. Add the sausage and sauerkraut and simmer until the flavors are blended. Taste and adjust seasoning as desired. Serve hot in warm soup bowls.

Fat Blaster

Float a lettuce leaf on top of soups. The leaf will absorb the fat and is easy to remove from the top of the soup. You can also remove fat by chilling soup in the refrigerator and skimming off the chilled fat layer that rises to the top.

Sausage and Kale Soup

1 tablespoon extra-virgin
   olive oil
2 pounds Italian sausage, sweet
   or hot, cut into 1-inch pieces
1 pound kale, leaves stripped
   from stems (stems reserved)

1 pound white mushrooms,
   trimmed and sliced
2 tablespoons minced garlic
2 tablespoons hot paprika
Salt, to taste
Freshly ground black pepper
4 cups water or beef stock

Serves 6

Carb Level: Moderate
Per serving:
Carbohydrate: 13g
Protein: 26g
Fat: 51g

1. Heat the olive oil in a large, deep nonstick skillet over medium-high heat. Add the sausage and cook without stirring until the sausage browns well on one side, about 5 minutes. Meanwhile, chop the stems of the kale into about ½-inch lengths and cut the leaves into ¼-inch strips.
2. Stir the sausage and let it brown a bit more; remove with a slotted spoon and transfer to a plate lined with paper towels to drain. Add the mushrooms to the skillet and cook until soft and lightly browned, stirring occasionally, about 8 minutes. Use a slotted spoon to transfer the mushrooms to a bowl and set aside.
3. Add the kale stems to the skillet and cook, stirring frequently, until they begin to brown, 3 to 4 minutes. Reduce the heat to medium and add the garlic, paprika, kale leaves, salt, and pepper; cook for about 1 minute, stirring to combine.
4. Return the sausage to the pan and add the water (or stock). Raise the heat to high and cook for about 5 minutes, stirring occasionally and scraping the bottom of the pan with a wooden spoon. Add more salt and pepper to taste and ladle into bowls, topping with the reserved mushrooms.

This soup can be on the spicy side if you use hot Italian sausage and hot Hungarian paprika, or you can tone it down with regular sausage and mild paprika.

Entertaining Tip

Lightly broil sausage slices and spear them on toothpicks. Serve with a hearty mustard as a simple supplementary hors d'oeuvre.

Purée of Cauliflower Soup with Two Cheeses

Serves 4

Carb Level: Moderate

Per serving:

Carbohydrate: 13g

Protein: 14g

Fat: 13g

The tangy goat cheese is a nice garnish—you can substitute blue cheese or even Parmesan if desired.

2 pounds cauliflower, cut into florets
3½ cups chicken stock
1 cup shredded sharp Cheddar cheese
1 teaspoon Worcestershire sauce
Dash hot pepper sauce
Salt, to taste
Freshly ground black pepper
¼ cup goat cheese crumbles
1 tablespoon snipped chives

1. In a medium-sized saucepan, combine the cauliflower and stock; bring to a simmer over medium-high heat. Reduce heat to medium and cook for about 20 minutes, or until the cauliflower is soft. Remove from heat.
2. Use a slotted spoon to transfer the cauliflower to a food processor fitted with the metal blade. Process until smooth, adding more stock if necessary. Return the soup to the pot and add the cheese and Worcestershire; whisk to completely incorporate. Season with the hot sauce, salt, and pepper to taste.
3. To serve, ladle the soup into shallow soup bowls and garnish with the goat cheese and chives. Serve hot.

CHAPTER 5
Simple Sides

Cauliflower Purée

Serves 4

Carb Level: Low
Per serving:
Carbohydrate: 9g
Protein: 3g
Fat: 3g

This dish
can replace
mashed
potatoes.

1 pound cauliflower florets,
    chopped
2 cloves garlic
⅓ cup vegetable stock

1 tablespoon butter
½ teaspoon salt
Freshly cracked black pepper
Snipped fresh dill, for garnish

1. Put the cauliflower, garlic, and stock in a medium-sized saucepan, cover, and simmer for about 10 minutes, until the cauliflower is tender.
2. Drain the cauliflower, reserving the cooking liquid.
3. Transfer the cauliflower to a food processor fitted with a metal blade. Process until smooth, adding the reserved cooking liquid as needed to reach the desired consistency. Add the butter and process. Season with salt and pepper to taste. Transfer to a serving bowl, garnish with dill, and serve immediately.

Zucchini Marinara

Serves 4

Carb Level: Low
Per serving:
Carbohydrate: 8g
Protein: 3g
Fat: 3g

Use your
favorite pack-
aged marinara
sauce for this
preparation.

2 tablespoons olive oil
½ cup chopped yellow onion
2 cups sliced zucchini (about
    ½-inch-thick rounds)
Salt, to taste

Freshly cracked black pepper
1 cup marinara sauce
¼ cup shredded mozzarella
    cheese
Chopped fresh parsley

1. Heat the oil in a medium-large nonstick skillet over medium-high heat. Add the onions and cook until soft, about 4 minutes.
2. Add the zucchini and salt and pepper to taste; cook, stirring frequently, for 4 minutes.
3. Add the marinara sauce and bring to a simmer; cook until the zucchini is tender when pierced with a fork.
4. Top with shredded mozzarella, cover, and heat until the cheese melts, about 3 minutes. Top with parsley and serve immediately.

Mediterranean Green Beans

1 pound fresh green beans, ends
   trimmed, cut into
   1-inch pieces
2 teaspoons minced fresh
   rosemary
1 teaspoon lemon zest

1 tablespoon olive oil
1 tablespoon, plus ½ teaspoon
   kosher salt
Freshly cracked black pepper, to
   taste

Serves 4

Carb Level: Low
Per serving:
Carbohydrate: 8g
Protein: 2g
Fat: 4g

This simple
recipe can be
served hot or
at room tem-
perature.

1. Fill a medium-sized saucepan with cold salted water and bring to a boil
   over high heat. Add the beans and cook until they are a vibrant green,
   just about 4 minutes.
2. Drain the beans and transfer to a large bowl. Add the remaining ingredients and toss to coat evenly. Serve warm or at room temperature.

Green Peas with Shiitake Mushrooms

1 tablespoon olive oil
2 scallions, thinly sliced
8 ounces shiitake mushroom
   caps, sliced
2 cloves garlic, minced
2 cups frozen peas, petite size

1 tablespoon water
1 teaspoon seasoned rice wine
   vinegar
¼–½ teaspoon seasoned salt
Freshly cracked black pepper, to
   taste

Serves 4

Carb Level: Moderate
Per serving:
Carbohydrate: 13g
Protein: 5g
Fat: 4g

The shiitakes
give this
recipe an
Asian flair.

1. Heat the olive oil in a medium-sized nonstick skillet over medium heat.
   Add the scallions and mushrooms and cook, stirring frequently, for
   about 7 minutes, until the mushrooms soften slightly.
2. Add the garlic and stir to mix. Cook for just about 1 minute, but don't
   let the garlic brown (it imparts a bitter taste). Add the peas and water
   and reduce heat. Cook until the peas are tender, about 4 minutes.
3. Stir in the rice wine vinegar, salt, and pepper. Serve hot.

Grilled Vegetable Stacks

Serves 4

Carb Level: Low
Per serving:
Carbohydrate: 6g
Protein: 2g
Fat: 14g

Drizzle your favorite vinaigrette over the vegetables for a different taste.

1 medium-sized zucchini
1 medium-sized yellow squash
¼ cup olive oil
½ teaspoon kosher salt
Freshly cracked black pepper

2 medium-sized tomatoes, ripe
  but not soft
¼ cup diced red pepper
¼ cup julienned fresh basil

1. Trim the zucchini and yellow squash and cut into ½-inch rounds. Place in a medium-sized mixing bowl and drizzle with half of the olive oil. Season with salt and pepper. Use a rubber spatula to toss until evenly coated with oil and seasonings.
2. Cut the tomatoes into ½-inch slices and transfer to paper towels for several minutes. Brush the tomato slices with the remaining oil and season with salt and pepper.
3. Preheat an oiled grill pan over medium-high heat. Grill the zucchini and yellow squash rounds, turning once, until just starting to soften, about 1 to 2 minutes per side. Transfer to a plate to keep warm.
4. Grill the tomato slices for just about 30 seconds per side, depending on ripeness. Transfer to the plate.
5. To assemble, place a slice of tomato on a plate, top with a zucchini slice, then a yellow squash slice, and sprinkle the diced red pepper and basil leaves on top. Serve warm or at room temperature.

Stovetop Grill Pans

Grill pans are an easy and convenient way to "grill" on your stovetop. The nonstick variety is the best type. The key tip is to make sure the pan is hot before adding the vegetables.

Indian Spiced Cauliflower

3 tablespoons vegetable oil
1 cup sliced red onion
½ teaspoon turmeric
3 cups cauliflower florets

2 green chilies, seeded and
   chopped
2 cups red and orange bell pepper
   strips (about ¼-inch strips)

1. Heat the oil in a nonstick skillet over medium-high heat. Add the red
   onion and cook until just soft, about 3 minutes. Add the turmeric, stir,
   and cook for 1 minute.
2. Add the cauliflower and reduce heat to medium; cook, stirring occasionally, for about 8 minutes.
3. Add the chilies and bell peppers, and cook for about 5 minutes, until
   the peppers are tender. Season with salt and pepper to taste. Serve hot.

Serves 4

Carb Level: Moderate
Per serving:
Carbohydrate: 14g
Protein: 3g
Fat: 10g

Turmeric
provides
intense color
and subtle
flavor to this
dish.

Creamed Spinach

2 tablespoons butter
1 pound baby spinach leaves
1 tablespoon water
½ teaspoon salt

Freshly cracked black pepper, to
   taste
2 tablespoons all-purpose flour
½ cup evaporated milk

1. Melt the butter in a medium-sized nonstick skillet over medium-high
   heat. Tip the skillet to coat the bottom with the melted butter.
2. Reduce heat to medium and add the spinach leaves. Add the water
   and stir. Cook until the leaves start to wilt, about 2 to 3 minutes. Season
   with salt and pepper.
3. Sprinkle the flour over the spinach and stir to evenly distribute. Add
   the evaporated milk and stir. Cook, uncovered, until the sauce starts to
   thicken, about 4 to 6 minutes. Serve hot.

Serves 4

Carb Level: Low
Per serving:
Carbohydrate: 9g
Protein: 5g
Fat: 3g

Garnish
with leftover
bacon or
bacon bits.

Sautéed Fennel with Olives and Arugula

Serves 4

Carb Level: Low

Per serving:

Carbohydrate: 8g

Protein: 1g

Fat: 4g

This pairs well with a fish entrée for a fall dinner.

1 teaspoon olive oil
1 pound fennel bulb, thinly sliced
½ cup thinly sliced leek (white and pale green parts only)
½ cup seeded and diced red bell pepper (about ½-inch dice)
¼ cup capers, rinsed and drained
¼ cup sliced kalamata olives
1½ cups arugula leaves (organic baby arugula leaves if possible)
½ teaspoon salt
Freshly cracked black pepper

1. Heat the oil in a large nonstick skillet over medium-high heat. Add the fennel, leek, red pepper, and capers; sauté until crisp-tender, about 3 to 4 minutes.
2. Add the olives and arugula leaves, and sauté until the leaves just start to wilt, about 1 minute. Season with salt and pepper. Serve hot.

Grilled Veggie Kebabs

Serves 4

Carb Level: Moderate

Per serving:

Carbohydrate: 12g

Protein: 3g

Fat: 15g

Easy to prepare ahead for a summer cookout.

8–12 (10-inch) skewers
1 green bell pepper, seeded and cut into 1-inch dice
1 pint cherry tomatoes
1 red bell pepper, seeded and cut into 1-inch dice
2 small zucchini, cut into ½-inch-thick rounds
8 ounces medium-sized button mushrooms, stemmed and cleaned
½ cup Italian or Greek salad dressing

1. Clean and oil grill grate and preheat grill to medium.
2. Assemble the kebabs by threading a piece of the green pepper, tomato, red pepper, zucchini, and mushroom on a skewer, repeating the process for each skewer.
3. Brush the skewers generously with salad dressing and cook over a medium-hot fire, continuing to baste with the remaining dressing until the vegetables are lightly charred, about 4 minutes per side. Season with salt and fresh cracked pepper. Serve immediately.

Green Beans with Roquefort Crumbles and Walnuts

1 pound green beans, ends
   trimmed and cut into 2-inch
   pieces
4 slices bacon

4 ounces Roquefort cheese
   crumbles
¾ cup walnut pieces, toasted
Freshly cracked black pepper

Serves 4

Carb Level: Moderate
Per serving:
Carbohydrate: 11g
Protein: 13g
Fat: 24g

Substitute sliced almonds or pecan pieces for the walnuts.

1. Bring a medium-sized saucepan of salted water to a boil. Add the beans and cook until crisp-tender, about 3 to 4 minutes. Drain and set aside.
2. Cook the bacon until crisp, drain, and cut or break into crumbles.
3. To assemble, place the beans on a serving platter and sprinkle bacon pieces, Roquefort crumbles, and toasted walnuts on top. Add a few twists of freshly cracked pepper and serve.

Braised Celery

2 bunches of celery (about
   1½ pounds)
2 tablespoons butter
¾ cup beef stock

½ teaspoon salt
Freshly cracked black pepper
2 tablespoons snipped fresh
   chives

Serves 4

Carb Level: Low
Per serving:
Carbohydrate: 7g
Protein: 2g
Fat: 6g

Add ¼ cup roasted red pepper strips as a garnish.

1. Trim the tops and stem ends from the celery and rinse the stalks to remove any sand and grit. Cut the stalks into 5-inch lengths.
2. Melt the butter in a medium-large nonstick skillet over medium heat. Add the celery stalks and sauté, stirring occasionally, for about 5 minutes.
3. Add the stock, cover, and cook over low heat until tender, about 10 to 12 minutes. Season with salt and pepper. Garnish with chives and serve hot.

Warm Mediterranean Cauliflower Salad

Serves 4

Carb Level: Low

Per serving:

Carbohydrate: 10g

Protein: 5g

Fat: 8g

This delicious vegetable dish is hearty and satisfying.

1 pound cauliflower florets, chopped
1 clove garlic, peeled and minced
⅓ cup vegetable stock
¼ cup pitted kalamata olives
1 tablespoon capers

¼ cup large-diced red bell peppers
½ cup feta crumbles
¼ cup Greek-style salad dressing
Salt, to taste
Freshly cracked black pepper

1. Put the cauliflower, garlic, and stock in a medium-sized saucepan, cover, and simmer for about 8 to 10 minutes, until the cauliflower is tender.
2. Drain the cauliflower, discarding the cooking liquid.
3. Transfer the cauliflower to a medium-sized mixing bowl and add the olives, capers, red peppers, and feta. Toss with salad dressing until evenly coated. Season with salt and pepper to taste. Transfer to a serving platter and serve warm.

Creamed Mushrooms

Serves 4

Carb Level: Low

Per serving:

Carbohydrate: 8g

Protein: 3g

Fat: 23g

A perfect accompaniment to grilled meat.

2 tablespoons butter
1 tablespoon minced shallots
2 teaspoons all-purpose flour
12 ounces mixed mushrooms, cleaned, stems trimmed

¾ cup heavy cream
¼ cup Madeira or port wine
½ teaspoon dried thyme
½ teaspoon salt
Freshly cracked black pepper

1. Melt the butter in a medium-sized nonstick skillet over medium heat and add the shallots; cook over low heat, stirring frequently, until tender, about 5 minutes. Sprinkle the flour over the shallots and stir.
2. Stir in the mushrooms, cream, wine, thyme, salt, and pepper. Simmer over medium-low heat, uncovered, until the sauce thickens slightly, about 20 minutes. Adjust seasoning to taste and serve hot.

Asian Snow Peas with Sesame

1½ tablespoons sesame oil
1 pound fresh snow pea pods,
   rinsed, stem ends trimmed
1 cup sliced scallions
¼ cup red pepper strips (about
   ¼-inch wide)

¼ cup pine nuts or chopped
   peanuts
1 tablespoon sesame seeds
½ teaspoon salt
Freshly cracked black pepper, to
   taste

1. Heat the sesame oil in a medium-sized nonstick skillet over medium heat. Add the snow peas, scallions, and red peppers; sauté over medium heat, stirring frequently, about 3 minutes.
2. Add the nuts, sesame seeds, salt, and pepper. Cook, stirring constantly, for about 2 minutes. Serve hot.

Serves 4

Carb Level: Moderate
Per serving:
Carbohydrate: 12g
Protein: 5g
Fat: 8g

You can substitute frozen snow peas.

Broccoli and Fried Shallots

3 cups broccoli florets
1 tablespoon olive oil
½ cup thinly sliced shallots

Salt, to taste
Freshly cracked black pepper, to
   taste

1. Bring a large saucepot of salted water to a boil. Add the broccoli and cook until vibrant green and crisp-tender, about 7 minutes. Drain and set aside.
2. Heat the oil in a large nonstick skillet over medium heat. Add the shallots and sauté, stirring until the shallots are just lightly browned, about 4 minutes.
3. Add the broccoli, salt, and pepper, and stir-fry for about 1 minute, until mixed. Serve hot.

Serves 4

Carb Level: Low
Per serving:
Carbohydrate: 6g
Protein: 2g
Fat: 4g

Broccoli is a good source of vitamins A and C.

Brussels Sprouts and Toasted Nuts

Serves 4

Carb Level: Low

Per serving:

Carbohydrate: 6g

Protein: 4g

Fat: 6g

Brussels sprouts are available year round, but fall is the best time.

2 cups quartered Brussels sprouts (ends trimmed)

¼ cup coarsely chopped un-salted dry-roasted peanuts

1 tablespoon olive oil

Salt, to taste

Freshly cracked black pepper, to taste

1. Add 1 inch of salted water to a medium-sized saucepan fitted with a vegetable steamer basket. Bring to a boil and add the Brussels sprouts. Cover and cook over medium heat until crisp-tender, about 7 minutes. Rinse under cold water and drain; set aside.
2. Add the peanuts to a large nonstick skillet. Toast the nuts over medium heat, tossing frequently for about 3 minutes. Add the sprouts, oil, salt, and pepper; sauté until heated through, about 5 minutes. Taste and adjust seasoning as desired and serve hot.

Sautéed Kale and Red Wine Vinaigrette

Serves 4

Carb Level: Moderate

Per serving:

Carbohydrate: 17g

Protein: 6g

Fat: 5g

Kale is higher in carbs than most greens but is a pow-erhouse when it comes to vitamins and nutrients.

1½ tablespoons olive oil

1 teaspoon Dijon mustard

½ teaspoon honey

2 teaspoons red wine vinegar

½ teaspoon salt

Freshly cracked black pepper

1½ pounds kale

1. Combine the olive oil, Dijon, honey, and vinegar in a small bowl and whisk to combine. Season with salt and pepper. Set aside.
2. Rinse the kale under cold, running water to remove any sand and grit hiding in the curly leaves. Pull off and discard the stems, and roughly chop the leaves.
3. Place the kale, with just the water that clings to the leaves, in a large nonstick skillet over medium heat. Cook, stirring constantly, until the kale wilts, about 5 minutes. Continue to cook until the leaves are crisp-tender, about 3 minutes. Add the olive oil mixture and stir to combine. Adjust seasoning to taste. Serve hot.

Escarole and Hot Pepper Oil

2 tablespoons olive oil
½ teaspoon red pepper
    flakes
1 clove garlic, minced

2 pounds escarole, washed,
    stemmed, and roughly
    chopped
½ teaspoon salt

1. Heat the oil and red pepper flakes in a large nonstick skillet over low heat. Cook, stirring frequently, for about 4 minutes.
2. Add the garlic and stir, making sure the garlic does not brown (it imparts a bitter taste). Add the escarole and salt and cook, stirring frequently, until the escarole starts to wilt, about 5 minutes. Continue to cook until the leaves are crisp-tender, about 3 to 4 more minutes. Adjust seasoning to taste. Serve hot.

Serves 4

Carb Level: Low
Per serving:
Carbohydrate: 9g
Protein: 5g
Fat: 4g

Top this dish with a few crumbles of crispy bacon, if desired.

Oven-Roasted Asparagus and Parmesan

1½ pounds asparagus, bottoms
    trimmed
1 tablespoon olive oil
½ teaspoon salt

Freshly cracked black pepper, to
    taste
¼ cup freshly grated Parmesan

1. Preheat oven to 450°.
2. In a large mixing bowl, combine the asparagus, olive oil, salt, and pepper. Toss to evenly coat the asparagus. Line a baking sheet with parchment paper and lay out the asparagus in a single layer.
3. Bake until crisp-tender, about 8 minutes, depending on the thickness. Sprinkle the cheese on top, and bake until the cheese melts, about 2 minutes. Taste and adjust seasoning as needed. Transfer to a serving platter and serve hot.

Serves 4

Carb Level: Low
Per serving:
Carbohydrate: 4g
Protein: 4g
Fat: 5g

Medium-sized stalks of asparagus work best for this recipe.

Oven-Braised Fennel with Goat Cheese

Serves 4

Carb Level: Low
Per serving:
Carbohydrate: 3g
Protein: 3g
Fat: 3g

This recipe
has few
ingredients,
so quality
is important.

*1 pound fennel bulbs, trimmed
and cut into ⅛-inch-thick
slices*

¼ cup chicken stock
¼ cup goat cheese crumbles
Freshly cracked black pepper

1. Preheat oven to 400°.
2. Place the fennel slices in an even layer in a medium-sized baking dish. Add the stock and cover with foil. Bake until crisp-tender, about 20 minutes.
3. Remove the foil and top the fennel with the goat cheese crumbles; bake until the cheese just starts to melt, about 3 minutes. Transfer to a serving platter, sprinkle with pepper, and serve immediately.

Roasted Zucchini

Serves 4

Carb Level: Low
Per serving:
Carbohydrate: 3g
Protein: 1g
Fat: 3g

Substitute
yellow squash
for half the
zucchini for
a variation in
color.

1 tablespoon olive oil
*2 cups zucchini rounds (about ½
inch thick)*
½ teaspoon salt

Freshly cracked black pepper
2 tablespoons minced red onion
1 garlic clove, minced
1 teaspoon lemon zest

1. Preheat oven to 425°.
2. Combine the olive oil, zucchini, salt, and pepper in an 8" x 8" baking dish with sides. Use a rubber spatula to stir to coat the zucchini evenly with the oil and seasonings. Bake, uncovered, for about 12 minutes, stirring once midway through cooking.
3. Add the red onion, garlic, and lemon zest, stirring to combine. Bake until the zucchini is tender, about 5 minutes. Transfer to a serving platter and serve hot.

Broiled Eggplant and Sunflower Seeds

1½ pounds eggplant
3 tablespoons olive oil
½ teaspoon kosher salt

Freshly cracked black pepper
¼ cup roasted sunflower seeds

1. Wash and dry the eggplant. Cut the eggplant into ½-inch-thick rounds. Brush both sides of the rounds with olive oil and season with salt and pepper.
2. Oil a broiler pan or rack and preheat the broiler. Broil the eggplant for about 6 to 8 minutes, until lightly browned on top. Turn the slices and broil until cooked through, about 4 minutes.
3. Top the slices with the sunflower seeds and broil for 1 minute. Transfer the eggplant slices to a serving platter and serve hot.

Serves 4

Carb Level: Low
Per serving:

Carbohydrate:	10g
Protein:	3g
Fat:	5g

The nuttiness and texture of the sunflower seeds works well with the eggplant.

Butternut Squash Purée

1 tablespoon butter
2 cups skinned, seeded, and
    cubed butternut squash
½ cup vegetable stock

½ cup heavy cream
1 teaspoon ground cinnamon
¼–½ teaspoon red pepper flakes
¼ cup almond slivers, toasted

1. Melt the butter in a medium-sized saucepan over medium-high heat.
2. Add the squash; cook, stirring occasionally, for about 5 minutes.
3. Add the stock and bring to a simmer; cover and cook until the squash is tender, about 15 to 18 minutes.
4. Use an electric mixer to whip the squash. Drizzle in the heavy cream while mixing until it is the consistency of mashed potatoes.
5. Add the cinnamon and red pepper flakes. Taste and adjust seasoning as desired. Transfer to a serving bowl and top with toasted almonds. Serve immediately.

Serves 4

Carb Level: Moderate
Per serving:

Carbohydrate:	11g
Protein:	3g
Fat:	22g

Butternut squash is a good source of beta-carotene and is loaded with vitamin A.

Sugar Snap Peas

Serves 4

Carb Level: Moderate

Per serving:

Carbohydrate: 16g

Protein: 6g

Fat: 4g

Fresh sugar snap peas only need to be cooked for a moment to bring out their flavor and color.

2 tablespoons water
1 pound sugar snap peas,
washed and stemmed
½ teaspoon salt

Freshly cracked black pepper
1 tablespoon olive oil
2 tablespoons snipped fresh dill

1. Heat the water in a medium-sized nonstick skillet over medium heat. Add the peas, salt, and pepper. Cook, stirring occasionally, until the peas turn bright green and are crisp-tender, just about 2 to 3 minutes.
2. Add the olive oil and dill, toss, and adjust seasoning as desired. Transfer to a serving platter and serve warm or at room temperature.

Chopped Broccoli with Lemon Zest

Serves 4

Carb Level: Low

Per serving:

Carbohydrate: 5g

Protein: 3g

Fat: 10g

A simple and easy summer dish with a clean, fresh taste.

¼ cup water
1–1½ pounds broccoli florets
3 tablespoons olive oil
¼ teaspoon lemon zest

Fresh-squeezed lemon juice, to
taste
½ teaspoon salt
Freshly cracked black pepper

1. Heat the water in a medium-sized saucepan over medium heat. Cook, stirring occasionally, until the broccoli turns bright green and is crisp-tender, about 5 to 6 minutes.
2. Add the olive oil, lemon zest, lemon juice, salt, and pepper; toss to mix, and adjust seasonings as desired. Transfer to a serving platter and serve warm or at room temperature.

Brie and Blue Spread

Serves 6

Carb Level: Low
Per serving:
Carbohydrate: 1g
Protein: 9g
Fat: 21g

Serve with whole-wheat crackers, sliced jicama chips, celery sticks, and carrot sticks.

7 ounces Brie cheese, rind removed, at room temperature
2 ounces blue cheese, at room temperature

3 tablespoons butter, at room temperature
¼ cup heavy cream
Freshly ground white pepper
Parsley sprigs, for garnish

1. Combine the cheeses and butter in a food processor fitted with a metal blade; process the cheeses and butter for 10 seconds. Add the cream and pepper, and process until smooth, stopping once to scrape down the sides of the bowl.
2. Transfer to a serving dish and garnish with parsley sprigs. Serve at room temperature. The spread can be prepared up to 3 days in advance, kept covered, and refrigerated. Bring to room temperature before serving.

Asian Beef Salad

Serves 4

Carb Level: Low
Per serving:
Carbohydrate: 5g
Protein: 17g
Fat: 43g

You can make this recipe even easier by using deli roast beef.

½ cup mayonnaise
2 tablespoons teriyaki sauce
¾ pound cooked beef tenderloin, trimmed, sliced, and cut into strips
½ cup sliced button mushrooms
¼ cup water chestnuts, rinsed and drained

¼ cup Chinese peapods, rinsed and stemmed
Red bell pepper, stemmed, seeded, and cut into matchsticks to yield ¼ cup
¼ cup thinly sliced scallions
Fresh cilantro leaves, for garnish

Mix together the mayonnaise and teriyaki sauce. Place all the remaining ingredients in a medium-sized bowl. Add about ¾ of the dressing mixture and toss to combine. If needed, add more dressing, 1 teaspoon at a time, until desired consistency is achieved. Taste and adjust seasoning as desired. Refrigerate until ready to serve. Garnish with fresh cilantro leaves.

Chicken Sauté with Vegetables and Herbs

4 (5-ounce) skinless, boneless
    chicken breast halves
¼ teaspoon seasoned salt
Freshly ground pepper
1 egg white
1 tablespoon cornstarch
2 tablespoons chicken stock
½ cup sliced white mushrooms
½ cup sliced zucchini

½ cup large-diced green pepper
    (about 1-inch pieces)
½ cup chopped scallions
1 cup chopped tomato
2 teaspoons tamari
1 teaspoon chopped basil
1 teaspoon chopped oregano
1 teaspoon chopped thyme

Serves 4

Carb Level: Low
Per serving:
Carbohydrate: 8g
Protein: 25g
Fat: 11g

This is a great one-skillet meal. You can add spicy chili sauce if you want to add some zip to the recipe.

1. Rinse the chicken and pat dry with paper towels. Line your work area with plastic wrap. Cut the breasts into thirds and place on the plastic wrap. Season the chicken lightly with salt and pepper. Cover with another layer of plastic wrap and lightly pound to a thickness of ½ inch.
2. Combine the egg white and cornstarch in a medium-sized bowl and whisk until smooth. Add the chicken and stir to coat evenly. Let rest for several minutes.
3. Heat the stock in a large nonstick skillet over medium-high heat. Add the chicken and cook for 3 to 4 minutes, just until the chicken is opaque throughout, stirring occasionally. Use a slotted spoon to transfer the chicken to a plate and tent with tinfoil to keep warm.
4. Add the mushrooms to the skillet and cook until softened, about 3 minutes. Add the zucchini, green peppers, scallions, tomatoes, tamari, and herbs. Bring to a simmer and cook, stirring frequently, until the vegetables are crisp-tender, about 5 minutes.
5. Add the chicken and any accumulated juices to the pan and heat through, about 2 minutes. To serve, use a slotted spoon to transfer the chicken and vegetables to warmed serving plates and drizzle a bit of the cooking juices over the meat. Serve hot.

Cream of Spinach Soup

Serves 6

Carb Level: Low

Per serving:

Carbohydrate: 10g

Protein: 6g

Fat: 10g

Pair with an entrée salad for a complete luncheon.

2 (10-ounce) packages frozen chopped spinach
1 cup chopped white onion
6 cups chicken stock
¼ teaspoon salt

Freshly cracked black pepper, to taste
Freshly grated nutmeg, to taste
2 cups half-and-half, at room temperature

1. Combine the spinach, onions, and stock in a large saucepan over medium-high heat. Bring to a low boil and reduce heat to a simmer. Cook until the spinach is tender, about 10 minutes, stirring occasionally. Remove from heat, add the salt, pepper, and nutmeg, and let cool for several minutes.
2. Transfer the mixture to a food processor or blender. Process until smooth.
3. Transfer the spinach mixture back to the saucepan and slowly add the half-and-half, stirring constantly to combine. Reheat gently until heated throughout, about 6 to 8 minutes; do not boil. Serve hot.

Whipped Goat Cheese with Chives and Lemon

Serves 4

Carb Level: Low

Per serving:

Carbohydrate: 2g

Protein: 18g

Fat: 28g

To use as a salad topping: roll in the shape of a log, wrap in plastic wrap, refrigerate; then slice.

8 ounces fresh goat cheese
⅓ cup heavy cream
Pinch salt

⅛ teaspoon black pepper
1 tablespoon snipped chives
½ teaspoon lemon zest

Transfer all the ingredients to a food processor fitted with a metal blade and process until soft and uniform, about 1 minute. Transfer to a serving bowl and serve.

Cooking Tip

Try using a hand blender to purée soups. It saves the step of transferring the soup to a food processor or blender.

Madras Deviled Eggs

2 extra-large eggs
2 tablespoons mayonnaise
1½ tablespoons sour cream
1½ teaspoons Madras Curry
 Powder
⅛ teaspoon (or to taste)
 cayenne

¼ teaspoon ground cumin
1 tablespoon minced Major
 Grey's Chutney
1 tablespoon chopped chives
1 tablespoon fresh-squeezed lime
 juice
Paprika, for garnish

Serves 2

Carb Level: Moderate
Per serving:
Carbohydrate: 16g
Protein: 16g
Fat: 40g

1. Place the eggs in a medium-sized saucepan and add enough cold water to cover the eggs by at least 1 inch. Bring to a medium boil over medium-high heat and cook for 12 minutes. Run cold water over the eggs to cool, then peel and cut in half lengthwise.
2. While the eggs are cooking, mix the filling ingredients. Combine the mayonnaise, sour cream, curry powder, cayenne, cumin, chutney, chives, and lime juice in a small bowl and use a fork to blend into a paste. Add the cooked egg yolks and blend. Use either a small scoop or a pastry bag fitted with a star tip to pipe the filling into the egg whites. Sprinkle with paprika. Place in an airtight container and refrigerate.

This is a flavorful twist to the traditional deviled eggs. If chutneys aren't available at your grocer, you can substitute a good-quality salsa.

Quick Tip

Use a small paring knife to slice a small disk of the egg white from the bottom on each egg half. It will help the egg sit flat and not roll over.

Pan-Seared Veal Chops with Spinach

Serves 4

Carb Level: Low

Per serving:

Carbohydrate: 1g

Protein: 34g

Fat: 29g

Use packaged baby spinach leaves, available in the produce section of your grocer, to save a prep step.

3 tablespoons extra-virgin olive oil

4 bone-in rib veal chops, 1 to 1¼ inches thick, trimmed of excess fat

Salt, to taste

Freshly ground black pepper, to taste

2 teaspoons vegetable oil

1 teaspoon minced garlic

2 teaspoons fresh-squeezed lemon juice

1 teaspoon lemon zest

2 tablespoons minced fresh parsley

8 cups baby spinach leaves

1. Heat the olive oil in a large nonstick skillet over high heat. Season the chops with salt and pepper. Cook the chops until golden on the underside, about 7 minutes. Turn the chops and cook until golden, another 6 to 7 minutes for medium. Transfer the chops to a plate and tent with tinfoil to keep warm.
2. Add the vegetable oil to the pan and heat through, about 1 minute. Add the garlic and cook for about 30 seconds, stirring to prevent scorching. Add the lemon juice, lemon zest, and parsley; sauté for 1 minute, stirring. Add the spinach and cook until just wilted, about 2 minutes. Season with salt and pepper.
3. To serve, equally divide the spinach between 4 warmed serving plates. Top the spinach with a veal chop and drizzle any accumulated juices over the chop.

Salty Tales

Types of salt: Table salt is a fine-grained refined salt with additives that allow it to flow freely. Iodized salt is table salt with added iodine. Kosher salt is an additive-free coarse-grained salt. Sea salt is available in both fine grain and coarse grain and is manufactured by evaporating seawater. Rock salt is somewhat gray in color and comes in large crystals. Pickling salt is an additive-free, fine-grain salt specifically used for brines.

Peppered Tuna Steaks

½ cup good-quality balsamic
   vinegar
2 tablespoons freshly cracked
   peppercorns
⅛ teaspoon kosher salt

4 (8-ounce) tuna steaks,
   1 inch thick
4 tablespoons unsalted butter,
   chilled
Lemon wedges, for garnish

Serves 4

Carb Level: Low
Per serving:
Carbohydrate: 2g
Protein: 53g
Fat: 23g

Use a high-quality sushi-grade tuna steak for this recipe. You can also use tricolored peppercorns to add to the presentation of this dish.

1. Heat the vinegar in a small nonreactive saucepan and bring to a boil. Lower heat and cook until the vinegar is reduced to about 3 table-spoons. Set aside.
2. Press the cracked peppercorns firmly into one side of each tuna steak. Sprinkle the tuna lightly with salt. Heat 1 tablespoon of the butter in a large nonstick skillet over high heat and cook the fish, peppered side down, until seared, about 3 minutes. Turn over and cook for 45 seconds to 1 minute, until the fish is still very pink in the center. Transfer the fish to a plate and tent with tinfoil to keep warm.
3. Add the remaining butter and the reduced vinegar to the pan. Whisking constantly, cook over high heat until thick, 1 to 2 minutes.
4. To serve, place a tuna steak, peppered side up, on each serving plate. Drizzle the sauce over the fish and allow the sauce to pool on one side of the fish. Garnish with lemon wedges and serve hot.

Cracking Up

To crack peppercorns, place them on a rimmed baking sheet. Use a small, heavy-bottomed skillet to "press" on the peppercorns to crack them. The rim on the baking sheet will keep the peppercorns in the work area.

Poached Salmon Italian-Style

Serves 4

Carb Level: Low

Per serving:

Carbohydrate:	4g
Protein:	36g
Fat:	7g

This recipe is so simple, and cleanup is easy since there's just one cooking pan. You can substitute your favorite fish for the salmon.

1 cup chicken stock
½ ripe tomato, chopped
¼ cup green peppers, stemmed, seeded, and cut into ¼-inch dice
½ cup thinly sliced yellow onion
1 cup thinly sliced mushrooms
½ cup thinly sliced zucchini
1 teaspoon minced garlic

2 teaspoons dried Italian seasoning
¼ teaspoon salt
⅛ teaspoon ground black pepper
4 (6-ounce) skinless salmon fillets, about 1 inch thick
2 tablespoons grated Parmesan cheese

1. Combine the stock, tomato, peppers, onion, mushrooms, zucchini, garlic, seasoning, salt, and pepper in a large skillet over medium-high heat. Cover and bring to a boil.
2. Use a spatula to move the vegetables aside and carefully add the salmon fillets. Reduce the heat to medium, cover, and gently simmer until the fish is opaque and firm throughout when tested with a fork.
3. Use a slotted spatula to transfer the salmon to serving plates. Spoon the vegetable mixture over the fish and sprinkle with Parmesan. Serve hot.

What Is the Difference Between a Simmer and a Boil?

A simmer starts at 190° and a gentle boil starts at 200°. A boil starts at 212°. A cooking thermometer will determine the actual temperature. Simmering is a gentler cooking method and won't cause the ingredients to break up. A hard boil is good for pasta but not for vegetables. Soups and stews are best when cooked at a simmer or gentle boil.

Sautéed Chicken Medallions with Gremolata

2 tablespoons roughly chopped garlic
2 teaspoons capers
4 tablespoons chopped parsley
2 tablespoons lemon zest
Pinch kosher salt
Freshly cracked black pepper

1 teaspoon, plus 4 tablespoons olive oil
4 (5- to 6-ounce) skinless, boneless chicken breast halves
3 tablespoons all-purpose flour
1 tablespoon fresh-squeezed lemon juice

Serves 4

Carb Level: Low
Per serving:
Carbohydrate: 8g
Protein: 39g
Fat: 21g

Gremolata is a perfect topping for simply prepared fish and chicken dishes.

1. Combine garlic, capers, parsley, zest, salt, pepper, and 1 teaspoon of the oil in the work bowl of a small food processor and process until finely chopped and evenly blended. Transfer to a bowl and set aside.
2. Rinse and dry chicken with paper towels. Line your work area with plastic wrap. Cut breasts into thirds and place on lined work area. Season chicken lightly with salt and pepper. Cover with another layer of plastic wrap and lightly pound to a thickness of ½ inch.
3. Place flour in a shallow bowl. Dredge chicken medallions in flour and shake off any excess.
4. Heat 2 tablespoons of the oil in a medium nonstick skillet over medium-high heat. Cook chicken medallions until golden, about 3 to 4 minutes per side. Add more oil if needed. Transfer cooked chicken to a plate and tent with tinfoil to keep warm. Allow chicken to rest for 4 to 5 minutes to allow juices to reabsorb.
5. To serve, place 3 medallions on a serving plate, drizzle with lemon juice, and top with a sprinkling of the gremolata.

Gremolata Topping

This is an easy and flavorful topping for soups and stews. In a mini–food processor, combine 2 tablespoons fresh parsley, 1½ tablespoons lemon zest, and 4 cloves of garlic. Add a pinch of kosher salt, a pinch of red pepper flakes, and 1 tablespoon of olive oil. Process until evenly blended. Use a generous 1-teaspoon serving of gremolata as a garnish. (Carbs: 1g per generous 1-teaspoon serving.)

Egg Salad with Bacon and Horseradish

Serves 4

Carb Level: Low

Per serving:

Carbohydrate: 7g
Protein: 17g
Fat: 35g

Hard-boiled eggs are a great high-protein snack and can easily be made into a luncheon salad. Microwave the bacon while you're preparing the other ingredients.

½ cup mayonnaise
3 tablespoons horseradish, lightly drained
¼ teaspoon salt
Freshly cracked black pepper
½ cup finely chopped fresh parsley, plus extra for garnish

6 hard-boiled eggs, peeled and cut into ¼-inch dice
⅓ cup finely diced celery
¼ cup thinly sliced scallions
½ cup crispy cooked bacon crumbles
2 teaspoons caraway seeds, if desired

1. Mix together the mayonnaise, horseradish, salt, and pepper in a small bowl.
2. Combine the remaining ingredients in a medium-sized mixing bowl and lightly toss to mix. Add half of the mayonnaise mixture and toss to coat. Add additional dressing 1 tablespoon at a time until desired consistency is achieved. Taste and adjust seasoning as desired. Refrigerate until ready to serve. Garnish with parsley just before serving.

Savory Salads

Savory salads have always been a quick and easy fix. There are several tips to achieve the best-tasting salad, which is versatile and low in carbs. Use a quality real mayonnaise as opposed to salad dressing. The jar will be labeled with the words "real mayonnaise." Serve salads in the center of a bed of greens garnished with colorful trimmed crispy vegetables.

Deviled Egg Salad

6 hard-boiled eggs, peeled
2 tablespoons Dijon mustard
¼ teaspoon seasoned salt
½ teaspoon paprika

Freshly cracked black pepper, to
taste
2 tablespoons chili sauce
1–2 tablespoons mayonnaise

1. Cut the eggs in half lengthwise and remove the yolks. Set aside the whites. Place the yolks in a small bowl and add the Dijon, salt, paprika, pepper, and chili sauce. Use a fork to blend into a pastelike consistency. Add the mayonnaise, teaspoon by teaspoon, until a somewhat creamy consistency is achieved.
2. Finely chop the reserved egg whites and season with salt and pepper. Use a rubber spatula to fold the whites into the yolk mixture. Refrigerate until ready to serve. Garnish with additional paprika if desired.

Entertaining Tip

There are a number of different creative serving "dishes" you can use for Deviled Egg Salad and similar recipes, including radicchio cups, hollowed-out orange halves, spears of Belgium endive arranged in a starburst pattern, hollowed-out red, green, or orange peppers, seeded cucumber boats, or hollowed-out pineapple halves. There are many attractive presentations that require little, if any plate garnishes.

Serves 3

Carb Level: Low
Per serving:
Carbohydrate: 2g
Protein: 12g
Fat: 17g

This is an old-time classic preparation. You can add a drop or two of hot sauce to add a little zip if you want.

Lancaster County Ham Salad

Serves 4

Carb Level: Low

Per serving:

Carbohydrate: 10g

Protein: 45g

Fat: 44g

Use a good-quality kraut for this Amish favorite, and rinse and drain it well.

1 pound deli ham
2–3 tablespoons mayonnaise
⅛ teaspoon seasoned salt
Freshly cracked black pepper
1 cup sauerkraut, rinsed, drained, and patted dry

¾ pound Swiss cheese, sliced and cut into ¼-inch dice
1 tablespoon caraway seeds
1 tablespoon chopped fresh dill

Grind the deli ham in a food processor fitted with a metal blade, or chop it very finely. Mix the ground ham with 2 tablespoons of the mayonnaise, the salt, and pepper. Add the sauerkraut, cheese, and caraway; mix to combine. If needed, add more mayonnaise, 1 teaspoon at a time, until desired consistency is achieved. Taste and adjust seasoning as desired. Refrigerate until ready to serve, and garnish with dill.

Classic Ham Salad

Serves 3

Carb Level: Low

Per serving:

Carbohydrate: 10g

Protein: 27g

Fat: 20g

Try different types of ham in this recipe to add variety.

1 pound deli ham slices
2–3 tablespoons mayonnaise
2 tablespoons dill pickle relish

1 tablespoon Dijon mustard
Salt, to taste
Freshly cracked black pepper

Grind the deli ham in a food processor fitted with a metal blade, or chop very finely. Combine all the ingredients in a medium-sized mixing bowl, using only 1 or 2 tablespoons of the mayonnaise, and blend with a fork. If needed, add more mayonnaise, 1 teaspoon at a time, to achieve desired consistency. Refrigerate until ready to serve.

German Sausage Salad

3 tablespoons cider vinegar

1 tablespoon strong deli-style or German mustard

2 tablespoons vegetable oil

¼ teaspoon garlic salt

¼ teaspoon paprika

Freshly cracked black pepper, to taste

½ teaspoon brown sugar or honey

¾ pound knockwurst, cooked, cooled, and cut into ⅓-inch dice

¼ cup finely chopped red onion

2 tablespoons finely chopped deli dill pickles

1 tablespoon capers, rinsed and drained

Snipped fresh dill, for garnish

Serves 4

Carb Level: Low
Per serving:
Carbohydrate: 3g
Protein: 10g
Fat: 41g

There are so many sausages available. Your local deli will offer several varieties already cooked.

1. Mix the vinegar, mustard, oil, garlic salt, paprika, pepper, and brown sugar or honey in a small mixing bowl. Taste and adjust seasoning.
2. Combine the knockwurst, onions, pickles, and capers in a medium-sized mixing bowl. Add half of the dressing mixture and toss to combine. If needed, add more dressing, 1 teaspoon at a time, until desired consistency is achieved. Taste and adjust seasoning as desired. Refrigerate until ready to serve. Garnish with fresh-snipped dill.

Cooking Tip

To soften brown sugar, place it in a microwaveable dish and add a slice of fresh bread. Cover tightly and microwave on high for 30 seconds. Discard the bread when done.

Chicken Salad with Cashews and Apples

Serves 4

Carb Level: Low
Per serving:
Carbohydrate: 9g
Protein: 26g
Fat: 48g

You can
substitute
almonds or
walnuts for
the cashews.

½ cup peeled and diced Granny
  Smith apples
2 tablespoons rice wine vinegar
3 cups shredded, cooked chicken
  meat
¾ cup finely chopped celery

½ cup roasted cashew pieces
Pinch celery salt
Freshly ground black pepper
⅓ cup sour cream
⅓ cup mayonnaise
1 tablespoon lemon juice

1. Combine the apples with the rice wine vinegar in a medium-sized non-reactive bowl; toss. Add the chicken, celery, cashews, celery salt, and pepper; mix to combine.
2. Mix together the sour cream, mayonnaise, and lemon juice in a small nonreactive bowl. Add ¾ of the dressing to the chicken mixture and mix well. If needed, add more dressing until desired consistency is achieved. Refrigerate until ready to serve.

Chicken and Blue Cheese Salad

Serves 4

Carb Level: Low
Per serving:
Carbohydrate: 8g
Protein: 52g
Fat: 31g

Garnish the
plate with a
few carrot
sticks and
cucumber
slices.

½ cup blue cheese dressing
2 tablespoons sherry vinegar
1 tablespoon Dijon mustard
¼ cup blue cheese crumbles
½ cup cooked crispy bacon,
  broken into small pieces

4 cups diced or shredded cooked
  chicken meat
½ cup diced ripe avocado (about
  ½-inch dice)
Seasoned salt, to taste
Freshly cracked black pepper

1. Combine the dressing, vinegar, and Dijon in a bowl and mix well.
2. Combine the blue cheese crumbles, bacon, and chicken in a medium-sized mixing bowl. Add ¾ of the dressing to the chicken mixture and mix well. If needed, add more dressing, 1 teaspoon at a time, until desired consistency is achieved. Add the avocado and lightly combine. Taste and adjust seasoning as desired. Refrigerate until ready to serve.

Tuna Salad Niçoise

2 (8-ounce) ahi tuna steaks, cut
   in half, crosswise
Kosher salt
Lemon pepper
2 tablespoons vegetable oil
1 tablespoon, plus 1 teaspoon
   fresh-squeezed lemon juice
⅓ cup olive oil
¼ cup sherry vinegar

¼ teaspoon dry mustard
1 teaspoon chopped fresh basil
¼ cup sliced black olives,
   drained
1 tablespoon capers, rinsed and
   drained
3 anchovy fillets, if desired
Fresh lemon wedges

Serves 4

Carb Level: Low
Per serving:
Carbohydrate: 3g
Protein: 29g
Fat: 33g

Canned tuna salad will always get you through in a pinch. Consider this upgraded version using ahi tuna steaks.

1. Pat the tuna steaks dry with paper towels. Lightly season with salt and lemon pepper. Heat the vegetable oil in a small, heavy-bottomed skillet over high heat until almost smoking. Add the tuna steaks and cook until the underside is golden, about 3 to 4 minutes. Turn the steaks and continue to cook until no redness appears in the center. Remove from heat and drizzle 1 tablespoon of the lemon juice over the steaks. Let cool to room temperature.

2. Combine the remaining teaspoon of lemon juice, the olive oil, vinegar, and dry mustard in a small bowl; whisk until emulsified. Set aside.

3. Transfer the tuna steaks to a clean work surface, reserving any accumulated pan juices. Using a fork, flake the tuna into large pieces and roughly chop into bite-sized pieces. Transfer the chopped tuna and any accumulated pan juices to a medium-sized mixing bowl. Add the basil, olives, and capers, and lightly toss. Add half of the dressing mixture and toss to combine. If needed, add more dressing, 1 teaspoon at a time, until desired consistency is achieved. Taste and adjust seasoning as desired. Refrigerate until ready to serve. Garnish with anchovy fillets, if using, and lemon wedges.

Shrimp Salad

Serves 4

Carb Level: Low
Per serving:

Carbohydrate: 5g
Protein: 26g
Fat: 31g

This is an elegant, savory seafood salad. You can substitute cooked crab or lobster for the shrimp, or try a combination.

1½ pounds cooked medium-sized shrimp, peeled and deveined, tail off (about 2 cups)
¾ cup finely chopped celery
¼ cup finely chopped shallot
½ cup peeled, seeded, and diced cucumber (about ¼-inch dice)
1 tablespoon snipped fresh dill
½ cup mayonnaise
½ cup sour cream
1 teaspoon lemon zest
2 tablespoons fresh-squeezed lemon juice
¼ teaspoon dry mustard
Dash hot pepper sauce
¼ teaspoon Old Bay Seasoning for seafood
⅛ teaspoon Kosher salt
Freshly cracked black pepper
Lemon wedges, for garnish

1. Combine the cooked seafood, celery, shallot, cucumber, and dill in a medium-sized mixing bowl. Refrigerate until ready to dress.
2. Combine the mayonnaise, sour cream, lemon zest, lemon juice, dry mustard, pepper sauce, seafood seasoning, salt, and pepper in a small bowl and whisk together until evenly blended.
3. Add two-thirds of the dressing mixture to the seafood mixture and toss to combine. If needed, add more dressing, 1 teaspoon at a time, until desired consistency is achieved. Taste and adjust seasoning as desired. Refrigerate until ready to serve. Garnish with lemon wedges.

Veggie Tips

All vegetables, with the exceptions of the obvious, like onions, should be thoroughly rinsed under cold, running water. There are several fruit and vegetable "'spray washes'" on the market designed to remove shipping wax and pesticides. Follow the directions on the product label.

Salmon Salad

2 tablespoons capers, rinsed and
  drained
3 tablespoons mayonnaise
2 tablespoons ranch dressing
1 tablespoon chopped fresh
  parsley
Seasoned salt, to taste

Freshly cracked black pepper
16 ounces cooked salmon,
  skinned, boned, dark vein
  removed, and cut into bite-
  sized pieces
2 tablespoons chopped red onion
Lemon wedges, for garnish

Serves 4

Carb Level: Low
Per serving:
Carbohydrate: 1g
Protein: 23g
Fat: 17g

This is a nice
way to use an
extra piece
of cooked
salmon. You
can substi-
tute your
own favorite
dressing or
spice blend
for the ranch.

1. Combine the capers, mayonnaise, ranch dressing, parsley, salt, and pepper in a small bowl; mix well.
2. Combine the salmon and red onion in a medium-sized bowl and lightly toss together.
3. Add two-thirds of the dressing mixture to the salmon mixture and toss to combine. If needed, add more dressing, 1 teaspoon at a time, until desired consistency is achieved. Taste and adjust seasoning as desired. Refrigerate until ready to serve. Garnish with lemon wedges.

Tasty Salad Additions

Looking for things to add to salads without adding a lot of carbs? Low-carb salad additions include shaved Parmesan, blue cheese crumbles, goat cheese crumbles, and crispy bacon bits, to name just a few.

Pan-Sautéed Sausages with Dijon Glaze

Serves 1

Carb Level: Moderate

Per serving:

Carbohydrate: 15g

Protein: 31g

Fat: 20g

Sample a few of the gourmet sausages and regional specialties that are available now.

6 ounces gourmet chicken and apple sausage
1 tablespoon Dijon mustard
1 teaspoon Worcestershire sauce
1 teaspoon minced garlic

1 tablespoon ketchup
1 tablespoon olive oil
Pinch garlic salt
Freshly cracked black pepper

1. Cut the sausage into 1½-inch pieces. Combine the Dijon, Worcestershire, garlic, and ketchup in a small bowl and mix until blended.
2. Heat the oil in a small nonstick skillet over medium heat. Add the sausage pieces and cook, stirring frequently, until just starting to brown, about 5 to 6 minutes. Add the Dijon glaze and stir to coat the sausages. Cook until heated through, about 2 minutes. Serve hot with the pan glaze.

Sautéed Chicken with Asparagus

Serves 1

Carb Level: Low

Per serving:

Carbohydrate: 9g

Protein: 27g

Fat: 17g

Use medium-sized asparagus stalks if possible.

4 ounces asparagus spears
1 (5-ounce) skinless, boneless chicken breast
⅛ teaspoon salt
Freshly cracked black pepper

1 tablespoon all-purpose flour
1 tablespoon olive oil
¼ cup sliced red pepper
1 teaspoon lemon zest
⅓ cup chicken stock

1. Rinse the asparagus under cold, running water and pat dry with paper towels. Snap off and discard the woody bases of the asparagus stems and bias-cut the spears into 1½-inch pieces.
2. Rinse the chicken under cold, running water and pat dry with paper towels. Season with salt and pepper and coat with flour. Heat the oil in a nonstick skillet over medium-high heat. Add the chicken and cook for about 4 minutes until golden brown. Turn the chicken and add the red pepper, lemon zest, and stock; bring to a simmer. Simmer until the chicken is tender and cooked through, about 8 minutes.

Broiled Swordfish Kebab

1 teaspoon fresh-squeezed lime
   juice
1 tablespoon olive oil
1 teaspoon Dijon mustard
1 teaspoon snipped chives
Salt, to taste
Freshly cracked black pepper

1 (5-ounce) swordfish fillet, about
   1 inch thick
¼ red onion
¼ red pepper
¼ green pepper
2 cherry tomatoes
1 (10-inch) skewer

Serves 1

Carb Level: Moderate
Per serving:
Carbohydrate: 11g
Protein: 29g
Fat: 19g

Buy the
freshest
swordfish
fillet pos-
sible—you
can substi-
tute tuna or
halibut if you
like.

1. Combine the lime juice, olive oil, Dijon, chives, and salt and pepper (to taste) in a small, nonmetal bowl. Cut the swordfish fillet into 4 even-sized pieces and add to the marinade, stirring once or twice to coat evenly. Refrigerate for 5 minutes.
2. Prepare the vegetables by cutting them into 1-inch squares. Oil broiler rack and place it about 4 inches from the heat source. Preheat broiler to medium-high.
3. Remove the fish from the marinade, reserving the marinade. Thread the vegetables and fish cubes onto the skewer, alternating the fish cubes with the vegetables. Brush the kebab with the reserved marinade.
4. Place the kebab on the oiled rack and cook for about 2 minutes per side, brushing with the marinade after each turn. Discard any remaining marinade. Cook about 10 to 12 minutes total, until the fish is cooked through and the vegetables are browned at the edges. Serve hot.

Sensitive Vitamins

Certain vitamins are sensitive to the elements. For example, vitamin C is sensitive to heat, air, and water. Vitamin D is sensitive to fat. What does it mean? Broil fish that is rich in vitamin D instead of pan-frying to retain the rich nutrients.

Ginger-Orange Chicken Breast

Serves 1

Carb Level: Low

Per serving:

Carbohydrate: 5g

Protein: 32g

Fat: 15g

Double the recipe and bring a chicken breast for your lunch. This is also great chilled, sliced, and served on a crispy green salad.

1 (5-ounce) skinless, boneless chicken breast
1 tablespoon butter
⅛ teaspoon seasoned salt
Freshly cracked black pepper

1 clove garlic, minced
2 teaspoons grated ginger
1 teaspoon orange zest
2 tablespoons orange juice

1. Rinse the chicken under cold, running water and pat dry with paper towels. Melt the butter in a small nonstick skillet over medium-high heat. Season the chicken with salt and pepper. Brown the chicken, turning it once, about 8 minutes per side. Transfer the chicken to a plate and keep warm.

2. Add the garlic to the pan and cook for about 1 minute, stirring frequently to prevent burning. Add the ginger, orange zest, and juice, and bring to a simmer. Add the chicken and any reserved juices and heat through, about 4 to 5 minutes. Cut through the bottom of the chicken to make sure it is cooked. Adjust seasoning to taste. Serve hot with the sauce.

Working with Chicken

Quick and easy cooking means using preprocessed products, especially chicken. Boneless, skinless chicken breasts are available in many forms: fresh, frozen, marinated, seasoned, and even precooked. Use fresh boneless, skinless breasts available in the meat section of your grocer. Use a good reputable brand and check the freshness date. Prior to cooking or preparing, always rinse the meat under cold running water and pat dry with paper towels.

Turkey Cutlets with Peach Salsa

1 (5-ounce) turkey cutlet
⅛ teaspoon garlic salt
Freshly cracked black pepper
1 teaspoon all-purpose flour
1 tablespoon olive oil

¼ cup quality chunky salsa
⅛ teaspoon red pepper flakes
¼ cup diced fresh peach (about
   ½-inch dice)
2 tablespoons chopped cilantro

1. Season the cutlet with the garlic salt and pepper. Sprinkle both sides of the cutlet with the flour. Heat the oil in a small nonstick skillet over medium-high heat. Sauté the cutlet until lightly browned, about 4 minutes per side. Transfer the cutlet to a plate and set aside.
2. Add the salsa, red pepper flakes, and peaches to the pan. Cook until heated through, about 2 minutes. Add the turkey and any juices; lightly simmer until heated through, about 2 more minutes. Taste and adjust seasoning as desired. Serve hot, garnished with fresh cilantro.

Serves 1

Carb Level: Moderate
Per serving:

Carbohydrate:	17g
Protein:	33g
Fat:	16g

Great flavors are blended for this easy, one-skillet preparation.

Tuscan Lamb Chops

2 lamb rib chops (about
   6–8 ounces total)
⅛ teaspoon garlic salt
Freshly cracked black pepper
1 tablespoon olive oil

1 clove garlic, minced
¼ cup marinara sauce
1 tablespoon balsamic vinegar
Chopped fresh rosemary, for
   garnish

1. Trim excess fat from the chops and season with the garlic salt and pepper. Heat the oil in a small nonstick skillet over medium-high heat. Add the chops and cook for about 4 minutes. Turn the chops and cook for another 4 minutes for medium. Transfer to a plate and keep warm.
2. Reduce heat to medium-low and add the garlic to the pan, stirring to prevent the garlic from browning. Add the marinara sauce and vinegar, and bring to a simmer; cook for about 2 minutes. Spoon the sauce over the chops and any accumulated juices. Garnish with fresh rosemary and serve hot.

Serves 1

Carb Level: Low
Per serving:

Carbohydrate:	7g
Protein:	23g
Fat:	51g

Try the fresh marinara sauces available in the refrigerated section of the supermarket.

Peanut-Glazed Chicken

Serves 1

Carb Level: Low

Per serving:

Carbohydrate: 8g

Protein: 40g

Fat: 18g

You gotta love recipes this simple and tasty.

1 (5-ounce) skinless, boneless chicken breast
Pinch seasoned salt
¼ cup plain yogurt

1 tablespoon creamy peanut butter
Pinch cayenne pepper
1 tablespoon chopped peanuts

1. Preheat oven to 375°.
2. Line a small baking pan with tinfoil. Rinse the chicken under cold, running water and pat dry with paper towels. Lightly season the chicken with salt and place in the center of the baking pan.
3. Combine the yogurt, peanut butter, and cayenne in a small bowl and mix until smooth. Spread on top of the chicken breast.
4. Bake the chicken, uncovered, until cooked through and juices run clear, about 17 to 20 minutes. Garnish with chopped peanuts.

Beef Tenderloin and Mushroom Stir-Fry

Serves 1

Carb Level: Low

Per serving:

Carbohydrate: 10g

Protein: 28g

Fat: 60g

Fillets may be expensive, but the convenience of no prep and no waste makes them a great one-skillet dinner.

1 (5-ounce) beef tenderloin fillet, 1 inch thick
Garlic salt, to taste
Freshly cracked black pepper
2 tablespoons olive oil, divided

1 teaspoon grainy mustard
4 ounces sliced mushrooms
¼ cup sherry wine
1 teaspoon chopped fresh thyme

1. Trim any visible fat from the fillet and cut into 5 even-sized chunks. Season the fillet with garlic salt and pepper. Heat 1 tablespoon of the oil in a small nonstick skillet over medium-high heat. Add the mustard and fillet pieces and stir-fry to desired temperature, about 7 minutes total for medium-rare. Transfer the meat to a plate and tent with tinfoil to keep warm.
2. Heat the remaining oil and add the mushrooms, and stir-fry for about 3 minutes. Add the sherry and simmer until reduced by ⅓, about 3 minutes. Add the thyme, and adjust seasoning to taste. Spoon mushroom sauce over the fillet pieces and accumulated juices. Serve hot.

Grilled Pepper Steak with Gorgonzola

1 (5-ounce) beef tenderloin fillet
⅛ teaspoon Kosher salt
Freshly cracked pepper
2 tablespoons olive oil
⅛ cup sliced yellow onion

¼ cup bell pepper strips,
*   assorted colors (thin strips)*
1 clove garlic, minced
¼ cup beef or chicken stock
1 tablespoon Gorgonzola
*   crumbles*

Serves 1

Carb Level: Low
Per serving:
Carbohydrate: 5g
Protein: 29g
Fat: 64g

1. Preheat grill or oven broiler to medium-high; lightly oil the grill or broiler rack. Season the fillet with salt and pepper.
2. Heat the oil in a small nonstick skillet over medium-high heat. Add the onions and pepper strips and cook for about 4 minutes, stirring frequently. Add the garlic and cook for about 30 seconds, stirring to prevent the garlic from scorching. Remove from heat and set aside.
3. Grill or broil the fillet, about 4 minutes per side for medium-rare. While the fillet is cooking, reheat the pepper mixture over medium heat and add the stock. Bring to a simmer and cook for about 2 minutes to allow the flavors to meld.
4. Transfer the steak to a warm plate and let rest for about 4 to 5 minutes before serving. To serve, ladle the pepper mixture over the steak and top with the Gorgonzola crumbles. Serve hot.

If you don't have a grill, broiling the steaks works just as well. Use the convenience of the salad bar for the onions and peppers.

Cleaning Tip
If you use a garlic press to mince garlic, use an old toothbrush to clean the grid. The small head of the toothbrush makes it easy to get into hard-to-reach areas. Pop the toothbrush into the dishwasher to clean it.

Chicken Paprika

Serves 1

Carb Level: Low

Per serving:

Carbohydrate: 6g

Protein: 34g

Fat: 30g

This is an old favorite. Serve alongside a simple cucumber side dish for a hearty, satisfying meal.

1 (5-ounce) skinless, boneless chicken breast

Pinch garlic salt

Freshly cracked black pepper, to taste

1 tablespoon olive oil

1 clove garlic, minced

1 teaspoon Hungarian paprika

⅓ cup chicken stock

¼ cup sour cream, at room temperature

2 tablespoons chopped parsley

1. Rinse the chicken under cold, running water and pat dry with paper towels. Season with garlic salt and pepper. Heat the oil in a small nonstick skillet over medium-high heat. Cook the chicken until lightly browned, about 4 to 5 minutes per side. Transfer the chicken to a plate and cover with tinfoil to keep warm.
2. Reduce heat to medium-low and add the garlic, paprika, and chicken stock, stirring to combine. Bring to a simmer and cook until slightly reduced, about 5 minutes. Reduce heat to low and add the sour cream, whisking constantly to blend.
3. Return the chicken and any accumulated juices to the pan and cook until the chicken is cooked through, about 5 minutes. Serve with sauce ladled over the chicken and garnished with parsley.

What Is Reduction?

Many dishes are flavored through a "reduction" method. Reduction is a cooking definition that means boiling a liquid until it is reduced by evaporation, thereby concentrating the flavor. The reduced liquids are usually stocks, wines, sauces, or bouillon mixtures.

Chicken with Curry and Apricot Sauce

1 (5-ounce) skinless, boneless
   chicken breast
⅛ teaspoon seasoned salt
Lemon pepper, to taste
1 tablespoon vegetable oil
¼ cup sliced red onion

1 clove garlic, minced
¼ cup chicken broth
½ teaspoon curry powder
¼ cup apricot preserves
¼ cup plain yogurt, at room
   temperature

Serves 1

Carb Level: Moderate
Per serving:
Carbohydrate: 17g
Protein: 34g
Fat: 16g

This dish
has a sweet
taste and the
apricot pre-
serves add a
nice texture
to the sauce.

1. Rinse the chicken under cold, running water and pat dry with paper towels. Season the chicken with salt and lemon pepper. Heat the oil in a small nonstick skillet over medium-high heat. Cook the chicken until lightly browned, about 4 to 5 minutes per side. Transfer the chicken to a plate and tent with tinfoil to keep warm.
2. Reduce heat to medium-low and add the red onion. Cook until soft, about 2 minutes, stirring occasionally. Add the garlic and stir to combine. Add the broth, curry powder, and apricot preserves; bring to a simmer and cook until thickened, about 5 minutes.
3. Return the chicken and any accumulated juices to the pan and cook until the chicken is cooked through, about 5 minutes. Transfer the chicken to a serving plate and keep warm. Add the yogurt to the pan and stir to combine. Ladle sauce over the chicken and serve.

Supermarket Convenience

If cooking for one, shop at stores that only sell fruit and vegetables in bulk, not pre-packaged, so you can purchase only what you need. Salad bars are also effective, as you'll have no waste and it saves preparation time.

Broiled Pork Chops with Dill

Serves 2

Carb Level: Low

Per serving:

Carbohydrate: 1g

Protein: 18g

Fat: 12g

Cook two of these delicious chops and save the extra for later for a quick dinner fix.

2 (10-ounce) boneless pork loin chops, ½ inch thick
⅛ teaspoon seasoned salt
Freshly cracked black pepper
1 tablespoon olive oil
½ teaspoon dry dill weed
Pinch garlic powder
1 teaspoon Worcestershire sauce

1. Oil a broiler rack and position about 4 inches from the heat source. Preheat oven broiler to medium-high.
2. Trim excess fat from the chops and pierce in several places with a fork. Season with salt and pepper. Combine the olive oil, dill weed, garlic powder, and Worcestershire in a medium-sized bowl and mix to combine. Add the chops and turn to coat evenly.
3. Broil the chops for about 4 minutes on each side, until cooked through. Transfer to a plate, tent with foil, and let rest for 3 to 4 minutes. Serve hot with any accumulated juices. Store remaining chop with juices tightly sealed in the refrigerator. Reheat, covered, in a preheated 375° oven for about 10 to 14 minutes, until warmed throughout.

What Is the Proper Temperature for Pork?

Pork is generally served at the medium-well stage, 155° to 160° internal temperature. Better methods of raising hogs have eliminated the threat of trichinosis, which is actually destroyed at 137°.

Baked Red Snapper Veracruz

1 tablespoon olive oil
¼ cup finely diced yellow onion
4 ounces canned whole tomatoes
½ jalapeño pepper, seeded and
  minced
⅛ cup pimento-stuffed olives

1 tablespoon fresh cilantro
1 (6-ounce) skinless red snapper
  fillet
Pinch kosher salt
Red pepper flakes, to taste

Serves 1

Carb Level: Low
Per serving:
Carbohydrate: 10g
Protein: 2g
Fat: 16g

If you're not
a snapper
fan, you can
easily sub-
stitute cod,
halibut, or
salmon—just
use the
freshest fish
available.

1. Preheat oven to 400°.
2. Heat the oil in a large nonstick skillet over medium-high heat. Add the onion and cook until soft, about 4 to 5 minutes, stirring frequently. Add the tomatoes, jalapeño, olives, and cilantro. Bring to a simmer and cook for about 3 minutes, until slightly thickened.
3. Lightly oil a small baking dish. Place the fish in the center of the pan and lightly season with salt and red pepper flakes. Fold the tail section under to make the fish consistent in thickness. Pour the tomato mixture evenly over the fish. Cover the pan with tinfoil and bake for 10 to 12 minutes, until the fish is opaque and flakes easily when tested with a fork. Use a spatula to transfer the fish to a serving plate and top with the tomato mixture. Serve hot.

Precautions

Jalapeños can burn your eyes and irritate your skin. Wear rubber gloves when prepping and make sure you don't touch your eyes. Wash your hands and work area thoroughly after prepping.

Chicken Salad with Southwestern Ranch-Style Dressing

1 (5-ounce) skinless, boneless chicken breast
¼ teaspoon chili powder
Seasoned salt, to taste
½ tablespoon vegetable oil

¼ cup quality ranch dressing
¼ cup Spicy Salsa (see page 228)
4 ounces mixed salad greens
¼ cup shredded Cheddar cheese
Freshly cracked pepper, to taste

1. Rinse the chicken under cold, running water and pat dry with paper towels. Cut the chicken into 1-inch pieces. Sprinkle with chili powder and seasoned salt. Heat the oil in a small nonstick skillet over medium-high heat. Add the chicken and sauté for about 6 to 8 minutes, until cooked through, stirring occasionally.
2. Mix together the ranch dressing and salsa until blended. To assemble, place the salad greens on a plate; top with chicken, drizzle with the dressing, and sprinkle the cheese and pepper over the top. Serve warm.

Brats and Red Cabbage

1 tablespoon olive oil
8 ounces bratwurst links
½ cup chopped white onion
½ cup cooked red cabbage, rinsed
⅛ teaspoon seasoned salt

Freshly cracked black pepper
½ teaspoon caraway seeds
¼ cup grated Gruyère cheese
2 tablespoons Dijon mustard

1. Heat the oil in a medium-sized nonstick skillet over medium heat. Add the brats and cook, turning occasionally, until just starting to brown, about 8 minutes. Add the onions and cook until soft, stirring frequently, about 5 minutes. Add the cabbage, salt, pepper, and caraway seeds (if using); stir and cook until heated through, about 4 minutes.
2. To serve, place half of the cabbage on a serving plate, top with a bratwurst, and sprinkle with the cheese. Serve the Dijon on the side. Store the remaining cabbage, bratwurst, and cheese in an airtight container and refrigerate.

Breaded Chicken Breast

1 (5-ounce) skinless, boneless
    chicken breast
Pinch seasoned salt
Freshly cracked black pepper
1 tablespoon Dijon mustard

1 tablespoon fresh lemon juice
1 teaspoon olive oil
1 teaspoon snipped chives
1 tablespoon minced shallots
2 tablespoons fresh bread crumbs

Serves 1

Carb Level: Low
Per serving:
Carbohydrate: 7g
Protein: 19g
Fat: 21g

Fresh bread-
crumbs add
something
special.

1. Preheat oven to 375°. Line a small baking pan with tinfoil. Rinse the chicken under cold, running water and pat dry with paper towels. Season the chicken with salt and pepper and set aside.
2. In a small bowl, mix together the mustard, lemon juice, olive oil, chives, and shallots.
3. Dip the chicken in the mustard mixture to coat evenly and place in the center of the lined baking pan. Press the bread crumbs in an even layer over the top of the chicken. Bake, uncovered, until the juices run clear and the topping is browned, about 17 to 20 minutes. Serve hot.

Chicken Apple Sausages with Dijon Glaze

6 ounces gourmet chicken and
    apple sausages
1 tablespoon Dijon mustard
1 teaspoon Worcestershire sauce
1 teaspoon minced garlic

1 tablespoon ketchup
1 tablespoon olive oil
Pinch garlic salt
Freshly cracked black pepper

Serves 1

Carb Level: Moderate
Per serving:
Carbohydrate: 15g
Protein: 31g
Fat: 20g

Try other
gourmet sau-
sages on the
market.

1. Cut the sausages into 1½-inch pieces. Combine the Dijon, Worcestershire, garlic, and ketchup in a small bowl and mix until blended.
2. Heat the oil in a small nonstick skillet over medium heat and add the sausage pieces; cook, stirring frequently, until just starting to brown, about 5 to 6 minutes. Add the Dijon glaze and stir to coat the sausages. Season with garlic salt and pepper. Cook until heated through, about 2 minutes. Serve hot with the pan glaze.

Easy Oven-Barbecued Chicken Thighs

Serves 1

Carb Level: Moderate

Per serving:

Carbohydrate: 11g

Protein: 31g

Fat: 27g

Chicken thighs are a flavorful chicken cut. You can substitute boneless, skinless chicken breasts if you prefer white meat.

2 boneless chicken thighs (about 7 ounces total)
Pinch seasoned salt
Freshly cracked black pepper
1 teaspoon Dijon mustard

1 tablespoon ketchup
1 teaspoon honey
½ tablespoon lemon juice
½ teaspoon lemon zest
1 teaspoon olive oil

1. Preheat oven to 375°.
2. Line a small baking pan with tinfoil. Rinse the chicken under cold, running water and pat dry with paper towels. Season the chicken with salt and pepper and place in the center of the baking pan.
3. In a small bowl, mix together the mustard, ketchup, honey, lemon juice, lemon zest, and olive oil.
4. Brush the chicken with the sauce and bake for 25 minutes, until the juices run clear. Halfway through cooking, baste with any remaining sauce. Serve hot.

Cooking Tip

You should taste and adjust seasoning several times throughout the cooking process. It is more effective to season a little several times instead of seasoning a lot at the end. Be aware of items with high sodium, like canned chicken stock.

Pan-Fried Catfish

1 egg white
1 (5-ounce) skinless catfish fillet
1 tablespoon cornmeal
Pinch cayenne pepper

Pinch seasoned salt
3 tablespoons vegetable oil
Lemon wedges, for garnish

1. Beat the egg white in a shallow bowl until foamy. Dip the catfish fillet in the egg and sprinkle both sides of the fish with cornmeal. Season with salt and pepper.
2. Heat the oil in a medium-sized nonstick skillet over medium heat. When the oil is very hot, but not smoking, carefully place the catfish in the pan. Cook until golden, about 2 to 3 minutes. Use a spatula to carefully turn the fillet and cook another 2 to 3 minutes until the fillet is golden on both sides and firm to the touch.
3. Transfer the fish to several layers of paper towels to absorb any excess oil. Transfer to a serving plate and garnish with lemon wedges.

When Is Hot Hot Enough?

How do you know when the oil is hot enough when you're pan-frying? Whatever you do, don't stick your finger in it to test! The oil should appear to be rippling in the pan, but not smoking. It's important to make sure the oil is hot enough, otherwise the food you are cooking will soak up the oil and be soggy and greasy.

Serves 1

Carb Level: Low
Per serving:
Carbohydrate: 7g
Protein: 27g
Fat: 35g

Serve this with sautéed greens with bacon and a slice of ice-cold watermelon for a true Southern treat.

Steamed Littleneck Clams
with Herbs and Butter

Serves 1

Carb Level: Moderate

Per serving:

Carbohydrate: 11g

Protein: 38g

Fat: 3g

Clams are generally pretty salty, so there is no need to add any additional salt in this recipe.

15–20 littleneck clams, the
smaller the better
½ cup dry white wine
1 tablespoon minced shallots
1 teaspoon minced garlic

1 teaspoon chopped fresh parsley
1 teaspoon chopped mint
¼ cup (½ stick) butter
Freshly cracked black pepper

1. Wash and scrub the clams very well under cold, running water. Heat the wine, shallots, garlic, parsley, and mint in a heavy-bottomed saucepan with a tight-fitting lid over high heat. Add the clams and cover; cook until the clams open, about 5 minutes, shaking the pan occasionally.
2. Transfer the clams to a shallow bowl and leave any clams that did not open in the pot (they may open yet). Lower the heat to medium and add the butter, 1 tablespoon at a time, until melted. Discard any clams that did not open. Pour the sauce over the clams and serve hot.

Littlenecks

Littleneck clams are the smallest hard-shell clams with a diameter of less than 2 inches. They are flavorful and tender; the smaller the shell, the younger and more tender the clam.

Pan-Sautéed Pork Chops with Stilton and Port

2 center-cut rib pork chops, about 1 inch thick
Pinch seasoned salt
Fresh-cracked black pepper
1 tablespoon olive oil
¼ cup port wine
⅓ cup chicken stock

¼ cup heavy cream, at room temperature
1 teaspoon minced fresh jalapeño, if desired
2 ounces Stilton or blue cheese crumbles

Serves 1

Carb Level: Low
Per serving:
Carbohydrate: 9g
Protein: 45g
Fat: 63g

Stilton cheese and port wine are paired together to create a deliciously rich and creamy sauce for these succulent chops.

1. Trim all visible fat from the chops and season lightly with salt and pepper. Heat the oil in a small nonstick skillet over medium-high heat. Add the chops and cook, turning as needed, until browned on both sides and cooked through, about 16 minutes total. Transfer the chops to a plate and tent with tinfoil to keep warm.
2. Pour out remaining fat in pan and add port and stock. Bring to a simmer over medium heat and cook until slightly reduced, about 4 minutes. Slowly add the cream, whisking constantly to incorporate. Cook until the sauce is shiny and bubbly, about 3 minutes.
3. Add jalapeños, if using, and cook for just a minute. Remove from heat and stir in the Stilton crumbles. Place the chops on a serving plate with any accumulated juices and pour the Stilton sauce over the chops. Serve hot.

Jalapeño Facts

This chili is named after Jalapa, the capital of Veracruz, Mexico. The heat in these little guys is located in the seeds and veins. They are available fresh or canned. When working with chilies, always wear rubber gloves and avoid touching your eyes. Scrub down your work area, as the oils from the peppers are easily transferred.

Pan-Seared Ahi Tuna with Wasabi Aioli and Seaweed Salad

Serves 1

Carb Level: Low

Per serving:

Carbohydrate: 10g

Protein: 41g

Fat: 25g

This is a simple preparation featuring Japanese seaweed salad.

2 tablespoons mayonnaise
1 tablespoon fresh lemon juice
1 tablespoon wasabi paste
1 (6-ounce) sushi-grade ahi tuna
   steak, 1 inch thick
Pinch seasoned salt
Pinch cayenne pepper
4 ounces seaweed salad

1. Combine the mayonnaise, lemon juice, and wasabi paste until evenly blended. Set aside until ready to serve.
2. Heat a heavy-bottomed nonstick skillet over high heat. Pat the tuna dry with paper towels. Season with salt and cayenne pepper on both sides. Quickly sear the tuna, just about 45 seconds on each side. Tuna should be very rare in the center. To serve, place the seaweed salad on a plate. Place the tuna on top and finish with a dollop of the wasabi aioli.

Lamb Loin Chops with Yogurt Sauce

Serves 1

Carb Level: Low

Per serving:

Carbohydrate: 5g

Protein: 21g

Fat: 36g

Lamb chops are nicely paired with the creamy tanginess of the yogurt sauce.

2 lamb loin chops, 8–10 ounces
Pinch garlic salt
Freshly cracked black pepper
2 teaspoons olive oil
¼ cup plain yogurt
1 garlic clove, minced
1 teaspoon chopped mint
1 tablespoon peeled, seeded, and
   finely diced cucumber
1 teaspoon fresh lemon juice

1. Season the chops with garlic salt and pepper. Heat the oil in a small nonstick skillet over medium-high heat and add the chops. Cook until browned on both sides, about 3 to 4 minutes per side for medium. Transfer to a plate and tent with tinfoil to keep warm.
2. Combine the remaining ingredients in a small bowl and mix until blended. To serve, transfer the chops to a serving plate and drizzle with any accumulated juices. Place a dollop of yogurt sauce on the side. Serve hot.

Asian Salmon Patties

1 egg, beaten
1 tablespoon chopped cilantro
1 teaspoon hoisin sauce
½ tablespoon mayonnaise
½ tablespoon chopped scallion
Pinch minced fresh ginger

1 garlic clove, minced
⅛ teaspoon seasoned salt
Freshly cracked black pepper
¼ pound skinless salmon fillet,
*   cut into ⅓-inch pieces*
3 tablespoons fresh bread crumbs

1. In a medium-sized bowl, mix together all the ingredients except the salmon and bread crumbs. Add the salmon and bread crumbs and lightly toss until blended.
2. Heat a small nonstick skillet over medium-high heat. Split the salmon mixture in half; place the 2 portions in the skillet, 1 inch apart. Cook the cakes until the underside is golden, about 1½ minutes. Carefully flip and cook for about 1 to 2 minutes more. Transfer the cakes to a plate and let rest for several minutes. Serve at room temperature.

Serves 1

Carb Level:
Per serving:
Carbohydrate: 8g
Protein: 41g
Fat: 17g

Serve this with the Asian Chili Aioli (see below).

Asian Chili Aioli

¼ cup mayonnaise
2 tablespoons Asian chili sauce

1 teaspoon tamari

Combine all the ingredients in a small bowl and mix until blended. Refrigerate until ready to serve.

Serves 2

Carb Level: Low
Per serving:
Carbohydrate: 1g
Protein: 1g
Fat: 23g

This easy sauce goes great with dishes with an Asian flair.

Soy Sauce Vs. Tamari

Tamari is a sauce brewed from soybeans. It has a mellow taste and flavor and is slightly thicker and milder than soy sauce. You can substitute soy sauce for tamari in the same amount.

Fried Ham Steak with Cider Glaze

Serves 1

Carb Level: Low
Per serving:
Carbohydrate: 9g
Protein: 46g
Fat: 21g

Use a good-
quality ham
steak from the
butcher.

1 (8-ounce) ham steak
2 tablespoons unsalted butter,
   divided
½ teaspoon brown sugar or
   equivalent sugar substitute

1 teaspoon Dijon mustard
2 tablespoons apple juice or cider
¼ cup chicken stock
1 teaspoon tamari
1 teaspoon chopped fresh thyme

1. Pat the ham steak dry with paper towels. Melt 1 tablespoon of the butter in a medium-sized nonstick skillet over medium heat. Add the ham steak and cook until just starting to brown, about 3 minutes per side. Transfer the meat to a plate and tent with tinfoil to keep warm.
2. Melt the remaining tablespoon of butter and add the brown sugar or sugar substitute, mustard, apple cider, stock, tamari, and thyme. Bring to a simmer and cook until syrupy, about 3 minutes, stirring occasionally. Add the ham along with any juices; heat through, about 1 minute. Serve hot.

Parmesan-Crusted Chicken Breast

Serves 1

Carb Level: Low
Per serving:
Carbohydrate: Trace
Protein: 34g
Fat: 5g

The Parmesan
actually forms
a crust on the
chicken. Use a
finely grated
cheese for this
recipe.

1 (5-ounce) skinless, boneless
   chicken breast
Pinch seasoned salt
Freshly cracked black pepper, to
   taste

1 tablespoon freshly grated
   Parmesan
1 tablespoon dry white wine

1. Preheat oven to 375°. Line a small baking pan with tinfoil.
2. Rinse the chicken under cold, running water and pat dry with paper towels. Season the chicken with salt and pepper and place in the center of the baking pan.
3. Combine the Parmesan and wine in a small bowl and mix to a paste-like consistency. Spread the mixture on top of the chicken breast. Bake the chicken, uncovered, until cooked through and juices run clear, about 17 to 20 minutes. Serve hot.

Crispy Shrimp Vegetable Salad

½ cup lightly chopped cooked
   shrimp, peeled, tail removed
¼ cup water chestnuts, drained
¼ cup peas, cooked
2 tablespoons thinly sliced
   scallions
1 tablespoon diced red bell
   peppers (¼-inch dice)

2 tablespoons mayonnaise
1 tablespoon quality seafood
   sauce
1 teaspoon fresh-squeezed lemon
   juice
Salt, to taste
Lemon pepper, to taste
4 ounces mixed greens

Serves 1

Carb Level: Moderate
Per serving:
Carbohydrate: 17g
Protein: 21g
Fat: 1g

This is a
great do-
ahead
dish—keep
refrigerated
and assemble
when you
have time to
sit and enjoy
a great meal.

1. In a medium-sized mixing bowl, combine the shrimp, water chestnuts, peas, scallions, and peppers.
2. In a small bowl, combine the mayonnaise, seafood sauce, lemon juice, salt, and lemon pepper; mix until blended. Taste and adjust seasoning as desired.
3. Add half of the dressing to the shrimp mixture and toss to combine, adding more dressing as needed to reach desired consistency. Chill in the refrigerator. To serve, place the greens in the center of a serving plate and top with shrimp salad.

Use of the Senses

Check the freshness of fish and seafood with your nose and eyes. If there is any trace whatsoever of an ammonia smell, get rid of it. If fish smells just a little bit strong, rinse it under cold water. If it still has an odor, don't use it. Fresh fish and shellfish should smell like the sea.

Chicken and Spinach Wrap

Serves 1

Carb Level: Moderate

Per serving:

Carbohydrate: 17g

Protein: 23g

Fat: 15g

This recipe takes advantage of store-bought rotisserie chicken and the beautiful selection of prepped veggies and greens at the salad bar.

1 (8-inch) low-carb wrap, flavor of your choice

2 tablespoons flavored cream cheese spread

⅓ cup sliced or shredded rotisserie chicken or cooked chicken breast

½ cup spinach leaves

¼ cup peeled and shredded carrots

1 tablespoon sliced black olives

1 tablespoon sliced red onions

Salt, to taste

Freshly cracked black pepper

1. Place the wrap on a clean, dry work surface. Spread the cream cheese on the upper quarter of the wrap, about 1 inch from the edge. This will be the "glue" to hold the wrap together when you roll it up.
2. Spread the chicken in an even layer on the lower quarter of the wrap, about 1 inch from the edge. Top with the spinach, carrots, olives, and onions, equally distributed across the wrap. Sprinkle with salt and pepper.
3. Fold the bottom edge of the wrap over the filling and compress carefully, without tearing the wrap. Roll upward, away from you, using the cream cheese to seal the wrap closed. Cut in half on the bias for serving or wrap halves airtight in plastic wrap for later.

Carrot Facts

Carrots are a great source of beta-carotene and vitamin A. Know that ¼ cup of regular carrots contains 3g of carbohydrates and ¼ cup of baby carrots contains 5g of carbohydrates. However, studies have shown that beta-carotene is most effective when derived from natural foods and not from supplements. Carrots are a carb expenditure well worth it.

Sicilian Chicken

Serves 4

Carb Level: Low

Per serving:

Carbohydrate: 6g

Protein: 32g

Fat: 17g

A great one-pan dish that makes cleanup a breeze. You can also buy most of the produce at the salad bar, already prepped.

4 skinless, boneless chicken
   breast halves
¼ teaspoon salt
Freshly cracked black pepper
4 tablespoons olive oil, divided
1 cup thinly sliced red onion

½ cup bell pepper strips,
   assorted colors (about ¼-inch
   strips)
2 garlic cloves, minced
⅓ cup chopped fresh basil
2 tablespoons balsamic vinegar
¼–½ teaspoon red pepper flakes

1. Rinse the chicken under cold, running water and pat dry with paper towels. Season with salt and pepper.
2. Heat 2 tablespoons of the oil in a medium-sized nonstick skillet over medium-high heat. Cook the chicken until golden brown, about 4 to 5 minutes per side. Transfer the chicken to a plate and tent with tinfoil to keep warm.
3. Add the peppers and onions to the skillet; sauté until soft, about 4 minutes, stirring frequently. Add the garlic and sauté for about 1 minute, stirring frequently. Add half of the basil, the vinegar, and red pepper flakes; stir to combine.
4. Add the chicken and any accumulated juices. Cover and reduce heat to medium. Simmer until the chicken is cooked through, about 4 to 6 minutes. Taste and adjust seasoning as desired. Serve hot, garnished with the remaining basil.

Food Safety Facts

Chicken must be cooked to the following internal temperatures to ensure food safety and proper elimination of bacteria. Boneless chicken must be cooked to an internal temperature of 165° for at least 15 seconds. Bone-in chicken pieces must reach 170° and ground chicken must reach 165° for at least 15 seconds. Bone-in whole chicken must reach 180°.

Chicken Cutlets with Grainy Mustard

4 skinless, boneless chicken
   breast halves, cut in thirds and
   lightly pounded
⅓ teaspoon salt
Freshly cracked black pepper
3 tablespoons butter

3 tablespoons grainy mustard
⅓ cup dry white wine
½ cup chicken stock
¼ cup heavy cream, at room
   temperature
2 tablespoons chopped parsley

Serves 4

Carb Level: Low
Per serving:
Carbohydrate: 1g
Protein: 33g
Fat: 16g

1. Rinse the chicken under cold, running water and pat dry with paper towels. Season with salt and pepper. Melt the butter in a large nonstick skillet over medium-high heat. Add the chicken pieces in a single layer; sauté until golden, turning once, about 6 minutes total. Transfer the chicken to a plate and set aside.
2. Add the mustard, wine, and stock to the pan and bring to a simmer, stirring and scraping up any browned bits from the bottom of the pan. Simmer for about 4 minutes, until slightly reduced. Reduce heat to medium-low and slowly add the cream, stirring constantly to incorporate. Simmer for about 2 minutes.
3. Add the chicken and any accumulated juices, and cook until the chicken is heated through, about 2 minutes. Taste and adjust seasoning as desired. Serve hot, garnished with chopped parsley.

There are a number of flavored mustards on the market, even at your local grocer. Use a whole-grain or coarse mustard with flavors you enjoy, such as tarragon or horseradish.

Cooking Tip

Lightly pounding chicken breasts reduces the cooking time. To prepare, start with boneless, skinless breast halves that have been rinsed under cold, running water and patted dry with paper towels. Cut each breast into 3 even-sized pieces and line a workspace with plastic wrap. Lay the chicken pieces in a single layer and top with another layer of plastic wrap. Use the flat side of a meat mallet or the bottom of a small, heavy skillet to lightly and evenly pound the pieces to flatten, starting from the center of each piece and working your way out to the ends. The pieces should end up about ½ inch thick. Transfer pieces to a tray and repeat with remaining chicken. When complete, sanitize the entire work area.

Chicken with Mushroom Cognac Cream Sauce

Serves 4

Carb Level: Low

Per serving:

Carbohydrate: 8g

Protein: 35g

Fat: 24g

This is an elegant dish, easy to fix with sliced mushrooms from the produce section or salad bar.

4 skinless, boneless chicken breast halves
¼ teaspoon salt
Freshly cracked black pepper, to taste
3 tablespoons butter
¼ cup thinly sliced shallots

1 pound assorted mushrooms, cleaned, trimmed, and sliced
3 tablespoons cognac
½ cup heavy cream, at room temperature
1 tablespoon chopped thyme

1. Rinse the chicken under cold, running water and pat dry with paper towels. Season with salt and pepper. Melt the butter in a medium-sized nonstick skillet over medium-high heat. Add the chicken and cook about 4 to 5 minutes per side, until golden. Transfer the chicken to a plate and set aside.
2. Add the shallots and mushrooms to the skillet and sauté until lightly browned, about 6 minutes, stirring frequently. Add the cognac and bring to a simmer. Add the cream in a slow stream, stirring constantly to incorporate. Add the thyme and chicken, along with any accumulated juices. Bring to a low simmer and cook until the chicken is cooked through and the sauce is slightly thickened, about 5 minutes. Serve hot.

What Mushrooms Work Best?

Button mushrooms work just fine with this dish, but using a blend of different exotics, such as shiitakes, chanterelles, and portobellos, will really enhance the flavors.

Turkey Cutlets with Home-Style Gravy

4 (5-ounce) turkey cutlets
¼ teaspoon seasoned salt
Freshly cracked black pepper
2 teaspoons dry poultry
   seasoning, divided
4 tablespoons butter, divided
¼ cup diced yellow onion

¼ cup diced celery
2 tablespoons chopped fresh
   parsley
1 teaspoon chopped sage
2 tablespoons all-purpose flour
1¾ cups chicken stock

Serves 4

Carb Level: Low
Per serving:
Carbohydrate: 6g
Protein: 31g
Fat: 11g

1. Season the cutlets with the salt, pepper, and 1 teaspoon of the poultry seasoning. Melt 2 tablespoons of the butter in a large nonstick skillet over medium-high heat. Sauté the cutlets until lightly browned, about 4 minutes per side. Transfer the cutlets to a plate and set aside.
2. Melt the remaining butter in the skillet and add the onions, celery, parsley, and sage; sauté until softened, about 2 minutes, stirring frequently. Sprinkle the flour over the onions and celery, and stir to mix. Add the stock and cook until the gravy is bubbling and thickened, stirring constantly. Add the turkey, along with any accumulated juices, and lightly simmer until heated through, about 3 minutes. Taste and adjust seasoning as desired. Serve hot.

Fresh turkey cutlets are available in the poultry section. The gravy is made in the same skillet, so cleanup is easy.

Entertaining Tip

You can use your dishwasher as a plate warmer in a pinch. Load clean dinner plates into an empty dishwasher and run it on the rinse cycle ½ hour before you're planning to serve dinner. Leave the dishwasher sealed and your plates will be clean, shiny, and hot for restaurant-style service.

Broiled Cod with Dijon Mustard

Serves 4

Carb Level: Low

Per serving:

Carbohydrate:　2g

Protein:　24g

Fat:　24g

You can substitute scrod, haddock, or pollack if the cod is not the freshest. To spice up the flavor, try using a flavored Dijon such as tarragon.

½ cup (1 stick) butter
2 tablespoons minced shallots
1 tablespoon fresh-squeezed
　lemon juice
1 teaspoon paprika
2 tablespoons Dijon mustard

¼ teaspoon seasoned salt
Freshly cracked black pepper, to
　taste
4 skinless cod fillets (about
　1½ pounds total)
Fresh chopped parsley

1. Place oven broiler rack about 4 inches from the heat source. Preheat broiler to high. Melt the butter in a small saucepan over medium-low heat. Stir in the shallots and cook until soft, about 1 to 2 minutes. Add the lemon juice, paprika, mustard, salt, and pepper. Remove from heat and whisk until creamy and evenly blended. Transfer the butter sauce to a shallow bowl.
2. Dip the fillets in the butter sauce, coating both sides. Place the fillets in a single layer in a shallow broiler pan. Spoon any remaining butter sauce over the tops of the fillets.
3. Broil the fish until browned and cooked through, about 4 to 5 minutes. Baste with the pan juices several times during the cooking process. To serve, use a spatula to transfer the fillets to a serving platter and ladle the pan juices over the fish. Garnish with parsley and serve hot.

Easy Cleanup Tip

Line baking sheets and baking pans with tinfoil for easy cleanup. You can oil the tinfoil as you would the baking pan and when you're done cooking, discard the tinfoil and you shouldn't need to scrub the pan.

Pan-Sautéed Pork Chops with Gravy

4 center-cut loin pork chops,
   1 inch thick
½ teaspoon garlic salt
Freshly cracked black pepper
3 tablespoons olive oil
8 ounces mushrooms, sliced
¼ cup sliced yellow onion

2 cloves garlic, minced
¼ cup beef stock
2 tablespoons ketchup
2 tablespoons sour cream,
   at room temperature
2 tablespoons chopped fresh
   parsley

Serves 4

Carb Level: Low
Per serving:
Carbohydrate: 7g
Protein: 23g
Fat: 25g

Make sure the oil is really hot so that the chops sear quickly. Searing helps reserve the juices so the chops stay tender and flavorful.

1. Season the chops with garlic salt and pepper. Heat the oil in a medium-sized nonstick skillet over medium-high heat; cook the chops for about 3 minutes per side. Transfer to a plate and tent with tinfoil to keep warm.
2. Add the mushrooms, onions, and garlic and sauté until soft, about 5 minutes, stirring frequently. Add the stock and ketchup, and bring to a simmer. Return the chops to the pan, cover, and cook over medium heat until the chops are thoroughly cooked, about 10 minutes.
3. Place the chops on serving plates. Add the sour cream to the skillet and whisk until evenly blended. Pour the gravy over the chops and garnish with parsley. Serve hot.

Quick Tip

To speed up the cooking time of chicken or pork, cut it into small pieces, place the pieces between layers of plastic wrap, and use the flat side of a meat mallet to lightly flatten the meat. It is important to always season meat before cooking to enhance the taste.

Tropical Chicken

Serves 4

Carb Level: Moderate

Per serving:

Carbohydrate:	19g
Protein:	32g
Fat:	17g

A great family dish—serve it over rice for a very traditional tropical chicken presentation.

4 (5-ounce) skinless, boneless chicken breasts
¼ teaspoon garlic salt
Freshly cracked black pepper
4 tablespoons vegetable oil
4 cloves garlic, minced
1 cup chicken stock
1 cup canned pineapple in light syrup

½ teaspoon lemon zest
1 teaspoon orange zest
1½ tablespoons honey
2 tablespoons ketchup
2 tablespoons rice vinegar
1 tablespoon tamari
Sliced scallions, for garnish

1. Rinse the chicken under cold, running water and pat dry with paper towels. Season the chicken with salt and pepper. Heat the oil in a medium-sized nonstick skillet over medium-high heat. Cook the chicken until lightly browned, about 4 to 5 minutes per side. Transfer the chicken to a plate and tent with tinfoil to keep warm.
2. Add the garlic and sauté for about 30 seconds, stirring constantly to keep the garlic from browning. Add the remaining ingredients except the scallions and bring to a simmer; cook until slightly thickened, about 5 minutes.
3. Add the chicken and any accumulated juices. Reduce heat to medium and simmer until the chicken is cooked through, about 4 to 5 minutes. Serve hot with the sauce ladled over the chicken and garnished with sliced scallions.

Food Processor Tips

To mince garlic in a full-sized food processor, peel the garlic cloves and trim the root end. If garlic is older, split the clove lengthwise and remove the center shoot, which can be somewhat bitter when cooked. Fit the metal blade in the work bowl. With the motor running, drop the garlic down the feed tube, 1 to 2 cloves at a time, until minced. Do not put all the garlic in at once, as it won't mince evenly.

Italian Sausage Skillet Casserole

2 tablespoons olive oil
1 pound Italian sausage, cut into
    1-inch pieces
1 cup sliced red onion
1 cup red and green bell pepper
    strips
1 cup sliced button mushrooms

12 ounces pizza sauce
¼ teaspoon garlic salt
1 cup grated mozzarella cheese
Red pepper flakes, to taste
Dried Italian seasoning,
    to taste

Serves 4

Carb Level: Moderate
Per serving:
Carbohydrate: 16g
Protein: 19g
Fat: 45g

This is a great family dinner—kids think of it as a pizza without the crust.

1. Preheat broiler to low.
2. Heat the oil in a medium-sized, ovenproof, nonstick skillet over medium-high heat. Add the sausage and cook until it starts to brown, stirring frequently, about 8 minutes. Add the onions, peppers, and mushrooms, and cook until soft, about 8 minutes. Remove from heat and stir in the pizza sauce and garlic salt. Top with the mozzarella.
3. Transfer the pan to the oven and broil until the cheese starts to brown, about 2 minutes. Remember that the handle will be very hot when taking the pan from the oven. Garnish with red pepper flakes and Italian seasoning and serve hot.

Preparing Cheese

To shred a soft or semisoft cheese, pop it in the freezer for about 30 minutes before grating to make it easier to handle. It also won't stick to the grater as much.

Stuffed Chicken Rolls with Pesto Sauce

4 skinless, boneless chicken breast halves
⅓ teaspoon salt
Freshly cracked black pepper
2 slices imported prosciutto, cut in half

2 slices mozzarella cheese, cut in half
3 tablespoons olive oil
⅓ cup chicken stock
1½ cups prepared pesto cream sauce

1. Rinse the chicken under cold, running water and pat dry with paper towels. Line a workspace with plastic wrap, lay the chicken pieces in a single layer, and top with another layer of plastic wrap. Use the flat side of a meat mallet or the bottom of a small, heavy skillet to lightly and evenly pound the pieces several times, starting from the center of each piece and working your way out to the ends. The pieces should end up about ½ inch thick. Season with salt and pepper.
2. Place one piece of the prosciutto and the cheese in the center of each chicken piece and roll into a cylinder, tucking in the ends. Repeat with remaining pieces. Use a toothpick to secure each roll, seam-side down.
3. Heat the oil in a medium-sized nonstick skillet over medium-high heat. Add the chicken pieces in a single layer. Sauté until golden, using tongs to turn each roll during the cooking process. Cook until almost done, about 12 minutes.
4. Add the stock and pesto cream sauce to the skillet and turn the chicken to make sure it's not sticking to the pan. Bring the sauce to a simmer, cover, and cook the chicken until done, about 5 minutes. To check for doneness, cut into a roll from the bottom and make sure the chicken is cooked through. Taste the sauce for seasoning and adjust as desired. Serve hot.

Grilled Veal Chops with Herbs and Lemon

4 tablespoons olive oil, divided
½ cup thinly sliced yellow onion
4 cloves garlic, minced
2 teaspoons chopped capers,
   rinsed and drained
1 teaspoon lemon zest
1 tablespoon fresh-squeezed
   lemon juice

1 tablespoon finely chopped fresh
   parsley
¼ teaspoon salt
Freshly cracked pepper
4 (1-inch-thick) veal chops,
   trimmed of excess fat

Serves 4

Carb Level: Low
Per serving:
Carbohydrate: 3g
Protein: 24g
Fat: 11g

Simple to
prepare and
a fine-tasting
dish. A great
adult meal
on a summer
night.

1. Heat 2 tablespoons of the oil in a small nonstick skillet over medium heat. Add the onion and cook until soft, about 4 minutes, stirring frequently. Add the garlic and capers, and cook until soft, about 1 minute, stirring frequently. Add the lemon zest, juice, and parsley, and stir to incorporate. Remove from heat and set aside.
2. Oil a grill or broiler rack and position it about 4 inches from the heat source. Preheat grill or broiler to medium-high.
3. Rub the chops with the remaining 2 tablespoons of oil and season with salt and pepper. Grill or broil to the desired temperature, turning once, about 4 to 6 minutes on each side for medium-rare. Transfer the meat to a warm plate to rest for 5 minutes before serving.
4. While the chops are resting, reheat the sauce to serving temperature over medium heat, about 1 to 2 minutes. To serve, place a chop on each plate and drizzle any accumulated juices over the chops. Spoon the heated herb-lemon sauce over each chop and serve.

Fresh Vs. Jarred Garlic

Prepared garlic is now available in many forms in the produce section. It is best to buy the jars of whole, peeled cloves. The cloves should be smooth and unblemished. The jars of minced garlic often lack flavor and the garlic doesn't "melt" during cooking like fresh garlic.

Curried Shrimp

Serves 4

Carb Level: Low

Per serving:

Carbohydrate: 3g

Protein: 29g

Fat: 8g

Use a quality curry powder for the best results. Purchase the shrimp already peeled and deveined as a time-saver.

1½ pounds medium shrimp, peeled and deveined
1½ tablespoons curry powder
⅛ teaspoon chili powder
3 tablespoons vegetable oil

¼ cup sliced scallions
½ cup chili sauce
¼ teaspoon seasoned salt
Freshly cracked black pepper, to taste

1. Pat the shrimp dry with paper towels and transfer to a medium-sized mixing bowl. Add the curry and chili powder, and toss to coat evenly.
2. Heat the oil in a large nonstick skillet over medium heat. Shake off excess curry and chili powder and add the shrimp and cook, stirring often, until the shrimp starts to turn pink, about 2 minutes. Add the scallions and stir to mix. Stir in the chili sauce. Cook until heated through, about 3 minutes. Season to taste with salt and pepper. Serve hot.

Chile Sauce Additions

There also are a variety of gourmet chili sauces on the market. Try several and find a brand that suits you best. You'll find it to be a great recipe addition when you need to add zip. You can also add a few drops of hot sauce if you're a lover of spicy food.

Pan-Seared Duck Breast

½ teaspoon Chinese five-spice
   powder
¼ teaspoon ground cinnamon
½ teaspoon seasoned salt
Freshly cracked black pepper

4 (8- to 10-ounce) boneless duck
   breasts
1 tablespoon butter
1 tablespoon vegetable oil

Serves 4

Carb Level: Low
Per serving:
Carbohydrate: Trace
Protein: 26g
Fat: 110g

1. Combine the five-spice powder, cinnamon, seasoned salt, and pepper
    on a flat plate and set aside.
2. Trim any visible fat from the duck breasts. Leave a patch of skin on
    each breast large enough to cover two-thirds of the surface. Lightly
    score the skin with a sharp knife in a repeating crisscross pattern,
    making each cut about ½ inch in length. Place the breasts, skin-side
    down, into the spice mixture.
3. Heat the butter and oil in a heavy, medium-sized skillet over medium-
    high heat. The pan should be very hot but not smoking. Add the duck,
    skin-side down, and sprinkle with the remaining spice mixture. Cook,
    uncovered, turning only once after the skin is browned, about 3 min-
    utes. Turn and cook for another 2 minutes for rare. Total cooking time
    for rare is about 5 to 6 minutes; medium rare is 8 to 9 minutes. Adjust
    cooking times for desired temperature. Serve the breasts whole or cut
    into thin slices on the bias.

The portions
are very gen-
erous, so plan
on using the
leftovers for
a salad with
sliced duck
the next day.

Cooking Duck Breasts

Duck breast can be an intimidating proposition. Make sure you use a heavy nonstick
skillet and make sure it's really hot before adding the duck. The goal is to quickly sear
the skin. Also, make sure you don't overcook the duck; otherwise it will be tough and
chewy. Remember, you can always put it back on the heat, but once it's overdone,
you're stuck with tough duck.

Lemon-Honey Shrimp with Prosciutto

Serves 4

Carb Level: Low

Per serving:

Carbohydrate: 5g

Protein: 29g

Fat: 13g

The saltiness of the prosciutto, the tartness of the lemon, and the sweet honey finish make this an elegant way to serve shrimp.

1¼ pounds shrimp (21–25 count), peeled and deveined

3 ounces prosciutto, very thinly sliced

3 tablespoons olive oil

½ cup vegetable or chicken stock

2 tablespoons lemon juice

1 tablespoon honey

Salt, to taste

Freshly cracked black pepper

1. Pat the shrimp dry with paper towels. Cut the prosciutto into strips about 1½ inches wide and 2½ to 3 inches long. Wrap a strip of prosciutto around the center of each shrimp, pressing lightly to seal.
2. Heat the oil in a large nonstick skillet over medium-high heat. Add the shrimp and cook, turning once, until the shrimp start to turn pink and the prosciutto starts to crisp, about 4 to 5 minutes. Season with pepper. Transfer the shrimp to a plate and tent with tinfoil to keep warm.
3. Add the stock, lemon juice, and honey to the pan and bring to a simmer. Add the shrimp and any accumulated juices to the pan and stir to coat the shrimp evenly, being careful not to damage the prosciutto wrapping. Heat through, about 1 to 2 minutes. Season to taste with salt and pepper, and serve hot.

Shrimp Sizes

Shrimp is classified as colossal with fewer than 10 pieces per pound; jumbo is 11 to 15 pieces per pound; extra-large is 16 to 20 pieces per pound. Large is the most popular, with 21 to 30 pieces per pound. Medium is 31 to 35 pieces per pound; small is 36 to 45 pieces per pound; and miniature is 100 pieces per pound.

Whitefish Fillets with Creamy Caper Sauce

4 skinless whitefish fillets (about
   1½ pounds total)
¼ teaspoon seasoned salt
Freshly cracked black pepper
4 tablespoons all-purpose flour
6 tablespoons butter, divided
1 tablespoon minced shallot

½ cup dry white wine
2 tablespoons capers, rinsed and
   drained
2 teaspoons whole-grain mustard
½ cup heavy cream, at room
   temperature

Serves 4

Carb Level: Low
Per serving:

Carbohydrate:	8g
Protein:	29g
Fat:	37g

Lake Superior whitefish is a delicate and mild white-fleshed fish. They are rather large, so cook the fillets two at a time for ease of handling.

1. Season each fillet with salt and pepper. Sprinkle both sides of each fillet with about 1 tablespoon of the flour. Melt 3 tablespoons of the butter in a large nonstick skillet over medium heat. Tip the pan to make sure the bottom is evenly coated with melted butter. Add 2 of the fillets, and cook until well browned and cooked through, about 2 minutes per side. Use a spatula to transfer the fillets to a plate and tent with tinfoil to keep warm. Melt the remaining butter and repeat the process with the remaining fillets.
2. Add the shallot to the pan after the fillets have been removed. Cook for about 1 minute, until soft but not browned, stirring frequently.
3. Add the wine, capers, and mustard, and bring to a simmer. Cook for 2 to 3 minutes, until the sauce starts to thicken.
4. Slowly add the cream, stirring constantly until incorporated. Cook for about 5 to 6 minutes until the sauce starts to thicken. Taste and adjust seasoning as desired. To serve, place a fillet on each plate and ladle about 2 tablespoons of sauce over each fillet.

Cooking with Cream

Whenever using heavy cream to finish a sauce, make sure it's at room temperature and add it very slowly, stirring or whisking constantly. This will ensure a smooth, velvety sauce. If it is added too fast, or if the cream is too cold, it will seize, and appear curdled. If this does happen, try rapidly whisking the sauce to bring it back to a presentable consistency. If whisking does not work, the last resort is to process it through a food processor, which sometime works.

Sunshine Salad

Carb Level: Moderate
Per serving:
Carbohydrate: 17g
Protein: 7g
Fat: 17g

This is a unique and tasty combination of greens, fruit, and nuts. It's great for a potluck dinner; keep the dressing separate and mix just before serving.

6 ounces plain yogurt
2 tablespoons sour cream
2 tablespoons mayonnaise
1 tablespoon lemon zest
¼ teaspoon red pepper flakes
⅛ teaspoon seasoned salt
6 cups baby spinach salad
  leaves
1 large cucumber, peeled, seeded,
  and sliced, about 2 cups
  (about ¼-inch slices, cut into
  half-moons)
1 cup canned mandarin oranges,
  drained
1 cup halved cherry tomatoes
½ cup roasted sunflower seeds

1. In a small bowl, combine the yogurt, sour cream, mayonnaise, lemon zest, red pepper flakes, and seasoned salt; mix until well blended. Taste and adjust seasoning as desired.
2. In a large bowl, combine the spinach, cucumbers, oranges, cherry tomatoes, and half of the sunflower seeds. Toss with half of the dressing, adding more a bit at a time to reach desired consistency. To serve, transfer the salad to a chilled bowl and top with the remaining sunflower seeds.

Mix It Up

When mixing salads, always start with just half of the dressing. It's easy to add more, tablespoon by tablespoon, until the desired consistency is achieved. However, if you use too much dressing up front, you're stuck with an overdressed salad. If this does happen, you can sometimes rescue it by adding more greens and lightly tossing to mix.

Polish Sausage with Sauerkraut

10 ounces quality Polish sausage
1 tablespoon olive oil
¼ cup diced Granny Smith apples
   (about ¼-inch dice)

20 ounces jarred sauerkraut,
   rinsed well
Garlic salt, to taste
Freshly cracked black pepper, to
   taste

Cut the sausages into 2-inch pieces on the bias. Heat the oil in a medium-sized nonstick skillet over medium-high heat and add the sausage pieces. Cook the sausages until they just start to brown, about 8 to 10 minutes, stirring frequently. Add the diced apple and cook for about 3 minutes, stirring to coat with pan drippings. Add the sauerkraut, garlic salt, and pepper, and stir to combine. Cook until heated through, about 6 minutes. Adjust seasoning to taste and serve hot.

Serves 4

Carb Level: Low
Per serving:
Carbohydrate: 8g
Protein: 21g
Fat: 48g

Garnish with caraway seeds and serve with a spicy mustard.

Island Grilled Pork Patties

1 pound lean ground pork
1 tablespoon lime zest
1 teaspoon jerk seasoning
½ teaspoon ground allspice

½ teaspoon cayenne pepper
¼ teaspoon garlic salt
2 tablespoons chopped fresh
   cilantro

Clean and oil grill rack and place it about 4 inches from the heat source. Preheat grill to medium-high. Lightly mix together all the ingredients and form into 4 patties, each about 4 ounces. Grill for 7 to 9 minutes per side, turning once, until cooked throughout. Transfer the burgers to a plate and tent with foil to keep warm. Let rest for 1 to 2 minutes to allow the juices to reabsorb. Serve hot.

Serves 4

Carb Level: Low
Per serving:
Carbohydrate: 1g
Protein: 19g
Fat: 24g

Top with your favorite salsa or chutney to finish.

Creole Cabbage with Spicy Andouille

4 slices bacon, cut into thirds
¾ pound andouille sausage, cut into 1-inch pieces
1 cup sliced yellow onion
4 cups sliced green cabbage (⅛-inch strips), rinsed

Sugar substitute equal to 1 teaspoon granulated sugar
2 tablespoons Creole seasoning
⅛ teaspoon seasoned salt
Red pepper flakes, to taste

1. Heat a large nonstick skillet over medium-high heat and add the bacon and sausage pieces. Cook, stirring frequently, until the bacon starts to crisp and the sausage pieces start to brown, about 10 minutes.
2. Add the onions and cook until soft, about 4 minutes. Add the cabbage, stir, and cook until wilted, about 4 minutes.
3. Add the sugar substitute, Creole seasoning, salt, and red pepper flakes to the skillet and stir to mix. Cover and cook until the cabbage is tender, about 6 minutes. Serve hot.

Working with Onions

Refrigerate onions before cutting them to keep your eyes from watering. The cooling helps reduce the gases from emitting and irritating your eyes.

Tarragon-Mustard Pork Tenderloins

1¼ pounds pork tenderloin,
 trimmed of fat and cut into
 4 even-sized pieces
¼ teaspoon garlic salt
Freshly cracked black pepper
1 tablespoon vegetable oil

½ cup finely diced shallots
½ cup chicken stock
2 tablespoons Dijon or flavored
 mustard
1 tablespoon chopped fresh
 tarragon

Serves 4

Carb Level: Low
Per serving:
Carbohydrate: 4g
Protein: 30g
Fat: 8g

1. Line a work area with plastic wrap. Lay the tenderloin pieces in a single layer on top of the wrap and cover with another layer of plastic wrap. Use the flat side of a meat mallet to lightly flatten the meat to ½-inch thickness. Season meat with salt and pepper.
2. Heat the oil in a medium-sized nonstick skillet over medium-high heat. Add the pork and cook until the meat starts to brown, about 4 to 5 minutes per side. Transfer the meat to a plate and tent with foil to keep warm.
3. Add the shallots to the pan and cook until soft, stirring frequently, about 4 minutes. Add the stock and bring to a simmer; cook until slightly reduced, about 4 minutes. Whisk in the mustard.
4. Return the pork and any accumulated juices to the pan. Reduce heat to medium-low and cook until the pork is no longer pink in the center, about 4 to 5 minutes. Taste and adjust seasoning as desired. To serve, transfer the pork to a serving platter, ladle the sauce over the meat, and garnish with tarragon leaves. Serve hot.

There are a variety of flavored mustards available at your local market. Tarragon mustard works well with pork but feel free to try others.

What Is a Shallot?

Shallots are a member of the onion family and have a distinct mild flavor. They are used as a flavoring agent in many sauces. Dry shallots are available year-round and should be stored as you would store onions. Fresh shallots are available in the spring and should be stored in the refrigerator.

Tilapia Florentine

Serves 4

Carb Level: Low
Per serving:
Carbohydrate: 5g
Protein: 28g
Fat: 5g

Tilapia is a very mild, white-fleshed fish that bakes and broils very well. Make sure all bones have been removed from the fish before assembling this dish.

10 ounces frozen spinach, thawed and squeezed dry
¼ cup minced shallots
⅓ cup chicken broth
⅛ teaspoon ground nutmeg
2 tablespoons butter
1 pound skinless tilapia fillets
½ cup buttermilk

2 eggs, beaten
⅛ teaspoon hot pepper sauce
2 tablespoons grated Romano cheese
Seasoned salt, to taste
Freshly cracked black pepper, to taste

1. Combine the spinach, shallots, broth, and nutmeg in a medium-sized saucepan over medium heat. Cook, covered, for about 4 minutes, stirring occasionally.
2. Melt the butter in a medium-sized ovenproof skillet over medium-high heat. Remove from heat and spread the spinach mixture in an even layer in the skillet. Place the tilapia fillets in a single layer on the spinach.
3. Combine the buttermilk, eggs, and pepper sauce in a small bowl and mix until blended. Pour the mixture over the tilapia and top with the grated cheese. Season with salt and pepper.
4. Preheat broiler to medium-high with the rack positioned about 6 inches from the heat source. Transfer the skillet to the oven and broil until the sauce is evenly browned and the fish is cooked throughout, about 12 minutes. Turn the skillet once or twice to prevent overbrowning in any areas, if needed. Remove from heat and let rest for 4 to 5 minutes. (Remember that the handle of the skillet is very hot.) Cut into 4 equal portions and use a spatula to serve.

Preheating the Oven

It's important to make sure your oven is preheated to the proper temperature. Cooking times are based on this assumption. Allow 15 to 20 minutes for your oven to reach the proper temperature.

Tuscan-Style Strip Steaks

Serves 4

Carb Level: Low
Per serving:
Carbohydrate: 2g
Protein: 41g
Fat: 46g

5 tablespoons extra-virgin olive oil

1 tablespoon fresh-squeezed lemon juice

2 garlic cloves, minced

1 tablespoon chopped parsley

1 tablespoon chopped fresh oregano

Seasoned salt, to taste

Freshly ground black pepper, to taste

1 tablespoon vegetable oil

2 pounds boneless strip steak (1 to 1¼ inches thick), trimmed of visible fat and cut into 4 pieces

3 ounces Parmesan cheese, cut into thin shavings

The basting sauce enhances the flavors and melds with the natural pan juices to create a simple Tuscan-inspired sauce for the steaks.

1. In a medium-sized bowl, mix together the olive oil, lemon juice, garlic, parsley, oregano, salt, and pepper. Add the steaks and turn to coat evenly.
2. Heat the vegetable oil in a medium-sized nonstick skillet over medium-high heat. Remove the steaks from the marinade and cook until starting to brown, about 8 minutes per side. Baste with the remaining marinade during the cooking process.
3. Transfer the steaks to a plate and tent with tinfoil to keep warm. Let rest for 5 minutes to allow the juices to reabsorb. To serve, place a steak on each plate, drizzle any accumulated juices over the steaks, and garnish with Parmesan shavings.

Storing Extra Cheeses

While freezing is not recommended for storing cheeses, most can be frozen without much loss of flavor and texture. To freeze cheese, wrap individual portions airtight in a double layer of plastic wrap. Only thaw what you'll be consuming in one sitting as many defrosted cheeses develop a bitter aftertaste after a day.

Cauliflower Waldorf Salad

Serves 4

Carb Level: Moderate

Per serving:

Carbohydrate: 12g
Protein: 6g
Fat: 25g

You can add 2 cups of sliced rotisserie chicken to top this salad and increase the protein to 26g per serving.

⅓ cup mayonnaise
1 tablespoon honey
1 teaspoon Dijon mustard
3 cups cauliflower florets, broken into bite-sized pieces
¼ cup finely diced celery
½ cup halved green seedless grapes
½ cup walnut pieces
¼ teaspoon seasoned salt
Freshly cracked black pepper

1. Combine the mayonnaise, honey, and mustard in a medium-sized mixing bowl and whisk until blended.
2. Add the cauliflower, celery, grapes, and walnuts, and toss until evenly coated.
3. Season with salt and pepper. Taste and adjust seasoning as desired. Serve in a chilled salad bowl or on a bed of crispy greens.

Cauliflower Facts

A ½-cup serving of cauliflower has 3g of carbohydrates. It is a cruciferous vegetable on the list of anticancer foods and is high in vitamin C.

Pan-Seared Sea Scallops

4 tablespoons butter
1¼ pounds large sea scallops,
    abductor muscle removed,
    rinsed and patted dry with
    paper towels
¼ teaspoon salt
Freshly cracked black pepper

¼ cup chopped shallots
½ cup chicken stock
2 tablespoons fresh-squeezed
    lemon juice
1 teaspoon lemon zest
1 tablespoon chopped fresh
    parsley

Serves 4

Carb Level: Low
Per serving:
Carbohydrate: 6g
Protein: 24g
Fat: 13g

Restaurant-quality sea scallops are now available to the general public. Ask for fresh diver sea scallops; large, sweet, and succulent, these are a true treat!

1. Melt 3 tablespoons of the butter in a large nonstick skillet over medium-high heat. Season the scallops with salt and pepper and cook until seared, about 3 to 4 minutes per side. Transfer the scallops to a plate and tent with tinfoil to keep warm.
2. Add the remaining tablespoon of butter to the pan. Add the shallots and cook until soft, about 4 minutes, stirring frequently. Add the stock and lemon juice and bring to a simmer. Cook until slightly reduced, about 4 minutes.
3. Add the lemon zest and parsley and simmer for about 1 minute. Taste and adjust seasoning as desired. Transfer the scallops to serving plates and drizzle with the pan sauce. Serve hot.

Butter Facts

Butter rapidly absorbs flavors like a sponge. Regular butter can be stored in the refrigerator for up to one month, wrapped airtight. Unsalted butter should be stored for no longer than 2 weeks in the refrigerator.

Mussels with Creamy Leek Sauce

Serves 4

Carb Level: Moderate

Per serving:

Carbohydrate:	19g
Protein:	42g
Fat:	30g

Cultivated mussels are now available year-round. This is an intimate light-supper idea, served with a large salad.

2 tablespoons butter
1 cup sliced leeks (rinsed; white and light green parts only)
3 pounds mussels
1 cup dry white wine

1 cup heavy cream
½ cup bottled clam juice
2 tablespoons chopped thyme
¼ teaspoon kosher salt
Freshly cracked black pepper

1. Melt the butter in a heavy-bottomed saucepan with a tight-fitting lid. Add the leeks and cook until soft, about 5 minutes, uncovered and stirring frequently. Add the mussels, then the wine, cream, clam juice, and half of the thyme. Lightly season with salt and pepper.
2. Bring to a simmer, reduce heat, and cover the pan. Cook until the mussels open, about 5 minutes. Shake the pan occasionally throughout the cooking process.
3. Equally divide the mussels between 4 shallow bowls. Discard any mussels that have not opened. Add the remaining thyme to the broth, taste, and adjust seasoning as desired. Bring the broth to a simmer and drizzle over the mussels. Serve hot.

Using Milk or Cream

Whenever adding heavy cream or milk to a hot soup or sauce, it should be "tempered" to prevent curdling. The easiest way to temper the cream is to heat it to about the same temperature as the soup and slowly add it while stirring to incorporate. Otherwise, have the cream at room temperature and add very, very slowly, stirring constantly to incorporate.

The Basic Burger

Serves 4

Carb Level: Low

Per serving:

Carbohydrate: 0g

Protein: 27g

Fat: 24g

Experiment
with your
basic burger
by trying out
the three dif-
ferent cooking
methods.

1¼ pounds ground round beef

½ teaspoon seasoned salt

Freshly cracked black pepper, to
taste

Lightly mix the ground round with salt and pepper and form into
4 evenly sized patties. Cook by your choice of the following methods.

To grill: Clean grill rack and lightly oil to prevent sticking. Preheat grill
to medium-high. Cook for about 5 minutes per side for medium, turning
once. Transfer burgers to a plate and tent with foil to keep warm. Let
rest for 1 to 2 minutes to allow the juices to reabsorb. Serve hot. If using
an indoor grill, follow manufacturer's directions.

To broil: Clean broiler rack and lightly oil to prevent sticking. Set
broiler rack 4 inches from heat source. Preheat broiler to medium-high.
Cook for about 5 minutes per side for medium, turning once. Transfer
burgers to a plate and tent with foil to keep warm. Let rest for 1 to 2
minutes to allow the juices to reabsorb. Serve hot.

On stovetop: Heat 2 tablespoons oil in a nonstick skillet over medium-
high heat. Cook for about 5 minutes per side for medium, turning once.
Transfer burgers to a plate and tent with foil to keep warm. Let rest for
1 to 2 minutes to allow the juices to reabsorb. Serve hot.

Getting the Basics Down

There are many versions of the basic burger; some contain egg yolk, bread crumbs,
and any other number of additions. This is the simplest basic burger; therefore, the
quality of the ground meat is key. Be sure not to overhandle meat when forming ham-
burger patties. Use a very light touch and make sure you don't compact the meat too
much. Don't use a spatula to press down on the patty while cooking, either, because
you'll press out the natural juices and you'll lose the juiciness and flavor to boot.

Seasoned Bistro Burgers

1¼ pounds ground round beef
¾ teaspoon seasoned salt
⅛ teaspoon lemon pepper
1 tablespoon chopped fresh
　parsley

3 tablespoons butter
1 tablespoon Dijon mustard
1 tablespoon fresh lemon juice
2 teaspoons quality steak sauce

Serves 4

Carb Level: Low
Per serving:

Carbohydrate:	1g
Protein:	27g
Fat:	33g

You can add
a different
blend of
herbs or use
a flavored
or seasoned
Dijon mus-
tard for a dif-
ferent twist.

1. Lightly mix the ground round with the seasoned salt, lemon pepper, and chopped parsley, and form into 4 evenly sized patties. Melt the butter in a medium-sized nonstick skillet over medium-high heat. Add the mustard and quickly blend to combine. Add the burgers to the skillet and cook for about 4 minutes per side, turning once. (Burgers will be returned to the pan for additional cooking.) Transfer the burgers to a plate and tent with foil to keep warm.
2. Add the lemon juice and steak sauce to the pan and blend to combine. Return the burgers and any accumulated juices to the pan and let simmer for 2 to 3 minutes while basting. Remove the pan from heat and allow the burgers to rest for 2 to 3 minutes. Serve with sauce ladled over the top; serve hot.

How to Handle a Burger

Use tongs or a spatula to turn burgers during cooking. The idea is to make sure you don't pierce the meat, because doing so will allow the flavorful juices to escape. Always make sure the pan or grill is hot before putting burgers on to cook. The goal is to quickly sear the outside so the flavorful juices are trapped inside during the cooking process.

Bacon Burgers

Serves 4

Carb Level: Low

Per serving:

Carbohydrate:	4g
Protein:	85g
Fat:	41g

A winning
combination
of flavors
including
bacon
and sharp
Cheddar with
a hearty basic
burger. This
is definitely
a grill-time
recipe.

1¼ pounds ground round beef
¾ teaspoon seasoned salt
⅛ teaspoon fresh cracked pepper

¼ cup crispy bacon crumbles
8 (1-ounce) slices sharp Cheddar
   cheese

Lightly mix the ground round with the seasoned salt, pepper, and bacon crumbles, and form into 4 evenly sized patties. Clean and oil grill rack and preheat grill to medium-high. Cook the burgers for about 5 minutes on each side for medium. Add 2 slices of cheese per burger during the last 2 minutes of cooking. Transfer the burgers to a plate and tent with foil to keep warm. Let rest for 1 to 2 minutes to allow the juices to reabsorb. Serve hot.

Nothing Beats a Good Burger on the Grill!

Lean burgers are a staple in the diet plan of many people who are controlling carbs, so we've created a few special recipes that you can show off to your friends. A bunless burger is really no different from the classic Salisbury steak preparation that was popular in the 1970s. It was named after a nineteenth-century physician who recommended that his patients reduce their starch intake and eat plenty of beef.

Wisconsin Burgers

1¼ pounds ground round beef
½ teaspoon seasoned salt
⅛ teaspoon fresh cracked pepper

¼ cup sauerkraut, rinsed and drained
8 slices Muenster cheese

Serves 4

Carb Level: Low
Per serving:
Carbohydrate: 1g
Protein: 40g
Fat: 41g

Lightly mix the ground round with the seasoned salt and pepper, and form into 4 evenly sized patties. Clean and oil grill rack and preheat grill to medium-high. Cook the burgers for about 5 minutes on each side for medium. During the last 2 minutes of cooking, top each burger with 1 tablespoon of the kraut and 2 slices of cheese per burger. Transfer the burgers to a plate and tent with foil to keep warm. Let rest for 1 to 2 minutes to allow the juices to reabsorb. Serve hot.

Before You Eat

It's best to let burgers "rest" on a warm plate for 1 or 2 minutes before serving. This allows the juices to release and reabsorb into the burger, which adds to the juiciness and tenderness.

Right from the heart of Milwaukee—sprinkle the kraut with a few caraway seeds, if desired. This recipe is great on the grill or stovetop.

Blues Burgers

Serves 4

Carb Level: Low

Per serving:

Carbohydrate: 1g

Protein: 30g

Fat: 34g

Let the burgers sit for a minute or two after mixing to make sure the meat binds with the cheese.

1¼ pounds ground round beef

½ teaspoon seasoned salt

⅛ teaspoon red pepper flakes

½ cup blue cheese crumbles

¼ cup thinly sliced scallions

2 tablespoons vegetable oil

Lightly mix the ground round with the seasoned salt, pepper flakes, blue cheese crumbles, and scallions, and form into 4 evenly sized patties. Heat the oil in a medium-sized nonstick skillet over medium-high heat. Cook for about 5 minutes per side for medium, turning once. Transfer the burgers to a plate and tent with foil to keep warm. Let rest for 1 to 2 minutes to allow the juices to reabsorb. Serve hot.

Be Sanitary!

Use disposable plastic or latex gloves when working with burgers. It's more sanitary and prevents the burger from sticking to your hands. Dip your gloved hand into cold water to prevent the meat from sticking to your gloves. Whenever dealing with meat that may be served at any temperature other than well done, it's worth the extra sanitation effort.

Feta Burgers

1¼ pounds ground round beef
½ teaspoon garlic salt

¼ teaspoon cayenne pepper
½ cup feta cheese crumbles

Lightly mix the ground round with the garlic salt, cayenne pepper, and feta cheese crumbles, and form into 4 evenly sized patties. Clean and oil grill rack and preheat grill to medium-high. Cook the burgers for about 5 minutes on each side for medium. Transfer the burgers to a plate and tent with foil to keep warm. Let rest for 1 to 2 minutes to allow the juices to reabsorb. Serve hot.

Serves 4

Carb Level: Low
Per serving:
Carbohydrate: 1g
Protein: 29g
Fat: 28g

It's best to cook these delicacies on the grill.

Pizza Burgers

1¼ pounds ground round beef
½ teaspoon garlic salt
¼ teaspoon red pepper flakes
½ teaspoon dried Italian
  seasoning

6 ounces pizza sauce
8 (1-ounce) slices mozzarella
  cheese

Serves 4

Carb Level: Low
Per serving:
Carbohydrate: 10g
Protein: 76g
Fat: 34g

Get the kids—this is a family favorite.

Lightly mix the ground round with the garlic salt, pepper flakes, and Italian seasoning, and form into 4 evenly sized patties. Clean and oil grill rack and preheat grill to medium-high. Cook the burgers about 5 minutes on each side for medium. During the last 2 minutes of cooking, top each burger with a generous tablespoon of the pizza sauce and 2 slices of cheese per burger. Transfer the burgers to a plate and tent with foil to keep warm. Let rest for 1 to 2 minutes to allow the juices to reabsorb. Serve hot.

South of the Border Burgers

Serves 4

Carb Level: Low
Per serving:
Carbohydrate: 5g
Protein: 55g
Fat: 31g

Spicy salsa
equals spicy
burgers; mild
salsa equals
mild burgers!
This recipe
works well
on the grill,
in the broiler,
or on the
stovetop.

1¼ pounds ground round beef
½ teaspoon garlic salt
¼ teaspoon red pepper flakes
4 (1-ounce) slices pepper jack
   cheese

1 cup quality salsa, such as
   Frontera Grill brand
¼ cup canned jalapeño slices
¼ cup chopped fresh cilantro

Lightly mix the ground round with the garlic salt and pepper flakes, and form into 4 evenly sized patties. Clean and oil grill rack and preheat grill to medium-high. Cook the burgers for about 5 minutes on each side for medium. During the last 2 minutes of cooking, top each burger with a slice of cheese. Transfer the burgers to a plate and tent with foil to keep warm. Let rest for 1 to 2 minutes to allow the juices to reabsorb. Serve hot, topped with the salsa, jalapeños, and cilantro leaves.

Indoor or Outdoor?

The little indoor grills that are popular these days, such as the George Foreman Grill, are a convenient and easy alternative to using the larger charcoal or gas grills.

Basic Chicken Wraps

*3 ounces cream cheese, at room
temperature*
1 tablespoon mayonnaise
1 tablespoon fresh lemon juice
¼ teaspoon seasoned salt
Freshly cracked pepper

*2 (8-inch) low-carb tortillas, at
room temperature*
*2 cups sliced or cubed cooked
chicken*
½ cup thinly sliced red onion
1 cup baby spinach leaves

1. Mix together the cream cheese, mayonnaise, lemon juice, salt, and pepper in a small bowl (or use a food processor to blend until smooth).
2. Place the tortillas on a clean work surface. Spread half of the cream cheese mixture on the upper third of each tortilla, about ½ inch from the edge. Place half of the chicken on the lower third of each tortilla. Top each with onions and spinach.
3. Roll up each wrap: Starting from the bottom, fold the tortilla over the filling and roll upward, compressing slightly to form a firm roll. Press at the top to "seal" the wrap closed with the cream cheese mixture. Cut the sandwich in half and wrap in plastic film. Refrigerate until ready to serve.

Wrap Favorites

Wrap sandwiches have long been a favorite for folks on the fly. Easy to prepare in advance and wrap in plastic film, these quick sandwiches are delicious and easy to eat.

Serves 4

Carb Level: Low
Per serving:
Carbohydrate: 9g
Protein: 27g
Fat: 17g

Cream cheese is the "glue" that holds a wrap together. It's very simple to flavor the cream cheese for a nice twist.

Beef and Blue Wraps

Serves 4

Carb Level: Low
Per serving:

Carbohydrate: 9g
Protein: 18g
Fat: 17g

Use a good-quality deli roast beef for this delicious and flavorful wrap. You can also add 1 tablespoon of bacon crumbles for an extra treat.

3 ounces cream cheese, at room temperature
1 tablespoon mayonnaise
2 ounces blue cheese crumbles
¼ teaspoon seasoned salt
Freshly cracked pepper, to taste

2 (8-inch) low-carb tortillas, at room temperature
⅓ pound lean deli roast beef, trimmed of visible fat, sliced, and cut into ½-inch strips
¼ cup diced roasted red pepper
1 cup chopped romaine hearts

1. Mix together the cream cheese, mayonnaise, blue cheese, salt, and pepper in a small bowl (or use a food processor to blend until smooth).
2. Place the tortillas on a clean work surface. Spread half of the cream cheese mixture on the upper third of each tortilla, about ½ inch from the edge. Place half of the roast beef on the lower third of each tortilla. Top each with peppers and lettuce.
3. Roll up each wrap: Starting from the bottom, fold the tortilla over the filling, compressing slightly to form a firm roll. Press at the top to "seal" the wrap closed with the cream cheese mixture. Cut the sandwich in half and wrap in plastic film. Refrigerate until ready to serve.

The Truth about Tortillas!

They're so thin, how bad can they be? If you're watching carbs or watching fat, it's important to read the label. A plain flour tortilla has 21g of carbs, 3g of protein, 4g of fat, and 2g of fiber. A tomato basil wrap has 36g of carbs, 8g of protein, 3g of fat, and 5g of fiber. A whole-wheat low-carb tortilla has 11g of carbs, 5g of protein, 2g of fat, and 8g of fiber.

Turkey Time

3 ounces cream cheese, at room temperature
1 tablespoon mayonnaise
2 tablespoons cranberry sauce
¼ teaspoon seasoned salt
Freshly cracked pepper
2 (8-inch) low-carb tortillas, at room temperature

⅓ pound honey-roasted turkey breast, sliced and cut into ½-inch strips
¼ pound Cheddar cheese, shredded
1 cup chopped mesclun greens

Serves 4

Carb Level: Moderate
Per serving:
Carbohydrate:	11g
Protein:	20g
Fat:	23g

Use a good-quality deli roast beef for this delicious and flavorful wrap. You can add a few bacon crumbles to this wrap for added flavor.

1. Mix together the cream cheese, mayonnaise, cranberry sauce, salt, and pepper in a small bowl (or use a food processor to blend until smooth).
2. Place the tortillas on a clean work surface. Spread half of the cream cheese mixture on the upper third of each tortilla, about ½ inch from the edge. Place half of the turkey on the lower third of each tortilla. Top each with Cheddar cheese and greens.
3. Roll up each wrap: Starting from the bottom, fold the tortilla over the filling, compressing slightly to form a firm roll. Press at the top to "seal" the wrap closed with the cream cheese mixture. Cut the sandwich in half and wrap in plastic film. Refrigerate until ready to serve.

Substitution Suggestions

Consider using smoked meats in place of regular meats. There are excellent smoked chickens, smoked pork tenderloins and chops, and smoked ducks available at specialty stores. Substituting with a smoked meat can add a whole new flavor to the old standby recipes.

Italian Favorites

Serves 4

Carb Level: Moderate

Per serving:

Carbohydrate: 11g

Protein: 13g

Fat: 22g

Substitute your favorite salami or Italian cheeses. You can also add a few roasted vegetables.

---

3 ounces cream cheese, at room temperature
1 tablespoon mayonnaise
1 tablespoon chopped oil-packed sun-dried tomatoes, with a little of the oil
2 teaspoons dried Italian seasoning
¼ teaspoon seasoned salt
Freshly cracked pepper

2 (8-inch) low-carb tortillas, at room temperature
⅛ pound each: Genoa salami, mortadella, and provolone cheese, sliced and cut into ½-inch strips
¼ cup chopped pepperoncini, rinsed and drained
1 cup chopped arugula leaves

1. Mix together the cream cheese, mayonnaise, sun-dried tomatoes, Italian herbs, salt, and pepper in a small bowl (or use a food processor to blend until smooth).
2. Place the tortillas on work surface. Spread half of the cream cheese mixture on the upper third of each tortilla, about ½ inch from the edge. Equally divide the salamis and cheese between the tortillas, placing the ingredients on the lower third of the tortillas. Top each with the pepperoncini and arugula.
3. Roll up the wraps: Starting from the bottom, fold the tortilla over the filling and roll upward, compressing slightly to form a firm roll. Press at the top to "seal" the wrap closed with the cream cheese mixture. Cut the sandwich in half and wrap in plastic film. Refrigerate until ready to serve.

Wrap It Up

There are a variety of options for wraps other than bread or tortillas. Some ideas: lettuce leaves, radicchio cups, large spinach leaves, grape leaves, dried cornhusks, and banana leaves. A little creativity produces a beautiful and unique presentation.

South of the Border Favorites

3 ounces cream cheese, at room
    temperature
1 tablespoon mayonnaise
¼ teaspoon seasoned salt
Freshly cracked pepper
2 (8-inch) low-carb tortillas, at
    room temperature
⅓ pound roasted chicken breast,
    sliced and cut into ½-inch strips

¼ pound pepper jack cheese,
    sliced and cut into ½-inch
    strips
¼ cup chopped cilantro
¼ cup Spicy Salsa (see page
    228), drained
1 cup chopped romaine hearts

Serves 4

Carb Level: Low
Per serving:
Carbohydrate: 8g
Protein: 16g
Fat: 21g

Try salsa-roasted turkey or sliced flank steak instead of chicken, too. Drain the salsa slightly to prevent dripping while you eat.

1. Mix together the cream cheese, mayonnaise, salt, and pepper in a small bowl (or use a food processor to blend until smooth).
2. Place the tortillas on work surface. Spread half of the cream cheese mixture on the upper third of each tortilla, about ½ inch from the edge. Place half of the chicken on the lower third of each tortilla. Top each with the cheese, cilantro, salsa, and lettuce.
3. Roll up each wrap: Starting from the bottom, fold the tortilla over the filling and roll upward, compressing slightly to form a firm roll. Press at the top to "seal" the wrap closed with the cream cheese mixture. Cut the sandwich in half and wrap in plastic film. Refrigerate until ready to serve.

Mexican Cheeses

Authentic Mexican cheeses really enhance your south-of-the-border entrées. Good melting cheeses are Chihuahua and quesadilla. Queso Cotija is a flavorful cheese used for grating or crumbling as a garnish for dishes. Cream-style Mexican cheeses include crema Mexicana, which is thicker than whipping cream and a flavorful addition where spicy chilies are used.

California-Style BLT Wraps

Serves 4

Carb Level: Low

Per serving:

Carbohydrate: 9g

Protein: 9g

Fat: 20g

Eliminate the avocado if you're going to make this in advance—it will oxidize and look unappealing.

3 ounces cream cheese, at room temperature
2 tablespoons mayonnaise
¼ teaspoon seasoned salt
Freshly cracked pepper
2 (8-inch) low-carb tortillas, at room temperature

6 slices smoked bacon, cooked
¼ cup diced avocado
¼ cup seeded and diced ripe tomato
1 cup chopped romaine hearts

1. Mix together the cream cheese, mayonnaise, salt, and pepper in a small bowl (or use a food processor to blend until smooth).
2. Place the tortillas on work surface. Spread half of the cream cheese mixture on the upper third of each tortilla, about ½ inch from the edge. Place half of the bacon on the lower third of each tortilla. Top each with the avocado, tomato, and lettuce.
3. Roll up each wrap: Starting from the bottom, fold the tortilla over the filling and roll upward, compressing slightly to form a firm roll. Press at the top to "seal" the wrap closed with the cream cheese mixture. Cut the sandwich in half and wrap in plastic film. Refrigerate until ready to serve.

Wrap Facts

These wrap recipes are based on 4 servings, which is derived from using 2 wraps to make a sandwich, each cut in half, for a total of 4 halves, or 4 servings. These are considered lunch-sized portions. It's best to have the wraps at room temperature for ease of handling. If needed, microwave them for 5 to 10 seconds until they're pliable. Cold wraps tend to crack.

Thai-Inspired Spicy Beef Lettuce Wraps

2 tablespoons peanut oil or
   vegetable oil
1½ pounds lean ground sirloin
¼ cup diced red pepper
¼ cup sliced scallions
¼ cup chopped cilantro, plus
   extra for garnish

½ cup peanut sauce
Asian chili sauce, to taste
Salt, to taste
12 Boston lettuce leaves
½ cup chopped unsalted peanuts

Serves 4

Carb Level: Moderate
Per serving:
Carbohydrate: 13g
Protein: 37g
Fat: 43g

Kids especially enjoy using Boston lettuce leaves to roll their sandwiches. Adjust the spiciness of the beef according to the likes of your family.

1. Heat the oil in a large nonstick skillet over medium-high heat. Add the sirloin, stirring to break up the meat into small pieces. Cook, stirring frequently, until the meat starts to brown, about 5 minutes. Use a small ladle to remove and discard excess fat.
2. Add the red pepper and stir to incorporate; cook for about 3 minutes. Add the scallions, cilantro, peanut sauce, chili sauce, and salt; stir to blend. Cook until heated through, about 3 to 4 minutes. Taste and adjust seasoning as desired.
3. To serve, arrange the lettuce leaves on a serving platter. Spoon the beef mixture into the center of each leaf and garnish with the peanuts and cilantro.

Grading Beef

Prime cuts are usually the most expensive, tender, and flavorful meat with the highest amount of marbling, which is the streaks of white fat throughout the meat that indicate tenderness and flavor. Choice cuts are slightly below prime in cost and marbling. Select cuts are the leanest meats and therefore the least tender and usually require slower cooking methods to make them tender.

Lettuce Wraps with Spicy Beef and Cucumber Raita

Serves 4

Carb Level: Low

Per serving:

Carbohydrate: 6g

Protein: 29g

Fat: 26g

You can adjust the spiciness by adjusting the quantity of Asian chili sauce—start mild and you can always add more to top your lettuce wrap.

8 ounces plain yogurt
1 tablespoon chopped fresh mint
¼ teaspoon honey
¼ cup peeled and diced cucumber
Salt, to taste
Freshly cracked black pepper
2 tablespoons olive oil

1½ pounds ground sirloin
¼ teaspoon garlic salt
Lemon pepper, to taste
⅛–¼ cup (to taste) Asian chili sauce
¼ teaspoon garam masala
12 Boston lettuce leaves

1. Prepare the raita by mixing together the yogurt, mint, honey, cucumber, salt, and pepper in a small bowl. Cover and refrigerate until ready to use.
2. Heat the oil in a large nonstick skillet over medium-high heat. Add the sirloin, stirring to break up the meat into small pieces. Add the garlic salt and lemon pepper. Cook, stirring frequently, until the meat starts to brown, about 5 minutes. Use a small ladle to remove and discard excess fat. Add the chili sauce and stir to incorporate; cook for about 3 minutes. Add the garam masala and stir to blend. Cook until heated through, about 3 minutes. Taste and adjust seasoning as desired.
3. To serve, arrange the lettuce leaves on a serving platter. Spoon the beef mixture into the center of each leaf and garnish with additional chili sauce, if desired.

Facts about Greens

Excess water actually hastens decay of the leaves, so dry greens if they're wet before storing.

CHAPTER 10
Marinades and Rubs

Curried Vinaigrette

Serves 8

Carb Level: Low

Per serving:

Carbohydrate: 2g
Protein: Trace
Fat: 18g

A great flavor for simple salads that accompany Indian-flavored entrées.

¼ cup seasoned rice wine vinegar
⅓ cup fresh lemon juice
Sugar substitute equal to 1 teaspoon granulated sugar (optional)
1 teaspoon grated fresh ginger

1 clove minced garlic
½ teaspoon salt
½ teaspoon freshly cracked black pepper
2 teaspoons curry powder
½ teaspoon dry mustard
⅔ cup quality vegetable oil

Combine the vinegar, lemon juice, sugar substitute (if using), ginger, garlic, salt, pepper, curry powder, and mustard in a container or jar with a cover and shake vigorously to combine. Add the oil and shake until emulsified. Alternatively, combine all the ingredients in a food processor and process until creamy. Use immediately or refrigerate overnight. Bring to room temperature before using.

Berry Vinaigrette

Serves 8

Carb Level: Low

Per serving:

Carbohydrate: 2g
Protein: Trace
Fat: 18g

You can substitute strawberries for the fresh raspberries.

⅓ cup raspberry vinegar
Sugar substitute equal to 1 teaspoon granulated sugar (optional)
½ teaspoon salt

½ teaspoon cracked black pepper
¼ cup crushed fresh raspberries
⅓ cup quality vegetable oil
⅓ cup extra-virgin olive oil

Combine all the ingredients in a food processor and process until creamy. Use immediately or refrigerate overnight. Bring to room temperature before using.

Creamy Vinaigrette

⅓ cup cider vinegar
Sugar substitute equal to
   1 teaspoon granulated sugar
   (optional)
½ teaspoon salt

½ teaspoon cracked black
   pepper
½ teaspoon dry mustard
¼ cup whipping cream, at room
   temperature
⅔ cup quality vegetable oil

Combine the vinegar, sugar substitute (if using), salt, pepper, and mustard in a container or jar with cover and shake vigorously to combine. Add the cream and oil and shake until emulsified. Alternatively, combine all the ingredients in a food processor and process until creamy. Use immediately or refrigerate overnight. Bring to room temperature before using.

Serves 8

Carb Level: Low
Per serving:
Carbohydrate: 1g
Protein: Trace
Fat: 21g

This vinaigrette is great for use on cabbages, kale, and romaine hearts.

Horseradish Vinaigrette

⅓ cup red wine vinegar
Sugar substitute equal to
   1 teaspoon granulated sugar
   (optional)
1 teaspoon Dijon mustard

½ teaspoon salt
½ teaspoon freshly cracked black
   pepper
1 tablespoon horseradish
⅔ cup extra-virgin olive oil

Combine the vinegar, sugar substitute (if using), mustard, salt, and pepper in a container or jar with cover and shake vigorously to combine. Add the horseradish and oil and shake until emulsified. Alternatively, combine all the ingredients in a food processor and process until creamy. Use immediately or refrigerate overnight. Bring to room temperature before using.

Serves 8

Carb Level: Low
Per serving:
Carbohydrate: 1g
Protein: Trace
Fat: 18g

You can add more horseradish if you want to add more zip.

Citrus Vinaigrette

Serves 8

Carb Level: Low
Per serving:
Carbohydrate: 2g
Protein: Trace
Fat: 18g

You can use it as a marinade for chicken or fish.

⅓ cup combined lemon and orange juice
Sugar substitute equal to 1 teaspoon granulated sugar (optional)
½ tablespoon lemon zest
½ tablespoon orange zest
½ teaspoon salt
½ teaspoon freshly cracked black pepper
⅔ cup extra-virgin olive oil

Combine the lemon and orange juices, sugar substitute (if using), zests, salt, and pepper in a container or jar with cover and shake vigorously to combine. Add the oil and shake until emulsified. Alternatively, combine all the ingredients in a food processor and process until creamy. Use immediately or refrigerate overnight. Bring to room temperature before using.

Greek Rub

Makes 4 servings

Carb Level: Low
Per serving:
Carbohydrate: 2g
Protein: Trace
Fat: Trace

This is a perfect pairing with chicken.

2 tablespoons chopped fresh parsley
2 teaspoons chopped fresh oregano
2 teaspoons chopped fresh rosemary
1 tablespoon lemon zest
1 teaspoon garlic powder
Freshly cracked black pepper, to taste

Combine all the ingredients in a small bowl and mix thoroughly. Can be made the day before and stored refrigerated in an airtight container until ready to use.

Turkish Rub

2 tablespoons chopped fresh mint
3 cloves garlic, minced
1 tablespoon grated
   fresh ginger

1 teaspoon ground cinnamon
1 teaspoon ground cumin
Freshly cracked black pepper

Combine all the ingredients in a small bowl and mix thoroughly.

Makes 4 servings

Carb Level: Low
Per serving:
Carbohydrate: 1g
Protein: Trace
Fat: Trace

For best results, pan-sauté or oven-roast the meat.

South of the Border Rub

2 tablespoons chili powder
3 cloves garlic, minced
2 tablespoons chopped
   fresh cilantro

¼ teaspoon ground red pepper
1 teaspoon ground cumin

Combine all the ingredients in a small bowl and mix thoroughly.

Makes 4 servings

Carb Level: Low
Per serving:
Carbohydrate: 4g
Protein: 1g
Fat: 1g

This dry rub packs a punch with the bite of the chili powder and red pepper.

From Dressings to Drinks

If you have any leftover limes or lemons from making citrus dressing or vinaigrettes, they're great additions to a glass of iced tea or water. Slice them up and remove any visible seeds. Lay them in a single layer on a tray lined with parchment paper and freeze. Store them in the freezer in a sealable plastic bag.

Simple Herb Rub

Makes 4 servings

Carb Level: Low
Per serving:
Carbohydrate: 2g
Protein: Trace
Fat: Trace

This is a delicate rub that is appropriate for fish or chicken.

3 tablespoons chopped fresh parsley
2 teaspoons chopped fresh thyme
3 cloves garlic, minced

2 tablespoons chopped fresh basil
¼ teaspoon ground red pepper

Combine all the ingredients in a small bowl and mix thoroughly.

Creole Rub

Makes 4 servings

Carb Level: Low
Per serving:
Carbohydrate: 5g
Protein: 1g
Fat: Trace

Goes great with seared ahi tuna, roasted pork, or chicken.

2 tablespoons paprika
2 teaspoons garlic powder
2 teaspoons onion powder
1 teaspoon dried thyme

1 teaspoon dried oregano
1 teaspoon ground red pepper
1 teaspoon ground black pepper

Combine all the ingredients in a small bowl and mix thoroughly. Store excess rub in an airtight container at room temperature for up to 3 months.

Italian Rub

3 tablespoons chopped fresh
  parsley
2 tablespoons chopped fresh
  basil
2 cloves garlic, minced

2 teaspoons grated lemon zest
½ teaspoon dried thyme
½ teaspoon dried oregano
½ teaspoon ground black pepper

Combine all the ingredients in a small bowl and mix thoroughly.

Makes 4 servings

Carb Level: Low
Per serving:
Carbohydrate: 5g
Protein: 1g
Fat: Trace

Use a few
teaspoons of
wine to give
it more of a
pastelike con-
sistency.

Five-Spice Marinade

⅓ cup chopped scallions
¼ cup tamari
¼ cup rice wine
1 teaspoon grated lime zest

2 tablespoons grated ginger
1 tablespoon vegetable oil
2 teaspoons Chinese five-spice
  powder

Combine all the ingredients in a small bowl and whisk until mixed
thoroughly.

Makes 6 servings

Carb Level: Low
Per serving:
Carbohydrate: 2g
Protein: 2g
Fat: 2g

A delectable
marinade
for chicken
breasts.

Marinade Tips

There are many delicious marinades you can use with meats. For best results, prepare
these in advance and give the meat the time it needs to absorb the flavors before
cooking, and reserve ¼ cup of the marinade to baste the meat during the cooking
cup reserved for basting.

Savory Cuban Marinade

Makes 6 servings

Carb Level: Low

Per serving:

Carbohydrate: 6g

Protein: 2g

Fat: 8g

The citrus tang blended with the spice mix is a great combination for grilled meats and fish.

¼ cup chopped scallions

⅛ cup chopped garlic

½ cup fresh-squeezed orange juice

¼ cup fresh-squeezed lime juice

¼ cup olive oil

2 teaspoons kosher salt

½ teaspoon cayenne

1 teaspoon ground cumin

1 teaspoon dried oregano

2 tablespoons chopped fresh cilantro

½ cup vegetable stock

1 teaspoon orange zest

1 teaspoon lemon zest

Combine all the ingredients in a glass bowl and mix well.

Savory Marinade for Meats, Fish, and Poultry

Makes 6 servings

Carb Level: Low

Per serving:

Carbohydrate: 3g

Protein: Trace

Fat: 10g

A basic flavorful marinade great for chicken, beef, and pork.

⅔ cup red wine vinegar

⅓ cup vegetable oil

2 tablespoons Dijon mustard

2 tablespoons Worcestershire sauce

2 cloves garlic, minced

1 tablespoon chopped fresh parsley

¼ teaspoon paprika

⅛ teaspoon ground black pepper

1 bay leaf broken into pieces

Combine all the ingredients in a glass bowl and mix well.

Basic Herb Marinade

½ cup fresh lemon juice
½ teaspoon red pepper flakes
1 teaspoon seasoned salt
1 teaspoon lemon zest

3 cloves garlic minced
¼ cup chopped fresh parsley
¼ cup chopped fresh basil
⅓ cup olive oil

Combine all the ingredients in a glass bowl and mix well.

Makes 12 servings

Carb Level: Low
Per serving:
Carbohydrate: 2g
Protein: Trace
Fat: 9g

You can substitute your favorite herbs for the basil and parsley.

Tropical Marinade

⅔ cup pineapple juice
⅓ cup vegetable oil
2 cloves garlic, minced
¼ teaspoon paprika
1 teaspoon ground cumin

¼ teaspoon ground ginger
⅛ teaspoon ground nutmeg
⅛ teaspoon ground allspice
⅛ teaspoon ground black pepper

Combine all the ingredients in a glass bowl and mix well. Reserve about ½ cup of the unused marinade and simmer for about 4 minutes to use as a glaze to finish the chicken just before serving.

Makes 12 servings

Carb Level: Low
Per serving:
Carbohydrate: 2g
Protein: Trace
Fat: 6g

The is a delicious marinade for poultry.

Chimichurri Marinade

Makes 12 servings

Carb Level: Low

Per serving:

Carbohydrate: 2g

Protein: Trace

Fat: 12g

The cayenne adds a great kick—adjust the amount of cayenne and add a little orange juice and a hint of sugar substitute if you want to tone down the heat.

½ cup olive oil

¾ cup sherry vinegar

2 tablespoons paprika

1 to 1½ tablespoons cayenne

4 garlic cloves, minced

2 teaspoons dried oregano

2 bay leaves, broken in several pieces

1 teaspoon kosher salt

Combine all the ingredients in a glass bowl and mix well.

The Best Vinegars for Vinaigrettes

It all depends on the recipe and your own personal taste. Most vinegars have 4g of carbohydrates for a ¼-cup measure. Cider vinegar is fruity and tart with apple overtones. Red wine vinegar is somewhat tart with medium body and works well for most vinaigrettes. Sherry vinegar is a very mild, rich vinegar with flavors of dry sherry.

CHAPTER 11
More Good Food Fast

Skewered Scallops with Prosciutto and Basil

Serves 4

Carb Level: Moderate

Per serving:

Carbohydrate: 9g

Protein: 28g

Fat: 7g

You can easily turn this into an appetizer by using one wrapped scallop per skewer. Soaking wooden skewers prevents them from catching fire.

4 ounces thinly sliced prosciutto
20 large fresh basil leaves
20 diver sea scallops, abductor muscle removed
Seasoned salt, to taste

Freshly cracked black pepper, to taste
1 tablespoon olive oil
2 tablespoons fresh-squeezed lemon juice

1. If using wooden skewers, soak them in water for 20 minutes before using. Place a prosciutto slice on a work surface and lay a basil leaf at one end. Top with a scallop. Wrap the prosciutto around the scallop and basil, tucking in the sides. Repeat the process to make 20 packets. Thread 5 wrapped scallops onto each skewer and season with salt and pepper.
2. Oil a stovetop grill-pan and heat on medium-high. Cook the skewers until the prosciutto begins to sizzle. Turn once and continue cooking, no more than 6 minutes total. Drizzle with the lemon juice and serve hot.

Deli Convenience

Delis slice meats and cheeses in the requested thickness and will also provide quantities in a specific weight or specific count. For example, 6 slices of thick-sliced pepper jack cheese versus 4 ounces of thick-sliced country ham.

Orange-Braised Pork Tenderloin

1 pound pork tenderloin, trimmed of all visible fat and cut into 4 pieces
⅛ teaspoon seasoned salt
Freshly cracked black pepper, to taste
2 tablespoons olive oil
1 cup thinly sliced red onions

1 tablespoon red-wine vinegar
4½ ounces canned mandarin oranges, drained
½ cup fresh-squeezed orange juice
½ cup chicken stock
Pinch dry sage, crumbled
Pinch dried thyme

Serves 4

Carb Level: Moderate
Per serving:
Carbohydrate: 12g
Protein: 26g
Fat: 11g

You can substitute chicken for the pork if desired. This is a good recipe for anyone with a sweet tooth.

1. Season the pork medallions with salt and pepper. Heat the oil in a heavy, medium-sized nonstick skillet over medium-high heat. Add the pork and sear on both sides until golden, about 3 minutes per side. Transfer the pork to a plate and tent with tinfoil to keep warm.
2. Add the onions to the skillet and cook until soft, about 2 minutes, stirring frequently. Add the vinegar, oranges, orange juice, stock, sage, and thyme; bring to a simmer. Add the pork and any accumulated juices back to the skillet, reduce heat to medium-low, and cover; cook for about 8 to 10 minutes, until the pork is cooked through.
3. Uncover and simmer for 2 minutes to allow the sauce to reduce slightly.
4. To serve, place a medallion on each serving plate and spoon the oranges and sauce over the top. Serve hot.

Seared Ahi Tuna Steaks with Garlic

Serves 4

Carb Level: Low

Per serving:

Carbohydrate: 6g

Protein: 54g

Fat: 21g

The success of this recipe depends on having fresh, high-quality fish. The simple olive oil sauce lets the tuna shine through.

4 (8-ounce) Ahi tuna steaks, 1 inch thick
½ teaspoon seasoned salt
Freshly cracked black pepper
3 tablespoons olive oil
4 tablespoons minced garlic
3 tablespoons Worcestershire sauce
Dash hot pepper sauce
1 tablespoon Dijon mustard
3 tablespoons fresh-squeezed lemon juice

1. Heat a heavy nonstick skillet over high heat until wisps of smoke start to appear. Pat the tuna steaks dry with paper towels and season with salt and pepper. Add the tuna steaks to the skillet and quickly sear until the underside is a rich golden brown, about 2 minutes. Flip the steaks and brown the other side. (The steaks will be very rare in the center.) Reduce heat and cook for several more minutes if you prefer the tuna less rare. Transfer the steaks to a plate and tent with tinfoil to keep warm.
2. Allow the pan to cool slightly and add the olive oil, garlic, Worcestershire, hot pepper sauce, and Dijon. Cook until the garlic is soft, but not brown, about 2 minutes. Stir in the lemon juice and any accumulated juices from the tuna. Adjust seasoning to taste.
3. To serve, place the tuna steaks on serving plates and drizzle the sauce on top. Serve hot.

Roasting Garlic

Roasted garlic can usually be substituted for fresh garlic in most recipes. To roast garlic, cut off the very top of a garlic bulb to expose the tips of the cloves. Sprinkle the bulb with a little olive oil, salt, and pepper, and wrap in tinfoil. Bake in a 350° oven for about 1 hour. Roasted garlic is a great spread on vegetables and a delicious flavor addition to sauces, soups, and stews. A full bulb will serve 4 adults and has 3g of carbohydrates per serving.

Lemon-Garlic Venison

1 tablespoon minced garlic
¼ cup finely chopped fresh
* parsley*
1 teaspoon lemon zest
1 teaspoon freshly cracked
* pepper*

2 tablespoons olive oil
¼ teaspoon salt
4 (4- to 5-ounce) venison
* tenderloin steaks*

Serves 4

Carb Level: Low
Per serving:
Carbohydrate: 1g
Protein: 33g
Fat: 10g

1. Combine the garlic, parsley, lemon zest, and pepper in a small bowl. Pat the steaks dry with a paper towel. Rub both sides of the steaks with the parsley mixture and let stand for several minutes at room temperature.
2. Heat the oil in a medium-sized nonstick skillet over medium-high heat. Sprinkle the salt over the oil. Add the steaks to the skillet and cook for 6 to 8 minutes per side for medium-rare. Transfer the steaks to a plate and tent with tinfoil to keep warm. Let the steaks rest for 5 to 6 minutes to allow the juices to reabsorb. Serve hot with any accumulated pan juices.

Thaw frozen venison in your refrigerator overnight. This recipe is much simpler than most recipes for game.

Quick Tip
Use a mini–food processor to mince garlic. Always mince a little (or a lot) extra and store in a ramekin under a thin layer of olive oil. Refrigerate and use as needed.

Chicken in Saffron-Tomato Cream Sauce

Serves 4

Carb Level: Moderate
Per serving:

Carbohydrate: 12g
Protein: 40g
Fat: 15g

This rich sauce really dresses up the simple chicken preparation. The saffron threads add both color and flavor.

4 (6-ounce) skinless, boneless chicken breast halves
¼ teaspoon seasoned salt
Freshly cracked black pepper
¼ cup all-purpose flour
⅛ teaspoon ground cinnamon
Pinch ground cloves
⅛ teaspoon freshly ground nutmeg
⅛ teaspoon ground cumin
3 tablespoons vegetable oil
1 cup finely chopped yellow onion
4 tablespoons minced garlic
1 (14½-ounce) can crushed tomatoes
¼ teaspoon saffron threads
½ cup half-and-half, at room temperature

1. Rinse the chicken under cold, running water and pat dry with paper towels. Line a workspace with plastic wrap, lay the chicken pieces in a single layer, and top with another layer of plastic wrap. Use the flat side of a meat mallet or the bottom of a small, heavy skillet to lightly and evenly pound the pieces several times, starting from the center of each piece and working your way out to the ends. The pieces should end up about ½ inch thick. Season with salt and pepper.
2. Place the flour in a shallow bowl. Dredge the chicken pieces in the flour, shaking off excess. In a small bowl, mix together the cinnamon, cloves, nutmeg, and cumin.
3. Heat the oil in a large nonstick skillet over medium-high heat and add the chicken medallions in a single layer and cook until golden on both sides, turning as needed, about 6 to 7 minutes per side. Add more oil 1 tablespoon at a time, if needed. Transfer the chicken to a plate and tent with tinfoil to keep warm.
4. Add the onions to the skillet and cook until softened, about 4 minutes. Add the spice mix and stir to combine. Add the garlic and tomatoes, and bring to a simmer; cook for about 6 minutes, stirring frequently. Add the saffron and half-and-half, stirring constantly to blend. Bring back to a simmer and cook until slightly thickened, about 7 minutes. Taste and adjust seasoning as desired. To serve, place the chicken medallions on a serving plate and ladle equal portions of the sauce over the chicken. Serve hot, garnished with parsley.

Clams and Chorizo

1 tablespoon olive oil

½ pound chorizo sausage, quartered lengthwise and cut into ⅛-inch slices

½ cup sliced yellow onion

2 tablespoons minced garlic

¾ cup dry white wine

1 (14½-ounce) can diced tomatoes, with juice

4 pounds littleneck clams, well scrubbed

2 tablespoons chopped fresh parsley

½ teaspoon kosher salt

Freshly cracked black pepper, to taste

Serves 4

Carb Level: Moderate
Per serving:
Carbohydrate: 18g
Protein: 73g
Fat: 26g

High-quality clams are available year round. Remember to discard any clams that do not open—never try to force them open.

1. Heat the oil in a large, heavy-bottomed skillet over medium-high heat. Add the chorizo and cook until the sausage browns, about 4 minutes, stirring occasionally. Use a slotted spoon to transfer the sausage to a plate lined with paper towels to drain excess fat.

2. Add the onion to the pan and cook until soft, about 3 minutes. Add the garlic and stir. Add the wine and tomatoes, along with the juices. Bring to a simmer and cook until slightly thickened, about 4 minutes. Add the clams and cooked chorizo, cover, and cook over medium-high heat until the clams open, about 7 to 8 minutes. Shake the pan occasionally while cooking.

3. Use a slotted spoon to transfer the clams to a shallow serving bowl. Add the parsley, salt, and pepper to the pan, and stir to mix. Taste and adjust seasoning as desired. Pour the sauce over the clams and serve hot.

Leftover Wine?

Freeze leftover red or white wine in ice cube trays. After the wine has frozen solid, store the cubes in a labeled plastic bag in the freezer. You can then just add 1 or 2 cubes when a recipe calls for wine.

Chicken Breasts Stuffed with Ham and Cheese

Serves 4

Carb Level: Low
Per serving:

Carbohydrate: 7g
Protein: 67g
Fat: 16g

This dish can be prepared in advance and refrigerated overnight. It will take longer to cook if put into the oven directly from the refrigerator.

4 (6-ounce) skinless, boneless chicken breasts
¼ teaspoon seasoned salt
Freshly cracked black pepper, to taste
4 teaspoons Dijon mustard
4 ounces Black Forest deli ham (about 4 slices), cut into 1½-inch-wide strips
2 ounces deli Swiss or Gruyère cheese (about 2 slices), cut into 1½-inch-wide strips
1 tablespoon olive oil
1 egg, beaten
½ cup panko (Japanese-style breading)
Chopped fresh parsley, for garnish

1. Butterfly the chicken breasts and season with salt and pepper. Brush the inside of each breast with 1 teaspoon mustard. Lay equal portions of the ham and cheeses over half of each breast, and fold back to the original shape. Secure the seam with a toothpick.
2. Preheat oven to 375°.
3. Line a medium-sized baking dish with tinfoil and brush with the olive oil. Place the stuffed chicken breasts seam-side down in the baking dish. Brush the chicken with the beaten egg and evenly coat each breast with an equal amount of the panko crumbs. Season with salt and pepper. Bake uncovered until done, about 20 to 22 minutes. To check for doneness, cut through the bottom of a stuffed breast; the chicken should be cooked throughout without a trace of pinkness, and the cheese filling should be melted.
4. Let the chicken rest for a few minutes to allow the filling to set. To serve, place a breast on each serving plate and garnish with parsley. Serve hot.

Chicken Medallions with Almonds

6 (5-ounce) skinless, boneless chicken breast halves,
trimmed and cut into thirds
¼ teaspoon seasoned salt
Freshly cracked black pepper, to
taste
½ cup all-purpose flour
5 tablespoons olive oil, divided

½ cup yellow onions, peeled,
sliced
½ teaspoon ground cardamom
⅛ teaspoon ground ginger
½ cup chicken stock
½ cup slivered blanched
almonds, lightly toasted
½ cup chopped cilantro

Serves 6

Carb Level: Low
Per serving:
Carbohydrate: 7g
Protein: 37g
Fat: 30g

You can
use whole
chicken
breasts, but
the medal-
lions cook
much more
quickly.

1. Rinse the chicken under cold, running water and pat dry with paper towels. Line a workspace with plastic wrap, lay the chicken pieces in a single layer, and top with another layer of plastic wrap. Use the flat side of a meat mallet or the bottom of a small, heavy skillet to lightly and evenly pound the pieces several times, starting from the center of each piece and working your way out to the ends. The pieces should end up about ½ inch thick. Season with salt and pepper.
2. Place the flour in a shallow bowl. Dredge the chicken pieces in the flour, shaking off excess. Heat 2 tablespoons of the oil in a large skillet over medium-high heat. Add the chicken medallions and cook until they begin to brown, about 2 minutes on each side. Use a slotted spoon to transfer the chicken to a plate and set aside.
3. Add the remaining oil to the skillet. Add the onions and reduce heat to medium; cook, stirring constantly, until the onions are soft, 6 to 8 minutes. Add the cardamom and ginger; stir to mix. Add the stock and simmer until slightly reduced, about 8 minutes.
4. Add the chicken and cook through, about 4 minutes. To serve, place 3 chicken medallions on a serving plate and ladle equal portions of the sauce over the chicken. Garnish with the almond slivers and cilantro leaves, and serve hot.

Salmon on a Bed of Watercress

Serves 4

Carb Level: Low

Per serving:

Carbohydrate: 1g

Protein: 46g

Fat: 25g

This is an elegant ladies luncheon dish or a hearty dinner offering. Reduce the salmon to 6-ounce portions if serving for luncheon entrée.

4 (8-ounce) center-cut salmon fillets (skin on), 1 inch thick

5 tablespoons extra-virgin olive oil, divided

½ teaspoon kosher salt

Freshly cracked black pepper

1 tablespoon fresh-squeezed lemon juice

2 cups fresh watercress leaves, stemmed (rinsed and patted dry with paper towels)

1. Brush both sides of the salmon with about 2 tablespoons of the olive oil and season with salt and pepper. Heat 2 tablespoons of the olive oil in a medium-sized nonstick skillet over medium-high heat. Add the salmon, skin-side up. Cook until golden brown on each side, about 5 minutes per side. Transfer the salmon to a plate and tent with tinfoil to keep warm.

2. Combine the lemon juice and the remaining tablespoon of olive oil in a medium-sized nonreactive bowl and whisk to combine. Season with salt and pepper. Add the watercress leaves and lightly toss to coat evenly. To serve, use tongs to transfer equal portions of the watercress leaves to 4 serving plates. Top each with a salmon fillet and drizzle with any dressing left over in the bowl from the watercress. Serve hot.

Something Smells Fishy

Sometimes the smell of cooking fish is a little overpowering. You can reduce the potential smell by adding a small amount of acidic aromatic flavoring such as lemon or other citrus juice or a flavored vinegar. This will reduce the potential odors.

Beef Tenderloin with a Trio of Mustards

6 (6-ounce) filet mignons
¼ teaspoon kosher salt
Freshly cracked black pepper
2 tablespoons butter
1 tablespoon vegetable oil
¼ cup dry white wine

2 tablespoons Dijon mustard
2 tablespoons yellow mustard
2 tablespoons whole-grain
   mustard
1 cup heavy cream, at room
   temperature

Serves 6

Carb Level: Low
Per serving:
Carbohydrate: 2g
Protein: 23g
Fat: 50g

Serve with a
hearty salad
and simple
vegetable
and you have
a great cou-
ples' dinner
party.

1. Season the steaks with salt and pepper. Heat the butter and oil in a medium-sized heavy skillet over medium-high heat. Add the filets in a single layer, with space between each. Cook the steaks for 5 minutes, turn, and cook for another 5 minutes for medium-rare. Transfer the steaks to a plate and tent with tinfoil to keep warm.

2. Pour out and discard any accumulated fat in the skillet. Add the wine and bring to a simmer, stirring and scraping the bottom of the pan to loosen any browned bits. Add the mustards and stir to combine. Slowly add the cream, stirring constantly to combine. Simmer for 2 minutes, until reduced slightly. Taste and adjust seasoning as desired.

3. To serve, place each filet on a serving plate and drizzle with equal amounts of any accumulated juices. Spoon equal portions of the sauce over the filets and serve hot.

Beef Temperatures and Doneness

Rare meat will be pink at the edges and red in the center, with an internal temperature of 140°. Medium-rare meat will be pink at the edges and dark pink in the center,
with an internal temperature of 145° to 150°. Medium-well meat will be brown at the
edges and pink in the center, with an internal temperature of 155° to 160°. Well-done
meat will have no pink showing, with an internal temperature of over 160°.

Warm Pepper Jack and Bacon Dip

Serves 4

Carb Level: Low

Per serving:

Carbohydrate: 3g

Protein: 29g

Fat: 55g

This recipe is so easy and can be used almost like a fondue.

5 ounces bacon

2 cups shredded pepper jack cheese

1 cup cream cheese, at room temp

¼ cup Madeira

⅓ cup sliced scallions (about ¼-inch slices)

1. Heat a medium-sized nonstick skillet over medium-high heat and add bacon. Cook until crispy, stirring frequently, about 8 minutes. Use a slotted spoon to transfer the bacon to paper towels to drain. When cool, crumble into small pieces.
2. Combine the pepper jack cheese, cream cheese, and Madeira in a microwave-safe serving dish. Microwave on high for 90 seconds or until bubbly (cooking time will vary according to microwave power). Stir in the bacon pieces, top with scallions, and serve with crispy vegetables, such as blanched asparagus spears or celery sticks, or beef or chicken skewers.

Mediterranean Topping

Makes 4 servings

Carb Level: Low

Per serving:

Carbohydrate: 2g

Protein: 2g

Fat: 10g

This is a great topping for fish and chicken.

⅓ cup feta cheese crumbles

½ teaspoon dried oregano

¼ cup sliced kalamata olives

1 tablespoon capers, rinsed and drained

¼ cup quartered cherry tomatoes

1 tablespoon olive oil

Pinch garlic salt

⅛ teaspoon lemon pepper

Gently mix together all the ingredients in a small nonreactive bowl. Taste and adjust seasoning as desired. Refrigerate until ready to serve.

Fresh Salsa Toppings

Fresh salsas are packed with flavor. They are easy to prepare in advance and are the perfect finish for the ever-popular chicken breast. None of these toppings requires any cooking and all use fresh ingredients.

Cucumber and Red Pepper Salsa

1 teaspoon fresh lime juice
1 teaspoon honey
2 tablespoons olive oil
¾ cup peeled, seeded, and diced
    cucumber

¼ cup diced red pepper
1 clove garlic, minced
2 tablespoons chopped dill
Pinch seasoned salt
Freshly cracked black pepper

Combine the lime juice, honey, and olive oil in a small nonreactive bowl and whisk until blended. Add the remaining ingredients and lightly toss to mix. Taste and adjust seasoning as desired. Refrigerate until ready to serve.

Makes 4 servings

Carb Level: Low
Per serving:
Carbohydrate: 3g
Protein: Trace
Fat: 7g

This salsa is a perfect topping for a spicy grilled chicken breast.

Avocado Salsa with Pineapple

2 tablespoons fresh-squeezed
    lime juice
3 tablespoons olive oil
Sugar substitute equal to ½
    teaspoon granulated sugar
¾ cup diced ripe avocado (about
    ½-inch dice)

¼ cup finely diced red onion
⅛ cup finely diced celery
2 tablespoons chopped fresh
    cilantro
Pinch salt
Freshly cracked black pepper,
    to taste

Combine the lime juice, olive oil, and sugar substitute in a small nonre-active bowl and whisk to combine. Lightly toss the avocado pieces to coat evenly. Add the remaining ingredients and lightly toss to combine. Taste and adjust seasoning as desired. Serve immediately.

Makes 4 servings

Carb Level: Low
Per serving:
Carbohydrate: 5g
Protein: 1g
Fat: 14g

Tossing the avocado in the lime and oil mixture will help prevent browning.

Spinach and Parmesan Topping

Makes 4 servings

Carb Level: Low

Per serving:

Carbohydrate: 3g

Protein: 3g

Fat: 16g

This salsa should be prepared just before serving, or the spinach and basil will wilt.

¼ cup extra-virgin olive oil
2 tablespoons balsamic vinegar
⅓ cup shredded Parmesan cheese
¼ cup julienned fresh basil
2 cloves garlic, minced

¼ cup diced roasted red pepper (about ¼-inch dice)
½ cup roughly chopped baby spinach leaves
¼ cup thinly sliced red onion
1 teaspoon red pepper flakes
Pinch seasoned salt

Combine the oil and vinegar in a medium-sized nonreactive bowl and whisk to blend. Add the remaining ingredients and lightly toss to combine. Taste and adjust seasoning as desired. Serve immediately.

Herb Salsa

Makes 4 servings

Carb Level: Low

Per serving:

Carbohydrate: 6g

Protein: 1g

Fat: 7g

This is a delicious topping featuring your favorite herbs.

1 teaspoon honey
2 tablespoons olive oil
1 tablespoon fresh lemon juice
1 teaspoon lemon zest
¼ cup finely diced red onion
¼ cup finely diced celery

1 cup chopped fresh herbs, such as parsley, basil, cilantro, mint, dill, tarragon, oregano, or thyme
⅛ teaspoon garlic salt
⅛ teaspoon kosher salt
Freshly cracked black pepper

Combine the honey, olive oil, lemon juice, and lemon zest in a medium-sized nonreactive bowl and whisk to combine. Add the remaining ingredients and lightly toss to combine. Taste and adjust seasoning as desired. Refrigerate until ready to serve.

Island-Style Shrimp Cocktail

Serves 4

Carb Level: Low

Per serving:

Carbohydrate: 7g

Protein: 19g

Fat: 4g

A nice twist on the traditional shrimp cocktail. And it's easy to pack up to take to summer outdoor barbecues.

1 teaspoon minced garlic
¼ teaspoon salt
1 tablespoon minced fresh ginger
3 tablespoons finely chopped scallions
1 tablespoon finely chopped jalapeño
¼ cup fresh-squeezed lime juice

Sugar substitute equal to 2 tablespoons sugar
1 tablespoon vegetable oil
1 pound extra-large (21- to 25-count) shrimp, peeled, tails left on
¼ teaspoon salt
¼ teaspoon ground black pepper
Lemon and lime wedges

1. Combine the garlic, salt, ginger, scallions, jalapeño, lime juice, and sugar substitute in a small serving bowl and set aside.
2. Heat the oil in a medium-sized, heavy-bottomed nonstick skillet over high heat until it starts to smoke. Season the shrimp with salt and pepper. Add the shrimp to the skillet and sauté until cooked through, about 2 minutes. Remove skillet from heat and immediately add 2 tablespoons of the jalapeño-lime sauce to the skillet; toss to coat the shrimp.
3. Transfer the shrimp to a baking sheet to cool for about 5 minutes. To serve, arrange the shrimp on a platter with the bowl of sauce. Garnish with lemon and lime wedges.

Is the Pan Hot Enough?

Hold your hand about 4 inches over the pan and count to 3. You shouldn't be able to keep your hand comfortably over the pan for more than 3 seconds.

Scallops Madras

1 teaspoon curry powder
1 teaspoon garam masala
1 teaspoon minced fresh garlic
2 tablespoons olive oil
1½ pounds diver sea scallops,
   abductor muscle removed

1 tablespoon ketchup
¼ cup coconut milk
¼ teaspoon kosher salt
⅛ teaspoon cayenne pepper
1 tablespoon fresh-squeezed
   lemon juice

1. Combine the curry powder, garam masala, garlic, and olive oil in a medium-sized mixing bowl. Add the scallops and toss to coat.
2. Heat a medium-sized nonstick skillet over medium-high heat. Add the scallops and sear until almost cooked through, about 2½ to 3 minutes, turning and tossing throughout. Whisk in the ketchup, coconut milk, salt, and pepper. Continue to cook until the sauce is reduced and the scallops are opaque in the center and cooked through, about 4 to 5 minutes. Stir in the lemon juice. Taste and adjust seasoning as desired. Serve hot.

Where to Buy Spices

The Spice House does a wonderful job in compounding special ethnic blends of spices and packing imported spice and herb delicacies. They have a mail-order business and can be reached at ✍www.thespicehouse.com. They carry a number of different curry powder blends and other specialties.

Serves 4

Carb Level: Low
Per serving:
Carbohydrate: 7g
Protein: 29g
Fat: 12g

Buy spices from a spice shop, if you are near one, to get the freshest curry powder and garam masala possible.

Soft Tacos with Spicy Chicken Breasts

Serves 2

Carb Level: Moderate

Per serving:

Carbohydrate: 15g

Protein: 47g

Fat: 26g

Chopping the vegetables is what takes the time for this recipe. Use precut veggies from the salad bar where possible as a time saver.

2 (6-ounce) skinless, boneless chicken breast halves
Garlic salt, to taste
Cayenne pepper, to taste
1 tablespoon vegetable oil
¾ cup Spicy Salsa (see page 228)
1 tablespoon chopped cilantro, plus extra for garnish

2 (8-inch) low-carb tortillas
¼ cup shredded pepper jack cheese
¼ cup seeded and diced tomato
½ cup shredded romaine lettuce leaves,
⅓ cup diced avocado
¼ cup sour cream

1. Rinse the chicken under cold, running water and pat dry with paper towels. Cut the chicken across the grain into ½-inch strips. Season with garlic salt and cayenne.
2. Heat the oil in a medium-sized nonstick skillet over medium-high heat. Cook the chicken until almost done, about 5 minutes, stirring frequently. Add ¼ cup of the salsa and stir to combine. Bring to a simmer and finish cooking the chicken, about 2 to 3 minutes. Remove from heat and stir in the cilantro.
3. To serve, place each tortilla on a serving plate. Equally divide the chicken between the tortillas. Top with equal amounts of cheese, tomato, lettuce, and avocado. Serve the remaining salsa and the sour cream on the side. Garnish with cilantro leaves.

How Much Spice Is Spicy?

The definition of spicy is a very personal preference. When preparing and serving spicy dishes, it's best to prepare the dish at a moderate spiciness and serve salsas and hot sauces on the side.

Spicy Italian Sausage Pizza Wraps

1 teaspoon olive oil
6 ounces spicy bulk Italian
  sausage
⅓ cup chopped yellow onion
1 teaspoon dried Italian
  seasoning
4 ounces pizza sauce

2 (8-inch) low-carb tortillas
½ cup shredded mozzarella
⅓ cup shredded Parmesan
  cheese
Red pepper flakes, to taste

Serves 2

Carb Level: Moderate
Per serving:
Carbohydrate: 16g
Protein: 13g
Fat: 43g

1. Heat the oil in a heavy nonstick skillet over medium-high heat. Cook the sausage, stirring and breaking up larger pieces, until cooked through, about 6 minutes. Use a slotted spoon to transfer the sausage to a bowl.
2. Remove and discard all but 1 tablespoon of the fat from the skillet. Cook the onion until soft, about 4 minutes stirring frequently. Add the Italian seasoning, pizza sauce, and the reserved sausage. Stir to combine and cook until heated through and starting to simmer, about 2 minutes. Taste and adjust seasoning as desired.
3. To serve, place each tortilla in the center of a serving plate. Place half of the sausage mixture on each tortilla, spreading it about ½ inch from the edges. Sprinkle the cheeses on top and add red pepper flakes to taste. Fold over and serve hot.

Tortillas are the crust for these satisfying pizza-like treats. It's too messy to eat flat or open-faced, so fold 'em over.

Is the Oil Hot Enough?

The oil should be shimmering with ripples. You can drop in a few bread crumbs and they should start to bubble and fry. If the oil is smoking, the oil is too hot and you should remove the pan from the heat immediately. Never put a hot pan under cold water to cool. It can result in a dangerous situation.

Dry-Rub Sausages with Peppers

Serves 6

Carb Level: Low

Per serving:

Carbohydrate: 7g

Protein: 17g

Fat: 43g

This is a different and unique way to serve traditional grilled sausages. Try using Spicy Jerk Dry Rub (see page 216) with it.

6 uncooked, mild Italian sausage links

2 tablespoons spicy dry-rub mix

2 tablespoons vegetable oil

3 cups red and green bell pepper strips

1 tablespoon minced garlic

Garlic salt, to taste

Fresh-ground black pepper

1. Cut diagonal slashes in the sausages about 1 inch apart and about ¼ inch deep. Stuff the slashes with equal amounts of the dry rub.
2. Heat the oil in a medium-sized nonstick skillet over medium-high heat. Cook the sausages until no longer pink in the center, about 12 to 14 minutes, turning occasionally. Transfer the sausages to a plate and tent with tinfoil to keep warm.
3. Add the peppers to the skillet and cook until crisp-tender, about 10 minutes, stirring occasionally. Add the garlic and stir. Lightly season with garlic salt and pepper.
4. Add the sausages and any accumulated juices back to the pan. Cook until the sausages are heated through, about 2 to 4 minutes. Taste and adjust seasoning as desired, and serve hot.

Red Pepper Facts

Red bell peppers are also a typical salad addition. Red bell peppers are rich in vitamin C and beta-carotene, and a ¼-cup serving contains 2g of carbohydrates.

Pan-Sautéed Grouper with Jalapeño Butter

¼ cup (½ stick) butter, at room
temperature
2 tablespoons finely chopped
jalapeño chilies
½ teaspoon salt, plus extra for
seasoning

4 red snapper fillets, skin on
(about 1½ pounds total)
Freshly cracked black pepper, to
taste
¼ cup all-purpose flour
3 tablespoons vegetable oil
Fresh lime wedges, for garnish

Serves 4

Carb Level: Low
Per serving:
Carbohydrate: 6g
Protein: 36g
Fat: 24g

1. Combine the butter, chilies, and salt in a small bowl or small food processor and blend to combine. Set aside.
2. Season the fillets with salt and pepper. Place the flour in a shallow bowl. Dredge the fish in the flour and shake off any excess.
3. Heat the oil in a large nonstick skillet over medium-high heat. Carefully add the fish, skin-side up, and cook until browned, about 3 to 5 minutes. Use a spatula to carefully turn the fish and cook for 3 to 4 minutes per side, until the fish is golden on both sides and flakes when pierced with a fork.
4. To serve, transfer the fish to warm serving plates and top each with a dollop of the butter mixture. Garnish with lime wedges.

Grouper is a white, firm-fleshed fish with a meaty texture and mild flavor. You can also substitute cod, haddock, monkfish, or red snapper.

Fish Cooking Tips

As a rule, you should allow 12 minutes of cooking time for each inch of thickness of fish. This applies to pan-sautéing and roasting. Microwave times should be per the recipe. Always watch fish closely when broiling it.

Filet Mignon with Horseradish Cream

Serves 2

Carb Level: Low

Per serving:

Carbohydrate:	2g
Protein:	31g
Fat:	67g

The extra dollop of horseradish is for those who like a little more zest with their steaks. Prepare the sauce in advance to save time.

¼ cup sour cream
2 tablespoons mayonnaise
1 teaspoon fresh-squeezed lemon juice
1 tablespoon bottled horseradish, slightly drained
Dash hot pepper sauce
1 teaspoon chopped parsley
Pinch seasoned salt
Freshly cracked pepper
1½ tablespoons olive oil
2 (6-ounce) filet mignons
Additional horseradish, for garnish

1. Mix together the sour cream, mayonnaise, lemon juice, horseradish, pepper sauce, parsley, salt, and pepper. Set aside.
2. Heat the oil in a small nonstick skillet over high heat. Season the filets with salt and pepper. Cook, searing quickly over high, until the underside is browned, about 4 to 5 minutes for medium-rare. Flip the filets and cook for another 4 to 5 minutes.
3. Transfer the filets to a plate and tent with tinfoil to keep warm. Let rest for 4 to 5 minutes to allow the juices to reabsorb.
4. To serve, place the steaks on serving plates and dollop the sauce on top. Garnish with additional horseradish, if desired.

Cut to the Chase

Always put a damp cloth or nonskid plastic mat under your cutting board. Sliding cutting boards are one of the main causes for accidental knife cuts.

Roasted Salmon Fillets
with Horseradish Dijon Butter

4 (6-ounce) center-cut salmon
  fillets (skin on), about 1 inch
  thick
2 tablespoons olive oil
1/8 teaspoon salt
Freshly cracked black pepper, to
  taste
6 tablespoons (3/4 stick) butter, at
  room temperature

3 tablespoons bottled
  horseradish, drained
2 tablespoons grainy Dijon
  mustard
1 tablespoon minced shallot
Snipped fresh chives,
  for garnish

Serves 4

Carb Level: Low
Per serving:
Carbohydrate: 2g
Protein: 35g
Fat: 30g

Use the finest
salmon avail-
able; quality
counts with
such a simple
recipe. You
can use a
flavored mus-
tard, such as
tarragon, if
desired.

1. Preheat oven to 375°.
2. Line a medium-sized baking dish with tinfoil. Place the salmon, skin-side down, in the prepared pan, evenly spaced. Drizzle the olive oil over the salmon and season with salt and pepper. Bake the salmon for about 10 to 12 minutes, until medium-well.
3. Combine the butter, horseradish, mustard, and shallot in a small bowl and blend with a fork. Season with salt and pepper and divide into 4 portions.
4. To serve, place the salmon fillets on serving plates and top each with a portion of the horseradish butter. Garnish with snipped chives, and serve hot.

Easy Cleanup Tip

Visit a local restaurant supply store and buy a small quantity of disposable foil baking pans. Use these pans for baking items that have sauces that may be messy or difficult to clean. These pans are also great for use during grilling; use a pan for raw foods and another pan for cooked foods. They can be easily run through the dishwasher and can also be discarded if they're too difficult to clean.

Caribbean Spicy Grilled Lamb Chops

Serves 4

Carb Level: Low

Per serving:

Carbohydrate: 5g

Protein: 44g

Fat: 78g

The rich taste of lamb chops is perfectly paired with the smoky grilled flavor.

8 (5- to 6-ounce) lamb chops, 1½ inches thick
Garlic salt, to taste
Freshly cracked black pepper, to taste
2 tablespoons vegetable oil
1 cup finely diced yellow onion
1 tablespoon chopped thyme
1 tablespoon minced garlic
2 tablespoons tamari
⅓ cup dry sherry
½–1 teaspoon (to taste) hot pepper sauce
1 teaspoon cornstarch
1 tablespoon water

1. Clean and oil grill rack. Preheat grill to medium-high. Pat the chops dry with paper towels and season with salt and pepper.
2. Heat the vegetable oil in a small saucepan over medium-high heat. Add the onion and cook until soft, about 4 to 5 minutes. Add the thyme, garlic, tamari, sherry, and hot pepper sauce; bring to a simmer. Cook until slightly reduced, about 5 minutes.
3. Grill the chops over medium-high heat, turning after the first 4 minutes. Brush the chops frequently with the sauce. Cook for a total of 12 to 14 minutes for medium. Transfer the chops to a plate and tent with tinfoil to keep warm. Let the chops rest for about 5 to 6 minutes to allow the juices to reabsorb.
4. While the chops are resting, bring the remaining sauce to a simmer over medium-high heat; simmer for 2 minutes.
5. Combine the cornstarch and water, mixing until smooth. Add the cornstarch mixture to the sauce and bring back to a simmer, stirring constantly until the sauce thickens to the desired consistency. Adjust seasoning to taste.
6. To serve, place 2 chops on each serving plate and ladle the sauce over the top. Serve hot.

Chicken with Pepper Cream Sauce

3 tablespoons olive oil
4 (5-ounce) skinless, boneless
 chicken breasts
½ teaspoon kosher salt
1 tablespoon butter
¼ cup diced roasted red
 peppers

1 cup grated Parmesan cheese
2 cups heavy cream, at room
 temperature
3–4 tablespoons (to taste) hot
 pepper sauce
2 tablespoons chopped fresh
 parsley

Serves 4

Carb Level: Low
Per serving:
Carbohydrate: 5g
Protein: 42g
Fat: 67g

---

1. Heat the oil in a medium-sized nonstick skillet over medium-high heat. Sear the chicken until cooked through, about 7 minutes per side. Transfer the chicken to a plate, sprinkle with the salt, and tent with tinfoil to keep warm.
2. Melt the butter over medium-low heat in the same skillet. Add the red peppers, Parmesan, cream, and pepper sauce. Bring to a simmer, whisking frequently. Cook until slightly reduced, about 10 minutes.
3. To serve, transfer the chicken breasts and any accumulated juices to individual serving plates. Top the chicken with the sauce. Garnish with the parsley, and serve hot.

Serve the sauce on the side. The sauce packs the kick; you can adjust the heat by adjusting the amount of hot pepper sauce.

Veggie Facts

Vegetables are a great source of antioxidants, vitamins, and beta-carotene. It's worth the effort to work fruits and veggies into every meal.

Homemade Pepper Sauce

Serves 24

Carb Level: Low

Per serving:

Carbohydrate: 3g

Protein: Trace

Fat: Trace

Achiote is the ground seed of the annatto tree. It is available in East Indian, Spanish, and Latin-American markets.

2 cups roughly chopped yellow onion

2 tablespoons roughly chopped fresh garlic

¼ cup tomato ketchup

1½ cups white vinegar

18 jalapeño peppers, halved, stems removed, seeded if desired

¼ teaspoon ground achiote

¾ teaspoon seasoned salt

½ teaspoon allspice

Combine all the ingredients in the bowl of a food processor fitted with a metal blade. Process until liquefied, about 1½ minutes. Carefully transfer the mixture to a medium-sized saucepan over medium heat. Bring to a simmer and cook for 1 to 2 minutes. Let cool to room temperature and transfer to an airtight container. Store in the refrigerator until ready to use. The sauce will keep for up to 1 month, properly stored.

Hot Peppers!

Take precautions when putting this sauce together. It is hot! Use rubber gloves when working with the peppers and avoid touching your face and eyes. The juice from the peppers can be quite an irritant. To make the recipe less hot, remove the seeds from the peppers.

Pan-Sautéed Salmon
with Wasabi Cream Sauce

4 (6-ounce) salmon fillets
(skin on)
⅛ teaspoon seasoned salt
2 tablespoons butter
¼ cup heavy cream, at room
temperature

1 tablespoon fresh-squeezed
lemon juice
2 tablespoons wasabi paste
Freshly cracked black pepper
Fresh snipped chives, for
garnish

Serves 4

Carb Level: Low
Per serving:
Carbohydrate: 1g
Protein: 34g
Fat: 17g

This is an
elegant dish
that works
well with
firm-fleshed
fish. If you're
not a salmon
fan, substi-
tute halibut,
snapper,
or haddock.

1. Season the salmon with salt. Melt the butter in a medium-sized non-stick skillet over medium-high heat. When the butter starts to bubble, add the salmon, skin-side down. Cook until the underside starts to brown, about 4 minutes. Carefully flip the salmon and cook for another 3 to 4 minutes. Transfer the salmon to a plate and tent with tinfoil to keep warm.
2. Add the cream and lemon juice to the pan and stir to blend with the pan juices. Bring to a simmer and cook for 2 minutes. Remove from heat and let cool for 2 minutes. Add the wasabi paste and stir to blend. Taste and adjust seasoning as desired.
3. Place the salmon on serving plates and drizzle the sauce over the top. Garnish with fresh cracked pepper and chives; serve hot.

Cleanup Tip

Place a baking sheet upside down on the half of the stovetop where you are not cooking. It's much easier to clean the sheet pan than the stovetop.

Sichuan-Style Chicken Wings

Serves 3

Carb Level: Moderate
Per serving:
Carbohydrate: 17g
Protein: 20g
Fat: 44g

Add more or less pepper flakes based on your personal tastes. This is an easy recipe to prepare ahead of time—finish on the stovetop just before serving.

2 pounds chicken wings, tips clipped
3 teaspoons dried red pepper flakes
1 tablespoon orange zest
½ cup fresh-squeezed orange juice
½ tablespoon peeled, minced fresh ginger
2 teaspoons minced garlic
1 tablespoon honey
3 tablespoons sesame oil
¼ cup soy sauce
¼ cup chopped scallion
¼ teaspoon garlic salt
¼ cup vegetable oil
2 teaspoons cornstarch
1 tablespoon water

1. Rinse the chicken under cold, running water and pat dry with paper towels. Combine the pepper flakes, orange zest, juice, ginger, garlic, honey, sesame oil, soy sauce, scallions, and garlic salt in a medium-sized bowl and mix to combine. Add the chicken wings and stir to coat. Refrigerate until ready to use. (The recipe can be made ahead of time up to this point, and kept refrigerated as long as overnight.)
2. Heat the vegetable oil in a large nonstick skillet over medium-high heat. Use a slotted spoon to transfer the wings from the marinade to the pan. Reserve the marinade.
3. Cook the wings until browned on both sides, about 5 to 6 minutes per side.
4. Mix the cornstarch with the water, stirring until smooth. Add the reserved marinade to the chicken wings and bring to a simmer over medium heat. Slowly stir in the cornstarch mixture and stir until blended. Simmer for 5 to 6 minutes until thick and bubbly. Taste and adjust seasoning as desired. Serve hot.

Quick Tip

When a recipe calls for citrus zest and juice, make sure you remove the zest before juicing. It's near impossible to remove the zest from a squeezed citrus half.

Spicy Chicken Burgers

1 pound ground chicken
¼ cup finely chopped yellow onion
¼ cup finely chopped red bell pepper
1 teaspoon minced garlic

¼ cup thinly sliced scallions
½ teaspoon hot pepper sauce
1 teaspoon Worcestershire sauce
Salt, to taste
Freshly cracked black pepper, to taste

Serves 4

Carb Level: Low
Per serving:
Carbohydrate: 4g
Protein: 35g
Fat: 19g

You can substitute ground turkey or pork for the chicken. Adjust the quantity of pepper sauce to control the spiciness.

1. Clean and oil broiler rack. Preheat broiler to medium.
2. Combine all the ingredients in a medium-sized bowl, mixing lightly. Broil the burgers for 4 to 5 minutes per side until firm through the center and the juices run clear. Transfer to a plate and tent with tinfoil to keep warm. Allow to rest 1 or 2 minutes before serving.

Hot Stuff about Hot Sauce

Tabasco Sauce is a trademarked name and product held by the McIlhenny family since the mid-1800s. It is produced in Louisiana and is manufactured from tabasco peppers, vinegar, and salt. The peppers are fermented in barrels for three years before being processed for the sauce.

Spicy Seafood Stew

Serves 6

Carb Level: Low

Per serving:

Carbohydrate:	10g
Protein:	30g
Fat:	34g

Use your favorite fish in this delicious spicy stew. Pick a combination of firm-fleshed fish that won't easily fall apart or over-cook.

2 tablespoons oil
½ cup chopped yellow onion
½ cup diced green pepper
1 tablespoon minced garlic
3 cups canned peeled, chopped tomatoes, undrained
½ cup coconut milk
1 teaspoon hot pepper sauce
¼ cup fresh-squeezed lime juice

Seasoned salt, to taste
¾ pound skinless firm-fleshed fish fillets, such as cod, center-cut salmon, and/or halibut
¾ pound medium-sized shrimp, shelled and deveined
½ cup thinly sliced scallions
½ cup chopped fresh cilantro

1. Heat the oil in a large nonstick skillet over medium-high heat. Add the onions, peppers, garlic, and tomatoes. Bring to a simmer, stirring occasionally, and cook for 3 to 4 minutes.
2. Add the coconut milk, pepper sauce, lime juice, and seasoned salt. Bring to a simmer and cook for 2 minutes. Add the fish and stir, being careful not to break apart the fillets. Cook until the fish is cooked through, about 8 minutes. Add the shrimp and cook until opaque and cooked through, about 5 minutes.
3. To serve, use a slotted spoon to transfer equal amounts of the fish and shrimp to 4 shallow serving bowls. Pour the sauce over the seafood and garnish with scallions and cilantro. Serve hot.

Fish Storage Facts

If you're unable to cook fresh fish on the day it is purchased, store the fish on a bed of ice in the coldest part of the refrigerator. The same applies for shellfish.

Tabasco Drumsticks

3 tablespoons butter
½ cup Tabasco sauce
2 tablespoons cider vinegar
½ cup chicken stock

16 chicken legs
Salt, to taste
1 cup ranch dressing

1. Preheat oven to 450°. Oil a glass baking dish.
2. Melt the butter in a small saucepan over medium heat and add the Tabasco, vinegar, and stock; bring to a simmer.
3. Rinse the chicken under cold, running water and pat dry with paper towels. Place the legs in a single layer in the prepared baking dish. Bake until the chicken starts to brown, about 6 to 8 minutes; turn the legs and cook for another 6 to 8 minutes.
4. Turn the legs again and pour the sauce over the top; cook for about 8 to 10 minutes, until the chicken easily pulls away from the bone. Season with salt if desired and serve on a platter accompanied by the ranch dressing.

A Side of Asparagus

A ½-cup serving of asparagus is only 3 grams of carbohydrates. Asparagus is easy to prepare by roasting, steaming, or blanching. Any of the following toppings add the perfect finish: a touch of orange zest with melted butter, 1 tablespoon of grated Parmesan cheese, a drizzle of sesame oil and toasted sesame seeds, or 1 tablespoon of olive oil with a hint of lemon zest, poppy seeds, and a few grinds of freshly cracked black pepper.

Serves 4

Carb Level: Low
Per serving:
Carbohydrate: 2g
Protein: 60g
Fat: 49g

This is a great midday snack for the guys or any group that likes 'em spicy. Serve with green onions, celery sticks, and carrot sticks.

Broiled Halibut with Pepper Sauce

Serves 6

Carb Level: Low

Per serving:

Carbohydrate: Trace

Protein: 47g

Fat: 9g

The marinade has a nice kick, which enhances the flavor of this hearty fish.

1½ tablespoons vegetable oil
1 tablespoon Homemade Pepper Sauce (see page 210)
1 tablespoon fresh lime juice
Seasoned salt, to taste

Freshly cracked black pepper, to taste
6 (8-ounce) halibut steaks, about ¾ inch thick

1. Combine the oil, pepper sauce, lime juice, salt, and pepper in a shallow glass baking dish. Add the halibut steaks and turn to coat both sides evenly in the marinade. Let the steaks stand for about 15 minutes.
2. Clean and oil the broiler rack, and position it about 4 inches from the heat source. Preheat broiler to high. Broil the fish for about 4 minutes per side. The fish is done when the flesh just starts to separate. Serve hot.

Spicy Jerk Dry Rub

Makes about ¼ cup (4 servings)

Carb Level: Low

Per serving:

Carbohydrate: 2g

Protein: Trace

Fat: Trace

This is an authentic Jamaican jerk seasoning mix.

2 teaspoons chili powder
1½ teaspoons ground allspice
½ teaspoon ground cinnamon
¼ teaspoon ground nutmeg
½ teaspoon cayenne pepper

Pinch ground cloves
Pinch garlic powder
1 tablespoon seasoned salt
1 tablespoon onion powder
Freshly ground black pepper

Combine all the ingredients in a small bowl and mix to combine. Store in an airtight jar at room temperature.

Andouille and Scallop Skewers with Sage Leaves

12 metal or bamboo skewers
¼ cup olive oil
2 tablespoons fresh lemon juice
12 slices smoked bacon
12 ounces andouille sausage

24 medium-sized diver scallops,
   abductor muscle removed
24 large fresh sage leaves
Freshly ground black pepper

Serves 6

Carb Level: Low
Per serving:
Carbohydrate: 3g
Protein: 24g
Fat: 37g

This is a great outside grill recipe. You can make the skewers half the size for a cocktail offering and use the Spicy Salsa (see page 228) as a dipping sauce.

1. If using bamboo skewers, soak in warm water for 20 minutes before using. Mix the olive oil and lemon juice in a small bowl. Brush the skewers on all sides with the oil mixture.

2. Place the bacon slices in a single layer on several layers of paper towels and cover with a paper towel. Microwave on medium until just starting to cook, but still soft and pliable, about 3 minutes. Turn the bacon halfway through the cooking process. Cut the par-cooked bacon slices in half for a total of 24 pieces.

3. Cut the andouille into 24 pieces, about ½ inch thick. Wrap each scallop with a piece of bacon and thread onto the skewers, alternating with the sausage pieces and sage leaves. You should have 2 of each per skewer. Sprinkle the skewers with pepper.

4. Clean and oil the grill or broiler rack. Preheat grill or broiler to medium-high. Cook the skewers for 1 to 2 minutes per side, until the bacon sizzles and the scallops are cooked through. The scallops should be opaque through the center. Serve hot.

Entertaining Planning Tip

Whenever serving items on a skewer, always provide a small bowl or other receptacle so your guests will have somewhere to dispose of the skewers. Place 1 or 2 skewers in the bowl so your guests will get the idea.

Grilled Rib-Eye Steaks with Chipotle Butter

Serves 4

Carb Level: Low

Per serving:

Carbohydrate: Trace
Protein: 34g
Fat: 46g

Rib-eyes are one of the most flavorful cuts for grilled steaks. The chipotle butter adds a nice amount of heat and flavor.

4 (8-ounce) rib-eye steaks, about ¾ inch thick
2 tablespoons olive oil
Salt, to taste
Freshly cracked black pepper
¼ cup butter, softened
1 tablespoon chipotles in adobo sauce

1. Clean and oil grill rack. Preheat grill to medium-high.
2. Pat the steaks dry with paper towels and brush both sides with the oil. Season the steaks with salt and pepper. Grill the steaks over medium-high heat until grill marks are evident, about 4 minutes per side for medium-rare. Transfer the steaks to a plate and tent with tinfoil to keep warm. Let rest for 4 to 5 minutes to allow the juices to reabsorb.
3. Combine the butter and chipotles in a small food processor and blend until evenly mixed.
4. To serve, place the steaks on serving plates and drizzle with any accumulated juices. Top each steak with a dollop of the chipotle butter, and serve hot.

Smoky Hot Stuff

Chipotles are actually dried, smoked jalapeños. They are available dried, pickled, or canned in adobo sauce.

Ahi Tuna Steaks
with Horseradish Butter

3 tablespoons bottled
horseradish, lightly drained
3 tablespoons butter, at room
temperature
Pinch lemon zest
1 tablespoon fresh lemon juice
Seasoned salt, to taste

Freshly cracked black pepper, to
taste
4 (6-ounce) sushi-grade ahi tuna
steaks, about 1¼ inches thick
2 tablespoons olive oil
Lemon wedges, for garnish

Serves 4

Carb Level: Low
Per serving:
Carbohydrate: 2g
Protein: 40g
Fat: 24g

Use the best
tuna avail-
able, and
make sure
the skillet is
really, really
hot when you
put on the
steaks.

1. Combine the horseradish, butter, zest, lemon juice, salt, and pepper in a small bowl and use a fork to blend. Set aside.
2. Heat a large, heavy-bottomed skillet over medium until very hot, about 3 minutes. Place the steaks on a plate, drizzle with the oil, and season with salt and pepper.
3. Make sure the oven exhaust fan is on. Add the steaks to the pan (they will sizzle and smoke). Cook until the underside has a golden crust, about 3 to 4 minutes for medium-rare. Turn and cook the other side until golden, about 3 to 4 minutes for medium-rare. Transfer the steaks to a plate and tent with tinfoil to keep warm. Let rest for 4 to 5 minutes to allow the juices to reabsorb.
4. To serve, place a tuna steak on each plate and drizzle with any accumulated juices. Top each steak with a dollop of the horseradish butter and serve with lemon wedges.

Fresh Vs. Jarred Horseradish

Prepared horseradish is stored in vinegar. You can substitute fresh horseradish if desired. Fresh horseradish should be wrapped in plastic film and stored in the refrigerator. It is best when grated.

Mussels with Tequila and Jalapeño

**Serves 4
(appetizer portions)**

Carb Level: Low
Per serving:
Carbohydrate: 10g
Protein: 18g
Fat: 26g

The jalapeños add a delicious kick to the sauce for the mussels. Wear gloves when prepping the jalapeños, as they can irritate skin and eyes.

1½ pounds mussels
½ cup butter
2 tablespoons minced garlic
½ cup halved and thinly sliced leek (white and light green part only)
½ cup seeded and diced ripe tomato
⅓ cup sliced jalapeño (¼-inch slices)
¼ cup tequila
2 tablespoons fresh-squeezed lime juice
⅛ teaspoon kosher salt
Freshly cracked black pepper, to taste
Chopped fresh parsley, for garnish

1. Rinse and scrub the mussels under cold, running water. Remove the "beards" from the mussels.
2. Melt the butter in a large, heavy-bottomed pot. Add the garlic and cook until soft, about 1 minute, stirring frequently. Add the leeks and cook until soft, about 4 minutes, stirring frequently.
3. Add the tomatoes, jalapeños, tequila, lime juice, salt, pepper, and the mussels. Cover and cook until the mussels open, about 8 minutes. Use a slotted spoon to transfer the mussels to a shallow bowl; discard any mussels that did not open.
4. Simmer the sauce, until slightly reduced, about 4 to 5 minutes. Taste and adjust seasoning as desired. To serve, pour the sauce over the mussels and sprinkle with chopped parsley. Serve hot.

Scrambled Eggs with Chorizo

8 ounces Mexican uncooked
chorizo sausage
10 large eggs
¼ cup whole milk
¼ teaspoon seasoned salt

Freshly ground black pepper, to
taste
1 cup Spicy Salsa (see
page 228)

(see page 228)

Serves 4

Carb Level: Low
Per serving:
Carbohydrate: 7g
Protein: 29g
Fat: 33g

There are
two types of
chorizo—a
Spanish
tapas variety,
which is
smoked and
precooked,
and the
Mexican ver-
sion, which is
not cooked.

1. Remove the casings from the sausage. Heat a large nonstick skillet over medium-high heat and cook the sausage until starting to brown, about 5 to 6 minutes, stirring frequently. Break up the larger pieces of meat while cooking.
2. Break the eggs into a medium-sized mixing bowl. Add the milk and whisk until blended. Season with the salt and pepper. Move the chorizo to one side of the pan and add the eggs to the open area. Stir into the chorizo. Cook until the eggs are scrambled and set, about 4 minutes. Serve hot with salsa on the side.

What Is Salsa?

Salsa is the Mexican word for "sauce," which can signify cooked or fresh mixtures. Salsa cruda is an "uncooked salsa" and salsa verde is a "green salsa" that is usually tomatillo based and includes chilies and cilantro. Commercial salsas range from mild to mouth searing. Find the level of spice that suits your personal taste.

Pork Medallions with Jalapeño Mustard

Serves 2

Carb Level: Moderate

Per serving:

Carbohydrate: 16g

Protein: 38g

Fat: 40g

Adjust the amount of jalapeños in this recipe to control the heat, and wear rubber gloves while working with them.

2 tablespoons Dijon mustard
½ tablespoon honey
1 teaspoon minced garlic
1 tablespoon fresh-squeezed lemon juice
1 tablespoon finely minced jalapeño pepper, seeded (if desired)
Garlic salt, to taste
1 (¾-pound) pork tenderloin, trimmed of excess fat
Salt, to taste
Freshly cracked black pepper
3 tablespoons all-purpose flour
3–5 tablespoons olive oil

1. Combine the Dijon, honey, garlic, lemon juice, jalapeño, and garlic salt in a small nonreactive bowl and mix to combine.
2. Cut the pork tenderloin into 1-inch-thick slices and lightly season with salt and pepper. Place the flour in a shallow bowl. Dredge the pork medallions in the flour, shaking off excess.
3. Heat 3 tablespoons of the oil in a medium-sized nonstick skillet over medium-high heat. Add the pork medallions and cook until both sides are golden brown, about 6 to 7 minutes per side. Add more oil if needed.
4. Add the jalapeño glaze to the pork and stir to coat the medallions. Cook until the pork is firm to the touch and no pink shows in the center, about 2 to 3 minutes. Remove the pan from heat, tent with tinfoil, and let rest for 4 to 5 minutes. Stir to blend the juices, and adjust seasoning to taste. Serve hot.

Put Down That Fork!

Never use a fork to turn meats. It pierces the meat and allows the flavorful juices to escape. Use a spatula or tongs to gently turn or flip meats.

Chicken Paprikash

4 (6-ounce) skinless, boneless
    chicken breast halves
Salt, to taste
Freshly ground black pepper
¼ cup all-purpose flour
4 pieces of smoked bacon, cut
    into thirds
½ cup thinly sliced yellow onion

4 tablespoons paprika
¼ teaspoon dried marjoram
½ cup dry white wine
1 (14½-ounce) can diced
    tomatoes, drained
½ cup sour cream
2 tablespoons chopped fresh
    parsley

Serves 4

Carb Level: Moderate
Per serving:
Carbohydrate: 17g
Protein: 44g
Fat: 15g

A delicious
dinner that
the whole
family will
love.

1. Rinse the chicken under cold, running water and pat dry with paper towels. Season the chicken with salt and pepper. Place the flour in a shallow bowl. Dredge the chicken in the flour so both sides are lightly coated, shaking off excess.
2. Heat a medium-sized skillet over medium-high heat and cook the bacon until crisp, stirring and turning occasionally. Transfer the bacon to a plate lined with paper towels to drain. Pour out all but 1 tablespoon of the bacon drippings. Add the chicken and cook until both sides are golden, about 7 minutes per side. Transfer the chicken to a plate and tent with tinfoil to keep warm.
3. Add the onions to the pan and cook until soft, about 4 minutes, stirring occasionally. Add the paprika, marjoram, white wine, and tomatoes. Bring to a simmer and cook until slightly reduced, about 5 minutes, stirring occasionally.
4. Add the sour cream to the pan and stir to combine. Bring to a simmer and add the chicken back to the pan. Cook until the sauce is reduced and the chicken is cooked through, about 5 minutes. Taste and adjust seasoning as desired.
5. To serve, place a chicken breast on each plate and ladle sauce over the top. Garnish with chopped parsley and serve hot.

Green Beans and Bacon with Pearl Onions and Horseradish Cream

Serves 8

Carb Level: Moderate

Per serving:

Carbohydrate:	15g
Protein:	5g
Fat:	18g

This is a very rich dish. Eliminate the bacon and pork rinds if you need a vegetarian side dish.

Salt, to taste

10 ounces frozen pearl onions, thawed

1½ pounds green beans, trimmed and rinsed

3 tablespoons horseradish

2 teaspoons all-purpose flour

⅛ teaspoon freshly ground nutmeg

½ cup heavy cream

¼ cup sour cream

3 tablespoons butter

¼ cup cooked crispy bacon crumbles

1 teaspoon chopped fresh thyme

½ cup fried pork rinds, broken into small pieces

1. Bring a large saucepot of salted water to a boil. Add the onions and cook until tender, about 5 minutes. Use a strainer to transfer the onions to a bowl; set aside. Bring the water back to a boil, add more salt, and add the green beans. Cook until the beans are crisp-tender and bright green, about 5 minutes. Drain the beans and add to the onions.

2. Combine the horseradish, flour, nutmeg, cream, and sour cream, and whisk until smooth. Melt the butter in a large nonstick skillet over medium-high heat. Add the vegetables and sauté until heated through, about 3 minutes. Add the cream mixture and cook until slightly reduced and thickened, about 3 minutes. Add the bacon bits and thyme, and stir to combine. Taste and adjust seasoning as desired.

3. To serve, transfer to a serving platter and top with the fried pork rinds.

Sodium Alert

It's easy to overlook the statistics on salt when you're counting everything else in your diet. Remember that 2,400 milligrams per day should be your upper limit for sodium intake.

Chicken and Chorizo with Lemon

8 chicken thighs (about 3¼
    pounds)
⅛ teaspoon cayenne pepper
Seasoned salt, to taste
1 tablespoon lemon zest
2 tablespoons vegetable oil

8 ounces chorizo sausage, sliced
    into ¼-inch rounds
4 tablespoons fresh-squeezed
    lemon juice
¼ cup chopped fresh cilantro

Serves 4

Carb Level: Low
Per serving:
Carbohydrate: 6g
Protein: 68g
Fat: 70g

This is a favorite recipe for fans of dark meat. The flavor of the chorizo and the lemon tang perfectly pair with the tender, juicy chicken thighs.

1. Rinse the chicken under cold, running water and pat dry with paper towels. Place the chicken in a large nonreactive bowl. Add the pepper, salt, and zest, and toss to mix evenly.
2. Heat the oil in a large nonstick skillet. Place the chicken and chorizo in the pan. Cook over medium-high heat until the chicken is golden, about 10 minutes. Turn over and cook until the chicken is cooked through and the chorizo is browned, about 10 minutes longer. Add the lemon juice and increase heat to high. Cook for 3 to 4 minutes more. (The lemon will thicken the pan juices.) Taste and adjust seasoning as desired.
3. Place 2 chicken thighs on each serving plate. Drizzle the pan sauce over the chicken and garnish with the cilantro.

The Skinny on Chicken

Always sear chicken on the skin side first. Also know that poultry dark meat takes longer to cook than white meat.

Chipotle and Pork Tenderloin Medallions

Serves 4

Carb Level: Low

Per serving:

Carbohydrate: 8g

Protein: 32g

Fat: 12g

Canned chipotles (dried, smoked jalapeños) are available in the ethnic section of most major grocers.

1 (1¼-pound) pork tenderloin, trimmed of excess fat
Kosher salt, to taste
1 tablespoon minced garlic

2 cups sliced red onions
2 tablespoons olive oil
⅓ cup chipotles in adobo sauce

1. Preheat oven to 375°.
2. Cut the tenderloin into 8 equal-sized medallions and gently pat flat with the palm of your hand. Season with salt and place in a medium-sized nonreactive bowl. Add the garlic, 1 cup of the onions, and the oil. Toss to combine.
3. Cut the chipotles into a fine dice (it is best to wear gloves when working with hot peppers). Add to the pork and toss to mix.
4. Transfer the pork medallions and marinade to the rimmed baking sheet of a shallow broiler pan. Slip the marinated onion slices under the pork. Bake for 18 to 20 minutes, or until the pork is cooked through. (Do not overcook; the pork should be juicy and moist.) Serve with the remaining 1 cup onions on top.

Hot Peppers

The Scotch bonnet chili is a small irregular-shaped pepper that ranges in color from yellow to orange to deep red. It is one of the hottest chilies available and should be used sparingly in cooking.

Albuquerque-Style Salisbury Steak

1½ pounds ground chuck beef
½ cup shredded pepper jack
   cheese
¼ cup chopped fresh cilantro
1 (4-ounce) can chopped mild
   green chilies
2 tablespoons minced scallions

2 teaspoons chili powder
1 teaspoon salt
2 tablespoons vegetable oil
Freshly cracked black pepper, to
   taste
1 cup Spicy Salsa (see page 228)

Serves 4

Carb Level: Low
Per serving:
Carbohydrate:	7g
Protein:	35g
Fat:	47g

Don't com-
press the
meat so
much that
the juices
don't have
room to cook
in the center.

1. Combine the beef, cheese, cilantro, chilies, scallions, chili powder, and salt in a medium-sized mixing bowl. Gently combine with a fork or your hands. Compress very lightly into 4 oval patties, about ¾ inch thick. Sprinkle with pepper.
2. Heat the oil in a nonstick skillet over medium-high heat. Add the steaks and cook until brown on both sides, about 6 minutes per side for medium-rare. Transfer the steaks to a plate and tent with tinfoil to keep warm. Let rest for 4 to 5 minutes to allow the juices to reabsorb.
3. To serve, place a steak on each serving plate and add a portion of the salsa on the side. Serve hot.

Make Steak Ahead

These steaks can be made a day ahead, wrapped in plastic wrap, and refrigerated. Allow the steaks to sit at room temperature for about 15 minutes before cooking for better control of internal temperatures.

Spicy Salsa

Serves 8

Carb Level: Low

Per serving:

Carbohydrate: 3g

Protein: 1g

Fat: Trace

This simple salsa makes a great topping for beef, fish, and poultry dishes. To avoid a clash of flavors, use it as a topping for simply prepared dishes.

1 cup seeded and diced ripe tomatoes

1 tablespoon minced jalapeño pepper

½ cup finely chopped red onion

1 tablespoon white vinegar

¼ cup chopped cilantro

1½ tablespoons minced garlic

¼ teaspoon garlic salt

Freshly cracked black pepper, to taste

Mix all the ingredients in a nonreactive dish and toss to combine. Cover and refrigerate until ready to use.

Tomato Facts

Whenever cooking tomatoes or tomato products, make sure that you are using a nonaluminum pan. The acid in tomatoes will cause "pitting" in the pan and cause the pan to oxidize. Many people also believe that it gives the tomatoes an "off" taste.

Baked Eggs with Smoked Trout and Leek

Serves 4

Carb Level: Low

Per serving:

Carbohydrate: 2g

Protein: 15g

Fat: 27g

Smoked trout is a true delicacy and pairs nicely with the eggs and creamed leek mixture.

3 tablespoons butter
⅓ cup halved and thinly sliced leek (white and light green parts only)
6 ounces smoked trout, finely flaked
½ cup whipping cream, at room temperature

4 large eggs
Salt, to taste
Freshly ground black pepper, to taste
1 tablespoon snipped fresh chives

1. Preheat oven to 325°. Fill a large saucepan with water and bring to a boil.
2. Meanwhile, melt the butter in a medium nonstick skillet and add the leeks; cover and cook until soft but not brown, about 3 minutes. Remove from heat.
3. Brush 4 small ovenproof ramekins or soufflé dishes with a little melted butter from the pan.
4. Add the trout and a third of the cream to the pan with the leeks and stir to combine. Spoon equal amounts of the leek mixture into the 4 ramekins.
5. Make a well in the center of the leek mixture in each dish. Break an egg into the center of each well and top with 1 tablespoon of cream, salt and pepper, and ½ teaspoon of the chives.
6. Place the ramekins in a baking dish or roasting pan and pour in enough boiling water to come halfway up the sides of the ramekins. Bake for 20 to 25 minutes, or until the whites are set and the yolks are cooked but still tremble when lightly shaken. Remove from water bath and place on serving plates. Sprinkle with the remaining chives. Serve hot.

Baked Salmon and Eggs

4 slices smoked salmon (about
    4 ounces total)
4 large eggs
Seasoned salt, to taste

Freshly cracked black pepper
¼ cup crème fraîche
2 teaspoons chopped fresh dill
Sprigs of fresh dill, for garnish

Serves 4

Carb Level: Low
Per serving:
Carbohydrate: 1g
Protein: 11g
Fat: 10g

Use a good-
quality
salmon for
this recipe.
Instead of
lox, use thin
slices from
whole sides
of cured
salmon.

1. Preheat oven to 350°.
2. Trim a thin 2-inch-long strip from each piece of salmon and reserve.
3. Line 4 ramekins with the salmon slices and crack an egg into each. Season with salt and pepper. Fill a large saucepan with water and bring to a boil.
4. Meanwhile, mix together the crème fraîche and chopped dill in a small bowl. Place equal portions of the dill mixture on top of the egg in each ramekin.
5. Place the ramekins in a baking dish or roasting pan and pour in enough boiling water to come halfway up the sides of the ramekins. Bake for 15 to 20 minutes, or until the whites are set and the yolks are cooked but still tremble when lightly shaken. Remove from water bath and place on serving plates. Garnish with the reserved salmon strips, shaping them into curls, and the dill sprigs. Serve hot.

Egg Facts

1 whole large egg equals 0.6 grams of carbohydrates and 6.3 grams of protein. The breakdown: 1 large egg yolk equals 0.3 grams of carbohydrate and 2.8 grams of protein.

Basic Scrambled Eggs and Bacon

Serves 2

Carb Level: Low

Per serving:

Carbohydrate: 1g

Protein: 21g

Fat: 31g

Some people prefer "soft" eggs, where the mixture is still somewhat moist.

4 slices bacon
2 teaspoons butter
3 large eggs

Dash heavy cream
Salt, to taste
Freshly ground black pepper

1. Cut the bacon strips in half. Heat a small nonstick skillet over medium-high heat. Add the bacon strips in a single layer and cook until starting to brown on the underside, about 3 minutes. Flip the slices and cook until crispy, about 2 minutes. Transfer the bacon to a plate lined with paper towels to drain.
2. Melt the butter in a medium-sized nonstick skillet over medium heat. Whisk the eggs and cream in a bowl and season to taste with salt and pepper. Pour the egg mixture into the skillet and cook to desired doneness, stirring occasionally. Equally divide the eggs and bacon onto 2 warm plates and serve immediately.

Basil Vegetable Frittata

Serves 6

Carb Level: Low

Per serving:

Carbohydrate: 5g

Protein: 12g

Fat: 9g

Substitute other favorite vegetables for the mushrooms if you like.

8 eggs
¾ cup whole milk
½ cup seeded and chopped
    tomato
6 ounces button mushrooms, sliced

2 tablespoons chopped basil
½ teaspoon salt
½ teaspoon ground black pepper
½ cup grated Parmesan cheese
Chopped fresh parsley

1. Preheat oven to 375°.
2. Combine the eggs and milk in a large bowl and whisk until well blended. Add the tomatoes, mushrooms, basil, salt, and pepper, and stir to combine.
3. Lightly butter a 9-inch square nonstick baking pan. Pour the egg mixture into the prepared pan and top with the Parmesan cheese. Bake for 20 to 22 minutes, or until lightly browned and eggs are set. Allow to rest for 1 or 2 minutes and serve hot, garnished with parsley.

Breakfast Custards

1 teaspoon butter
2 large eggs
¾ cup half-and-half
Pinch salt

4 tablespoons shredded smoked cheese
Dash cayenne or nutmeg

Serves 2

Carb Level: Low
Per serving:
Carbohydrate: 6g
Protein: 14g
Fat: 24g

1. Preheat oven to 350°. Fill a medium-sized saucepot with water and bring to a boil. Butter two 6- or 8-ounce ramekins.
2. Combine the eggs and half-and-half in a medium-sized bowl and beat lightly. Season with salt and stir in the cheese. Pour the mixture into the prepared ramekins and top with cayenne or nutmeg.
3. Place the ramekins in a baking dish and pour in enough boiling water to come about halfway up the ramekins. Bake for 20 minutes. Serve warm.

Shell Shock

Is there a difference between brown-shelled eggs and white-shelled eggs? The shell color does not affect the nutritional value, cooking characteristics, or quality. Eggshell color is determined by the breed of the chicken.

The smoked cheese gives this dish personality. Smoked mozzarella or provolone will melt nicely—smoked Gouda gives a great flavor but doesn't always melt smoothly.

Breakfast Kebabs

Serves 4

Carb Level: Low

Per serving:

Carbohydrate: 6g

Protein: 27g

Fat: 43g

The kebabs can be assembled in advance and held at room temperature before broiling. You can add small slices of precooked sausages if desired.

12 strips bacon (not thick sliced)
2 ounces Gruyère cheese
16 cherry tomatoes
16 button mushrooms
1 tablespoon vegetable oil
1 teaspoon tomato paste

1 teaspoon Worcestershire sauce
1 teaspoon Dijon mustard
1 teaspoon soy sauce
¼ teaspoon garlic salt
Freshly cracked black pepper, to taste

1. Clean and oil broiler rack. Preheat broiler to medium-high. If using wooden skewers, soak in warm water for about 15 or 20 minutes before using.
2. Cut the bacon slices in half, widthwise. Cut the cheese into 24 small chunks and wrap a piece of bacon around each.
3. Thread the bacon rolls, tomatoes, and mushrooms alternately onto the skewers, starting and ending with a bacon roll.
4. Mix together all the remaining ingredients in a small bowl. Brush the mixture over the kebabs. Broil for 5 to 7 minutes, turning frequently and brushing with any extra sauce. Serve hot.

Brunch Buffet Tip

Use hollowed-out colorful bell peppers as a bowl for sauces. You can also use unsliced bread loaves to serve sauces; rounds work best. Use a sharp knife to cut out the center, insert a bowl, and fill with the sauce.

Brie and Asparagus Open-Faced Omelet

4 large eggs
2 tablespoons freshly grated
* Parmesan cheese*
1 tablespoon butter
Seasoned salt, to taste
Freshly cracked black pepper, to
* taste*

1 tablespoon sour cream
Pinch ground nutmeg
½ cup 1½-inch pieces asparagus,
* cooked and cooled*
2 ounces Brie cheese, sliced
Parsley sprigs, for garnish

Serves 2

Carb Level: Low
Per serving:
Carbohydrate: 3g
Protein: 20g
Fat: 20g

1. Preheat broiler to medium. Oil a baking sheet.
2. In a large bowl, beat the eggs and Parmesan cheese. Melt the butter in a medium-sized nonstick skillet over medium-high heat. Pour in half of the egg mixture and lightly season with salt and pepper. Cook, without stirring, until just set. Transfer the omelet to the prepared baking sheet. Repeat with the remaining egg mixture.
3. Combine the sour cream, nutmeg, salt, and pepper in a small bowl and set aside.
4. Arrange the asparagus pieces on top of each omelet and top with the sliced Brie. Broil for 1 minute, until the cheese melts.
5. Place omelets on serving plates and garnish with the parsley sprigs. Serve with nutmeg sour cream on the side. Serve hot.

The rind on the Brie is edible but is usually trimmed off and dis-carded. Slightly freeze the cheese to make slicing easier.

Egg Storage

Fresh eggs in their shells will last 3 weeks. Raw yolks/raw whites will last 2 to 3 days and hard-cooked eggs will last 1 week.

Egg, Cheese, and Italian Sausage Pie

Serves 4

Carb Level: Low

Per serving:

Carbohydrate:	2g
Protein:	24g
Fat:	36g

If you don't have a pie pan you can use a medium-sized ovenproof skillet. Use hot sausage and pepper jack cheese for a spicy wake-up call.

1 tablespoon butter
8 ounces Italian sausage (mild or hot, or a mixture)
8 eggs, beaten
2 tablespoons chopped fresh parsley

Salt, to taste
Freshly ground black pepper, to taste
¾ cup grated Cheddar cheese

1. Preheat oven to 350°. Lightly oil a 9-inch pie pan or glass baking dish.
2. Heat the butter in a medium-sized nonstick skillet over medium heat. Add the sausage and cook until fully browned, about 7 minutes. Let cool slightly.
3. Press the sausage into the pie pan, spreading it in an even layer over the bottom. Pour the eggs over the sausage and sprinkle with parsley, salt, and pepper. Bake for 7 or 8 minutes, or until the eggs are almost set. Remove from oven.
4. Sprinkle the cheese over the top of the eggs and return to the oven until the eggs are done and the cheese is melted, about 6 or 7 minutes.

Put It to the Test

To tell if an egg is old or fresh, place the egg in a bowl of salted water. If it sinks, it's fresh. Older eggs will float, as the air cell inside the shell expands with age.

Eggplant Slices Broiled with Ham and Cheese

1 (1-pound) eggplant,
   cut into ½-inch slices
Kosher salt, to taste
4 tablespoons olive oil

8 ounces country ham,
   thinly sliced
8 ounces mozzarella cheese, cut
   into ¼-inch slices
Cayenne pepper, to taste

Serves 4

Carb Level: Low
Per serving:
Carbohydrate: 7g
Protein: 23g
Fat: 31g

You can also add fresh herbs between the layers for an added treat. Basil and thyme are good choices.

1. Clean and oil broiler rack, and position it about 6 inches from the heat source. Preheat broiler to medium-high.
2. Sprinkle both sides of the eggplant with salt. Heat 2 tablespoons of the oil in a medium-sized nonstick skillet over medium-high heat. Add the eggplant and cook until soft, about 7 minutes. Transfer the eggplant to a tray lined with paper towels to drain.
3. Arrange the eggplant slices on a baking sheet and brush with some of the remaining olive oil. Broil until lightly browned on the top, about 8 minutes. Turn the pieces over, brush with the remaining oil, and broil for another 5 minutes.
4. Cover the eggplant with the ham slices and top with the cheese. Return to the broiler until cheese melts and is bubbly. Sprinkle with cayenne and serve.

Save the Date

You can mark the date of a hard-cooked egg right on the shell. If you boil your eggs with a bit of balsamic vinegar in the cooking water, it will color the shells a light brown so you'll be able to tell hard-cooked eggs from raw eggs.

Eggs Béarnaise

Serves 4

Carb Level: Low

Per serving:

Carbohydrate: 5g

Protein: 13g

Fat: 9g

This recipe isn't as complicated as it seems, and when you taste the finished product, you'll know it was worth it.

2 teaspoons olive oil

4 slices Canadian bacon

2 tablespoons orange juice

½ teaspoon salt, plus extra to taste

1 tablespoon vinegar

4 large eggs

1 cup Béarnaise Sauce (see page 239)

4 slices tomato

Freshly ground black pepper, to taste

4 ounces alfalfa sprouts

1. Heat the oil in a small nonstick skillet over medium-high heat. Add the Canadian bacon slices in a single layer and cook until starting to brown, about 2 minutes. Turn the bacon and cook for about 1 minute. Add the orange juice and stir to loosen the brown bits from the bottom of the pan. Cook until the juice is reduced and syrupy, about 2 minutes. Remove pan from heat.

2. Fill a medium-sized skillet with about 2 inches of water and add the ½ teaspoon salt and the vinegar; bring to a low boil over medium heat. Break each egg individually into a small custard cup or saucer. Carefully slide one egg at a time into the boiling water. Cook until set, about 3 to 5 minutes, depending on desired doneness. Carefully remove the eggs with a slotted spoon.

3. Gently warm the Béarnaise Sauce in a small nonstick pot. Heat the Canadian bacon on low to just warm through.

4. To assemble, place a tomato slice on each serving plate and top with a slice of the Canadian bacon. Top the bacon with the poached egg and season with salt and pepper. Pour the Béarnaise sauce over the egg and top with alfalfa sprouts. Serve hot.

Béarnaise Sauce

¼ cup wine vinegar
¼ cup dry white wine
1 tablespoon minced green onion
½ tablespoon dried tarragon
¼ teaspoon salt

⅛ teaspoon pepper
1 teaspoon chopped fresh parsley
Dash chervil
½ cup (1 stick) butter
3 egg yolks

Serves 4

Carb Level: Low
Per serving:
Carbohydrate: 7g
Protein: 10g
Fat: 108g

This is a classic rich and creamy sauce that is a delicious accompaniment for eggs, meat, or fish.

1. Combine the vinegar, white wine, green onions, tarragon, salt, pepper, parsley, and chervil in a small nonstick saucepan over medium-high heat. Boil until the liquid is reduced to 2 to 3 tablespoons, about 12 minutes. Strain into a small nonreactive bowl and reserve.
2. While the vinegar mixture is cooking, melt the butter in a small saucepan and keep warm. Place the egg yolks in the upper half of a double-boiler. The water in the bottom should not touch the upper pan. Beat the yolks until they look creamy and lemony. Turn heat to medium and add the melted butter, drop by drop, stirring constantly. After all the butter has been added, add the vinegar reduction and mix. Stirring continuously, cook until the sauce starts to thicken. Taste and adjust seasoning as desired. Serve warm.

Did You Know?

Salmonella bacteria does not come from the shell or cracks in the shell but from the yolk itself. You can have a perfectly clean, crack-free egg that contains salmonella.

Poached Eggs on Escarole with Bacon and Blue Cheese

Serves 4

Carb Level: Low

Per serving:

Carbohydrate: 8g

Protein: 18g

Fat: 34g

This is an elegant presentation and delicious blend of flavors.

3 tablespoons white wine vinegar

1 tablespoon fresh-squeezed lemon juice

¼ cup extra-virgin olive oil

2 tablespoons sour cream

2 teaspoons Dijon mustard

⅛ teaspoon ground black pepper

¾ teaspoon salt

8 lightly packed cups escarole, washed, dried, and torn into pieces

4 large eggs

3 ounces bacon strips, cooked until crispy, drained, and crumbled

2 cups halved cherry tomatoes

2 ounces blue cheese, crumbled

1. Combine 1 tablespoon of the vinegar, the lemon juice, oil, sour cream, mustard, pepper, and ¼ teaspoon of the salt in a small bowl. Toss the escarole with the vinaigrette in a large bowl and arrange the escarole on 4 individual serving plates.
2. Fill a medium-sized skillet with about 2 inches of water and add ½ teaspoon of the salt and the remaining 2 tablespoons of vinegar; bring to a low boil over medium heat. Break each egg individually into a small custard cup or saucer. Carefully slide one egg at a time into the boiling water. Cook until set, about 3 to 5 minutes, depending on desired doneness.
3. Carefully lift and drain each egg over the skillet using a slotted spoon. Gently place an egg on top of the escarole on each plate. Sprinkle the salads with the bacon, tomatoes, and cheese. Serve immediately.

Baked Eggs with Spinach

1 tablespoon butter, plus extra for
   greasing
1 cup chopped frozen spinach,
   thawed and well-drained
¼ cup whole-milk ricotta cheese
1 tablespoon grated Parmesan
   cheese, plus extra for garnish

Salt, to taste
⅛ teaspoon white pepper
⅛ teaspoon ground
   nutmeg
2 large eggs, at room
   temperature

Serves 2

Carb Level: Low
Per serving:
Carbohydrate: 5g
Protein: 13g
Fat: 15g

---

1. Preheat oven to 350°. Lightly butter 2 4-inch ovenproof ramekins.
2. Melt the butter in a small nonstick skillet over medium heat. When the butter starts to foam, stir in the spinach and cook until the spinach is heated through, about 2 minutes. Transfer to a small mixing bowl.
3. Add the ricotta cheese, Parmesan, salt, pepper, and nutmeg, and mix well. Equally divide the mixture between the 2 ramekins. With the back of a spoon, make a well in the center of the spinach in each ramekin. Break the eggs individually and slide one into each well without breaking the yolk. If desired, sprinkle about ½ teaspoon Parmesan cheese over each egg. Bake until the eggs are set, about 10 to 15 minutes. Serve hot.

You can prepare the spinach mixture in advance to save some time before serving. Bringing the eggs to room temperature will reduce the cooking time.

Frozen Vs. Fresh

Don't hesitate to use canned or frozen vegetables if you're in a pinch. Studies have shown that frozen and canned veggies can hold their own with fresh produce when it comes to good nutrition.

Fresh Fruit Kebabs
with Vanilla Yogurt Sauce

Serves 4

Carb Level: Moderate

Per serving:

Carbohydrate: 17g

Protein: 3g

Fat: 7g

Use only the freshest, ripest fruits available.

4 skewers
1 cup diced cantaloupe (1-inch dice)
1 cup diced pineapple (1-inch dice)
1 cup strawberries
1 cup blueberries
¾ cup vanilla whole-milk yogurt

¼ cup heavy cream
Sugar substitute equal to 2–4 tablespoons granulated sugar (to taste)
½ teaspoon vanilla extract

1. On each skewer thread a piece of cantaloupe, a piece of pineapple, a strawberry, and 2 blueberries.
2. Whisk together the yogurt, heavy cream, sugar substitute, and vanilla extract in a small bowl. Pour into a serving dish. Serve the kebabs with the dipping sauce on the side.

Herb-Baked Eggs

Serves 4

Carb Level: Low

Per serving:

Carbohydrate: 3g

Protein: 17g

Fat: 15g

This is a great recipe for experimenting.

Butter, for greasing
3 ounces ham, thinly sliced
3 large eggs
1 teaspoon Dijon mustard
¼ cup plain yogurt

¾ cup shredded Cheddar cheese
2 teaspoons chopped fresh chives
2 teaspoons chopped fresh parsley
Herb sprigs, for garnish

1. Preheat oven to 375°.
2. Lightly grease 4 6-ounce ramekins with the butter. Line the ramekins with the ham slices.
3. Combine the eggs, Dijon, and yogurt, and mix well. Stir ¼ cup of the cheese into the egg mixture. Add half of the chives and parsley to the egg mixture, and stir well. Spoon the mixture into the prepared ramekins. Sprinkle with the remaining cheese and herbs.
4. Bake for 20 to 25 minutes, until golden and set. Garnish with herb sprigs and serve hot.

Frittata with Pancetta and Chives

*4 ounces pancetta, cut into
¼-inch-thick slices*
1 teaspoon olive oil
8 extra-large eggs
3 tablespoons whole milk
¼ teaspoon salt
Freshly ground black pepper
¼ cup snipped fresh chives

Serves 4

Carb Level: Low
Per serving:
Carbohydrate: 2g
Protein: 22g
Fat: 13g

1. Cut the pancetta into ¼-inch dice. Heat the oil in a medium-sized non-stick skillet over medium heat. Add the pancetta and reduce heat to low; cook until the fat is rendered and the pancetta begins to get crisp, but not brown, about 7 to 9 minutes.
2. Preheat broiler. Combine the eggs, milk, salt, and pepper in a large mixing bowl and whisk until well mixed.
3. Pour the beaten eggs into the pan with the pancetta on low heat. Add the chives. Stir briefly with a wooden spoon and then let the eggs cook slowly, without stirring. After 1 minute, cover the pan and cook the eggs until almost firm, about 7 minutes.
4. Place the frittata under the broiler for 30 seconds to 1 minute, just until set and firm and starting to brown on top. Cut into wedges and serve hot.

If pancetta isn't available, use prosciutto or spicy Italian sausage—increase the cooking time if using raw sausage instead of a cured meat.

Pure Olive Oil Vs. Extra-Virgin

Don't use the expensive extra-virgin olive oil for frying or sautéing. The flavors tend to break down when exposed to high heat. Use pure olive oil, which contains both refined and virgin or extra-virgin. It is more economical.

Jalapeño-Cheddar Frittata

Serves 10

Carb Level: Low

Per serving:

Carbohydrate: 2g

Protein: 16g

Fat: 19g

This is a terrific brunch dish.

12 extra-large eggs
¼ cup half-and-half
½ teaspoon seasoned salt
Freshly cracked black pepper

½ cup sliced pickled jalapeños
2 tablespoons butter
2½ cups shredded Cheddar
    cheese

1. Preheat oven to 350°.
2. Combine the eggs, half-and-half, salt, and pepper in a medium-sized mixing bowl. Use an electric mixer to beat until very light.
3. Pat the jalapeño slices dry with a paper towel. Melt the butter in a medium-sized nonstick skillet over medium heat. Scatter the jalapeños evenly on the bottom of the pan. Sprinkle evenly with the cheese.
4. Pour the eggs over the cheese in a pan. Place the pan on a rimmed baking sheet and bake for 20 to 25 minutes, until just firm. Let cool for several minutes, until set, before removing from the pan. Cut into wedges and serve hot.

Jicama Salad with Mango and Black Beans

Serves 4

Carb Level: Moderate

Per serving:

Carbohydrate: 15g

Protein: 3g

Fat: Trace

A great brunch dish, easy to increase in quantity.

1 cup peeled and diced jicama
    (about ½-inch dice)
⅓ cup diced ripe mango (about
    ⅓-inch dice)
½ cup canned black beans,
    drained and rinsed
½ cup diced red onion (about ⅛-
    inch dice)

⅓ cup mandarin oranges,
    drained
2 tablespoons fresh lime juice
2 tablespoons fresh orange juice
2 tablespoons finely chopped
    cilantro
¾ teaspoon seasoned salt
Freshly cracked black pepper

1. Combine the jicama, mango, black beans, red onion, and mandarin oranges in a medium-sized bowl and toss to mix.
2. Mix together the lime juice, orange juice, cilantro, salt, and pepper in a bowl. Pour over the jicama mixture and toss well. Let stand at room temperature for 10 minutes to allow the flavors to blend, and serve.

Prosciutto with Figs

4 ounces prosciutto, thinly sliced
4 fresh figs, quartered
1 teaspoon honey
2 tablespoons fresh-squeezed
lemon juice

2 tablespoons extra-virgin olive
oil
Freshly cracked black pepper,
to taste
Pinch salt
16 toothpicks for serving

1. Trim any excess fat from the prosciutto and cut in half lengthwise.
2. Wrap each of the fig pieces with a piece of the prosciutto. Place a fig
quarter in each prosciutto nest.
3. Combine the remaining ingredients in a small bowl and whisk well.
Spoon over the figs and serve with picks.

Serves 4

Carb Level: Low
Per serving:
Carbohydrate: 7g
Protein: 8g
Fat: 9g

Figs should
be firm to the
touch and the
skin should
be unblem-
ished.

Radicchio Cups with Ham and Eggs

1 teaspoon olive oil
¾ cup cubed ham (about
¼-inch cubes)
8 large eggs
¼ cup half-and-half

¼ teaspoon seasoned salt
Freshly cracked black pepper
2½ cups shredded Cheddar cheese
4 radicchio leaves
Snipped fresh chives, for garnish

1. Heat the oil in a small nonstick skillet over medium-high heat and
sauté the ham. Combine the eggs, half-and-half, salt, and pepper in a
medium-sized mixing bowl and beat until smooth. Add the eggs to the
ham and cook for about 1 minute. Gently stir as curds form, and cook
to desired doneness. Taste and adjust seasoning as desired. Add the
cheese and lightly stir while the pan is still on the heat.
2. Form each radicchio leaf into the shape of a cup and place on serving
plates. Spoon in equal parts of the egg and cheese mixture. Garnish
with snipped chives, and serve hot.

Serves 4

Carb Level: Low
Per serving:
Carbohydrate: 4g
Protein: 37g
Fat: 39g

The radicchio
cups add a
nice element
to the presen-
tation.

Salami and Melon Stack

Serves 4

Carb Level: Low
Per serving:
Carbohydrate: 7g
Protein: 10g
Fat: 18g

If you find "stacks" difficult to eat, fan the salami and melon slices across the top of the tomato.

1 tablespoon mayonnaise
1 tablespoon sour cream
Salt, to taste
Freshly cracked black pepper
4 large ripe tomato slices

12 thin slices Genoa salami
12 thin slices cantaloupe, peeled and seeded
1 teaspoon capers, rinsed and drained

1. Combine the mayonnaise, sour cream, salt, and pepper in a small bowl and mix well.
2. Place a tomato slice on each serving plate. Top with equal portions of the mayonnaise mixture. Top with 3 slices each of salami and melon in an alternating pattern.
3. To serve, sprinkle with capers and freshly cracked pepper.

Shirred Egg

Serves 1

Carb Level: Low
Per serving:
Carbohydrate: 1g
Protein: 9g
Fat: 17g

Small 4- to 6-ounce ramekins or custard cups work best.

1 teaspoon butter
1 extra-large egg
1 tablespoon heavy cream
1 tablespoon shredded Cheddar cheese

Pinch salt
Freshly cracked black pepper, to taste

1. Preheat oven to 325°.
2. Use a bit of the butter to lightly grease a 4- to 6-ounce ovenproof ramekin dish. Break the egg into the ramekin, being careful to leave the yolk intact. Sprinkle cream on top and dot the remaining butter on top. Season with salt and pepper and top with shredded cheese.
3. Bake, uncovered, to desired doneness, about 15 to 18 minutes. (The white should be set and the yolk soft.) Serve hot.

Smoked Salmon and
Cream Cheese Frittata

8 large eggs
½ cup whole milk
¼ cup chopped fresh chives
¼ cup chopped fresh basil
½ teaspoon black pepper
⅛ teaspoon salt

2 teaspoons vegetable oil
2 ounces cold cream cheese, cut
　　into ½-inch pieces
3 ounces thinly sliced smoked
　　salmon, chopped

1. Combine the eggs, milk, chives, basil, pepper, and salt in a medium-sized bowl and mix until smooth.
2. Position broiler rack about 6 inches from the heat source. Preheat broiler to medium.
3. Heat the oil in a medium-sized, ovenproof nonstick skillet over moderate heat until hot but not smoking. Pour the egg mixture into the skillet and sprinkle the cream cheese pieces on top. Cook, using a spatula to lift up the cooked egg around the edges to let raw egg flow underneath. Cook for 3 to 5 minutes, until the frittata is set on bottom and the eggs are almost set but still moist on top.
4. Remove from heat and sprinkle the salmon over the frittata, lightly pressing the salmon into the frittata.
5. Broil the frittata until set, slightly puffed, and golden in patches, about 1 to 1½ minutes.
6. Let cool for 5 minutes. Loosen the edge with a spatula and slide the frittata onto a large plate. Cut into wedges and serve at room temperature.

Serves 4

Carb Level: Low
Per serving:
Carbohydrate: 　3g
Protein: 　17g
Fat: 　18g

You can use a flavored cream cheese, such as chive, to add a little zest to this dish.

Strawberry Yogurt Frappé

Serves 4

Carb Level: Low

Per serving:

Carbohydrate: 10g

Protein: 2g

Fat: 1g

You can use frozen strawberries (unsweetened) if desired. Make sure the ingredients are well chilled before you start.

1½ cups cubed cold cantaloupe
1 cup ripe strawberries, hulled
½ cup strawberry yogurt

¼ cup blueberries, for garnish
4 tiny mint sprigs, for garnish

1. Combine the cantaloupe and strawberries in a blender and process until smooth. With the blender running, add the yogurt through the feed tube and process until smooth.
2. Equally divide into 4 portions in chilled glasses. Add several blueberries in the center of each glass and place mint sprigs between the berries for garnish. Serve immediately.

Almond Cookies

Serves 24
(about 72 cookies)

Carb Level: Low
Per serving:
Carbohydrate: 5g
Protein: 1g
Fat: 2g

Great alone
or with a fruit
dessert. Store
in an airtight
container. To
crisp, put in a
low-temp oven
for one or two
minutes.

*Sugar substitute for baking equal
to 7 tablespoons granulated
sugar*
*3 egg whites, at room
temperature*

*½ cup finely ground blanched
almonds*
⅓ cup cake flour
1 teaspoon Cointreau
¼ teaspoon vanilla extract

1. Preheat oven to 425°. Oil 2 17" x 14" baking sheets or line with parchment paper.
2. In a large bowl, stir together the sugar substitute and egg whites until the whites are frothy and the sugar substitute is dissolved. Add the remaining ingredients and whisk until the batter is somewhat smooth.
3. Place rounded teaspoon-sized dollops of dough on the prepared baking sheets, leaving a 1-inch space between each cookie.
4. Bake in the oven for 5 to 6 minutes or until the edges turn golden. Remove from oven and transfer the cookies to a wire rack. Let cool completely.

Sweet Tooth

Adding sweet spices such as cinnamon, nutmeg, or cardamom will enhance the perception of sweetness in your desserts.

Almond Cream Cheese Dip

8 ounces cream cheese, at room
  temperature
1 cup sour cream
¼ cup brown sugar or 2
  tablespoons honey
1 teaspoon vanilla extract

¼ cup finely chopped toasted
  almonds
1⅓ teaspoons Amaretto or
  almond liquor
Finely chopped toasted almonds,
  for garnish

Serves 10

Carb Level: Low
Per serving:
Carbohydrate: 6g
Protein: 3g
Fat: 15g

Combine all the ingredients (except the garnish) in a food processor fitted with a metal blade and process until well mixed. Transfer to a serving bowl and garnish with chopped almonds.

For Something Different

Dip apple and pear slices in a mixture of 2 tablespoons rice wine vinegar and 1 teaspoon honey. The acid in the vinegar will keep the apples and pears from browning. This flavor is much nicer and complements the natural sweetness of the fruits. It's better than using lemon-acidulated water.

This is a delicious dip for fruits. Serve this accompanied by sliced apples, sliced pears, strawberries, and grapes.

Berries and Cantaloupe

Serves 4

Carb Level: Moderate
Per serving:
Carbohydrate: 19g
Protein: 1g
Fat: Trace

Make sure
you use a ripe
cantaloupe.

1 tablespoon fresh-squeezed
  orange juice
1½ tablespoons honey
Pinch ground cinnamon

1 cup blueberries
2 cups diced cantaloupe (about
  1-inch dice)
Fresh mint leaves, for garnish

1. Combine the orange juice, honey, and cinnamon in a large bowl and mix well.
2. Pick over the blueberries, rinse under cold water, and drain on paper towels.
3. Add the fruit to the orange juice mixture and lightly toss to coat evenly. Garnish with fresh mint leaves and serve.

Cantaloupe Rings with Blueberries and Lemon Cream

Serves 4

Carb Level: Moderate
Per serving:
Carbohydrate: 11g
Protein: 1g
Fat: 4g

Make sure the
cantaloupe is
ripe and pick
over the ber-
ries to make
sure all stems
have been
removed.

½ cup heavy cream
⅛ teaspoon Wyler's light, sugar-
  free lemonade
  drink mix

4 (1-inch-thick) cantaloupe slices,
  peel on, seeded
2 cups fresh blueberries
Fresh mint leaves, for garnish

1. Combine the cream and lemonade mix in a medium-sized bowl and use an electric mixer to beat until soft peaks form.
2. Place a cantaloupe ring in the center of each dessert plate. Equally divide the blueberries in the center of each melon ring. Top with equal portions of the lemon cream and garnish with fresh mint leaves. Serve chilled.

Caramelized Pears with Toasted Almonds

3 pears, ripe but firm, quartered, cored, and thinly sliced
1 packed tablespoon brown sugar

2 tablespoons sliced almonds
½ cup vanilla yogurt
Fresh mint leaves, for garnish

Serves 4

Carb Level: Moderate
Per serving:
Carbohydrate: 17g
Protein: 2g
Fat: 4g

Use pears that are ripe but still firm. Overly ripe pears will cook too quickly.

1. Clean and oil broiler rack. Preheat the broiler to medium-high.
2. Fan the pear slices in concentric circles in a shallow ovenproof dish. Sprinkle the brown sugar over the pears.
3. Broil until the sugar is caramelized, but not burned, about 4 to 5 minutes. Sprinkle the almonds on top and broil for 1 more minute, until golden.
4. To serve, divide the pears among 4 serving plates. Top each with equal parts of the yogurt and garnish with mint leaves. Serve immediately.

Chocolate Fudge Mousse with Coffee Whipped Cream

1 package Jello sugar-free/fat-free instant chocolate fudge pudding mix
2 cups cold skim milk
¾ cup heavy cream, chilled

Sugar substitute equal to 2–3 tablespoons granulated sugar
1 tablespoon prepared, very strong coffee, chilled
Fresh strawberry slices

Serves 4

Carb Level: Low
Per serving:
Carbohydrate: 9g
Protein: 1g
Fat: 18g

You can use instant coffee crystals to make the coffee.

1. Combine the pudding mix and milk in a medium-sized mixing bowl. Use an electric mixer to beat for about 1½ minutes, until smooth. Equally divide the mixture between 4 parfait cups. Set aside for 5 to 7 minutes.
2. Put the cream in a medium-sized mixing bowl. Beat the cream until it just holds its shape. Sift the sugar substitute over the cream and continue to beat until soft peaks form. Stir in the coffee and mix just until blended. Refrigerate until ready to serve.
3. To serve, top the pudding with equal amounts of coffee whipped cream. Served chilled. Garnish with fresh strawberries, if desired.

Grilled Pineapple with Coconut

Serves 6

Carb Level: Low

Per serving:

Carbohydrate: 10g

Protein: Trace

Fat: 3g

This is a great recipe for an outdoor cookout.

½ ripe medium-sized pineapple
3 tablespoons dark rum
1 tablespoon brown sugar

1 cup nondairy frozen topping (such as Cool Whip)
¼ cup shredded coconut

1. Clean and oil grill rack, and position it about 6 inches from the heat source. Preheat grill to medium.
2. Peel the pineapple and cut crosswise into 6 slices about ¾ inch thick. Drizzle the rum over both sides and sprinkle with brown sugar.
3. Grill the pineapple, with the cover on, for 10 minutes total, turning once. Transfer the pineapple to serving plates. Top with whipped topping and sprinkle with shredded coconut.

Strawberry Parfait

Serves 4

Carb Level: Moderate

Per serving:

Carbohydrate: 19g

Protein: Trace

Fat: 3g

This is a simple preparation that takes full advantage of ripe strawberries.

1 cup strawberries, rinsed, dried, and hulled
1½ cups nondairy whipped topping (such as Cool Whip), thawed

½ cup light, sugar-free strawberry preserves
4 whole strawberries
Fresh mint leaves, for garnish

1. Slice the strawberries lengthwise and divide equally between 4 chilled martini glasses or ramekins.
2. Combine the whipped topping with the preserves in a medium-sized mixing bowl and stir until evenly blended. Dollop the mixture on top of the fruit or use a piping bag to top each with a rosette. Garnish each with a whole strawberry and a fresh mint leaf.

Lime Almond Tarts

½ cup, plus 1 tablespoon slivered
  blanched almonds, toasted
1 tablespoon lime zest
Sugar substitute equal to
  ½ cup granulated sugar
2 large eggs

6 tablespoons butter, plus extra
  for greasing
3 tablespoons fresh-squeezed
  lime juice
½ cup heavy cream, whipped

Serves 8

Carb Level: Low
Per serving:
Carbohydrate: 8g
Protein: 4g
Fat: 20g

---

1. Preheat oven to 350°.
2. Place the ½ cup almonds in a food processor fitted with a metal blade and pulse until the almonds are finely ground. Transfer the almonds to a bowl and set aside.
3. Using the same food processor bowl, combine the lime zest and sugar substitute, and process until evenly mixed, about 1 minute. Add the eggs, butter, lime juice, and the reserved ground almonds; pulse 2 to 3 times, then process for 8 to 10 seconds, until well mixed.
4. Lightly butter the inside of 8 4- or 6-ounce ovenproof ramekins. Equally divide almond mixture between the ramekins. Lightly press the mixture into the bottoms of the ramekins and smooth the surface. Place on a baking sheet and bake until lightly browned, about 15 minutes.
5. Remove from oven and transfer the ramekins to a wire rack to cool. To serve, top the tarts with the whipped cream and sprinkle with the remaining toasted almonds.

Ground almonds add a delicious texture to this tart. Toast the slivered almonds for the best flavor and results.

Pleasing Presentation

Use hollowed-out halves of oranges and grapefruits as bowls for servings of fresh-cut fruits and berries. Use hollowed-out halves of lemons and limes as bowls for any sauces. Cut a small disk from the bottoms to keep the bowls sitting flat.

Pine Nut and Almond Macaroons

¼ cup Marsala wine
3 tablespoons dried currants
½ cup toasted slivered almonds
½ cup toasted pine nuts
Sugar substitute for baking equal
    to ½ cup granulated sugar

1 tablespoon all-purpose flour
1 large egg white
⅛ teaspoon almond extract
½ cup untoasted pine nuts

1. Preheat oven to 350°. Line a large cookie sheet with foil.
2. In a small, heavy saucepan, cook the Marsala and currants over medium heat until the liquid evaporates, about 5 minutes.
3. In a food processor, finely grind the almonds, the toasted pine nuts, the sugar substitute, and flour. In a separate bowl, mix together the egg white and almond extract. Add the egg mixture to the food processor with the nuts and blend until the dough forms into a ball.
4. Place the dough in a bowl and mix in the currants. Shape the dough into ¾-inch balls. Roll the balls in the untoasted pine nuts to cover, pressing gently so the nuts adhere.
5. Flatten the balls into 1½-inch rounds and place on the prepared cookie sheet, making sure that they are spaced at least 1 inch apart. Bake until golden brown, about 15 minutes. Let cool slightly and remove from foil using a metal spatula.

Healthy Sweet Treat

Use sugar-free beverage mixes to flavor whipped cream or nondairy whipped toppings. The flavors are very intense, so start with a pinch at a time until you have the right ratio for your taste.

Sabayon Sauce over Fresh Peaches

3 pounds fresh ripe peaches
Sugar substitute equal to
   ¼ cup granulated sugar
3 large egg yolks, at room
   temperature

2 tablespoons water
¼ cup Marsala wine

Serves 8

Carb Level: Moderate
Per serving:
Carbohydrate: 14g
Protein: 2g
Fat: 2g

1. Halve the peaches and remove the pits. Cut the peaches into ⅛-inch slices. Fan the peach slices in an attractive pattern on each serving plate.
2. Combine the sugar substitute and yolks in the top of a double boiler over medium heat. Use an electric mixer and beat the mixture until frothy. Add the water and wine. Continue to cook over simmering water, beating constantly with an electric mixer at medium speed until the temperature reaches 160°.
3. To serve, pour equal amounts of the sauce over the peaches and serve hot.

Make a Great-Tasting Sauce

Use a pinch of a sugar-free drink mix in a glass of ice-cold ginger ale for a refreshing sparkling sauce over berries and cantaloupe chunks.

Don't be intimi-dated by this classic French prep-aration. It's really quite easy—just make sure your equip-ment is lined up and ready to go.

Sliced Strawberries with Custard Sauce

Serves 6

Carb Level: Moderate

Per serving:

Carbohydrate: 12g

Protein: 3g

Fat: 3g

You can substitute blueberries or raspberries if desired. You can eliminate the Grand Marnier or substitute your favorite liquor.

1¼ cups whole milk
1 vanilla bean, split
1 strip orange zest
1 large egg
Sugar substitute for baking equal to 3 tablespoons granulated sugar

1 tablespoon Grand Marnier
3⅓ cups hulled and sliced strawberries
Fresh mint leaves, for garnish

1. Rinse a heavy saucepan with cold water and shake dry to help prevent sticking. Combine the milk, vanilla bean, and orange zest in the saucepan over medium heat. Bring to a simmer and remove from heat.
2. Combine the egg and sugar substitute in a small mixing bowl and beat until smooth but not fluffy. Temper the mixture by slowly mixing a little of the hot milk mixture into the egg. Add a little more of the hot milk, mix, add the remaining milk, and whisk until combined.
3. Cook over medium heat, stirring constantly with a wooden spoon. Cook until the custard is thick enough to coat the back of a wooden spoon, about 8 minutes. Do not boil or the sauce will curdle.
4. Strain the sauce into a clean bowl set on ice. Discard the orange zest. Scrape the seeds from the vanilla bean and put them back into the sauce. Add the Grand Marnier and continue to stir the sauce until the sauce is chilled. Add more ice if needed to chill quickly.
5. To serve, divide the strawberries equally between 6 ramekins. Drizzle the custard sauce over the berries and top with fresh mint leaves. Serve chilled.

SAMPLE MENUS

A Grecian Feast

Dish	Carbs	Protein	Fat
Herbed Goat Cheese and Black Olive Cucumber Cups	5g	18g	22g
Greek Islands Feta and Herb Spread	3g	6g	13g
Sautéed Fennel with Olives and Arugula	8g	1g	4g
Mediterranean Green Beans	8g	2g	4g
Lamb Loin Chops with Yogurt Sauce	5g	21g	36g
Almond Cookies	5g	1g	2g

A Quick and Easy Appetizer Party with Friends

Dish	Carbs	Protein	Fat
Curry Cayenne Peanuts	8g	10g	18g
Hot Crabmeat Dip	2g	7g	11g
Beef Tenderloin Bites with Creamy Horseradish Sauce	2g	11g	29g
Sausage Bites with Mascarpone Pesto	2g	12g	39g
Grapes with Roquefort	11g	7g	21g

A Vegetarian Dinner

Dish	Carbs	Protein	Fat
Ginger Cashews	11g	5g	16g
Endive Spears with Hummus and Sprouts	6g	3g	3g
Asparagus Soup with Truffle Oil	8g	4g	9g
Grilled Vegetable Stacks	6g	2g	14g
Broccoli and Fried Shallots	6g	2g	4g
Cauliflower Purée	9g	3g	3g

A Formal Dinner for Company

Dish	Carbs	Protein	Fat
Shrimp Skewers with Pineapple	5g	9g	Trace
Petite Salami Tortas	1g	5g	13g
Curried Cauliflower Soup	12g	4g	4g
Lemon-Honey Shrimp with Prosciutto	5g	29g	13g
Oven-Roasted Asparagus and Parmesan	4g	4g	5g
Braised Celery	7g	2g	6g
Strawberry Parfait	19g	Trace	3g

A Formal Dinner for Company

Dish	Carbs	Protein	Fat
Trio of Caviar	16g	13g	13g
Ham Pinwheels with Ricotta and Almonds	3g	15g	19g
Creamy Avocado Soup with Chives	17g	6g	23g
Tuscan-Style Strip Steaks	2g	41g	46g
Creamed Mushrooms	8g	3g	23g
Green Beans with Roquefort Crumbles and Walnuts	11g	13g	24g
Cantaloupe Rings with Blueberries and Lemon Cream	11g	1g	4g

A Formal Dinner for Company

Dish	Carbs	Protein	Fat
Oysters with Horseradish	2g	2g	6g
Water Chestnuts and Bacon	1g	9g	14g
Greek Feta Salad	17g	12g	44g
Whitefish Fillets with Creamy Caper Sauce	8g	29g	37g
Broiled Eggplant and Sunflower Seeds	10g	3g	5g
Chopped Broccoli with Lemon Zest	5g	3g	10g
Sabayon Sauce over Fresh Peaches	14g	2g	2g

A Great Date

Dish	Carbs	Protein	Fat
Fall Endive Spears	5g	3g	6g
Cucumber Rounds with Smoked Salmon	1g	5g	3g
Fennel Salad with Garlic Oil	3g	1g	27g
Sautéed Kale and Red Wine Vinaigrette	17g	6g	5g
Butternut Squash Purée	11g	3g	22g
Filet Mignon with Horseradish Cream	2g	31g	67g

A Great Date

Dish	Carbs	Protein	Fat
Cocktail Pecans	5g	2g	21g
Bacon, Lettuce, and Tomato Cups	4g	7g	18g
Watercress, Basil, and Goat Cheese Salad	2g	7g	15g
Zucchini Marinara	8g	3g	3g
Parmesan-Crusted Chicken Breast	Trace	34g	5g

A Great Date

Dish	Carbs	Protein	Fat
Sweet and Spicy Mixed Nuts	13g	6g	22g
Island-Style Shrimp Cocktail	17g	19g	4g
Iceberg Lettuce with Blue Cheese Dressing	6g	5g	14g
Creamed Spinach	9g	5g	3g
Pan-Sautéed Pork Chops with Gravy	7g	23g	25g
Chocolate Fudge Mousse with Coffee Whipped Cream	9g	1g	18g

A Great Date

Dish	Carbs	Protein	Fat
Endive Spears with Herb Cheese	3g	3g	12g
Oysters with Horseradish	2g	2g	6g
Warm Cabbage Bacon Slaw with Roquefort	16g	24g	41g
Asian Snow Peas with Sesame	12g	5g	8g
Grilled Veal Chops with Herbs and Lemon	3g	24g	11g
Caramelized Pears with Toasted Almonds	17g	2g	4g

A Seafood Extravaganza

Dish	Carbs	Protein	Fat
Herb-Broiled Oysters	6g	10g	8g
Smoked Whitefish Mousse on Cucumber Slices	1g	8g	5g
Warm Calamari Salad with Tomatoes	8g	19g	19g
Seafood Salad	1g	24g	28g
Pan-Seared Sea Scallops	6g	24g	13g
Salmon on a Bed of Watercress	1g	46g	25g

A Mexican Fiesta

Dish	Carbs	Protein	Fat
Spicy Roasted Garbanzos	14g	3g	4g
Warm Pepper Jack and Bacon Dip	3g	29g	55g
Spinach Salad with Shrimp and Roasted Pepper Vinaigrette	11g	26g	32g
Jicama and Red Cabbage Salad	6g	1g	7g
Quick Gazpacho	6g	1g	2g
Grilled Rib-Eye Steaks with Chipotle Butter	Trace	34g	46g
Mussels with Tequila and Jalapeño	10g	18g	26g
Grilled Pineapple with Coconut	10g	Trace	3g

Turn Up the Heat

Dish	Carbs	Protein	Fat
Five-Spice Tuna with Wasabi Aioli	Trace	14g	15g
Sichuan-Style Chicken Wings	17g	20g	44g
Indian Spiced Cauliflower	14g	3g	10g
Escarole and Hot Pepper Oil	9g	5g	4g
Chicken with Pepper Cream Sauce	5g	42g	67g
Berries and Cantaloupe	19g	1g	Trace

An Elegant Asian Dinner

Dish	Carbs	Protein	Fat
Sesame Shrimp with Seaweed Salad	1g	12g	3g
Asian Sesame Chicken Skewers	1g	20g	4g
Asian-Style Eggplant on Spinach	8g	4g	14g
Green Peas with Shiitake Mushrooms	13g	5g	4g
Pan-Seared Ahi Tuna with Wasabi Aioli and Seaweed Salad	10g	41g	25g
Almond Cookies	5g	1g	2g

Brunch for a Bunch

Dish	Carbs	Protein	Fat
Party Cheese Spread with Blue Cheese and Olives	3g	5g	16g
Farmers' Market Radishes with Watercress Butter	Trace	Trace	5g
Grilled Veggie Kebabs	12g	3g	15g
Mixed Greens with Garlic Ranch-Style Dressing	3g	1g	12g
Baked Eggs with Spinach	5g	13g	15g
Chilled Zucchini Squash Soup with Basil	6g	3g	13g
Pan-Sautéed Salmon with Wasabi Cream Sauce	1g	34g	17g
Andouille and Scallop Skewers with Sage Leaves	3g	24g	37g
Sliced Strawberries with Custard Sauce	12g	3g	3g

Index